CHRISTOLOGY AND MYTH
IN THE
NEW TESTAMENT

GERAINT VAUGHAN JONES

CHRISTOLOGY AND
MYTH IN THE
NEW TESTAMENT

AN INQUIRY INTO
THE CHARACTER, EXTENT AND
INTERPRETATION
OF THE
MYTHOLOGICAL ELEMENT
IN
NEW TESTAMENT
CHRISTOLOGY

———

LONDON
GEORGE ALLEN & UNWIN LTD

*Printed in Great Britain
in 11pt. Baskerville type
by Purnell and Sons, Ltd.
Paulton (Somerset) and London*

PREFACE

This enquiry is a contribution to the current theological discussion of the problem of the demythologizing of the New Testament. The spearhead of the controversy is, of course, Professor Rudolf Bultmann, who has so far received little support in theological quarters. Yet whatever may be one's views about Bultmann's method of solving the problem, the issues raised are of immense importance, for they involve the major questions of the interpretation and the validity of biblical thinking and the terminology in which it is expressed. For if this thinking does not express statements which are factually true, what is its meaning? How far are we committed to accepting all the New Testament affirmations in their present form? How far does religious 'truth' require 'mythological thinking' for its expression? What do the New Testament terms really mean, not only for those who used them but for modern Christians and for those whose task it is to make the faith acceptable or intelligible to the so-called 'modern' man? Questions such as these do not permit of evasion; and while Bultmann and others may be criticized for attributing too much importance to the modern man (whose modernity is neither the final word nor incapable of change) it is, after all, to the modern man of any age that the New Testament speaks. It may with justice, therefore, be urged that it should speak to him in terms which he can understand and not through an obsolete cosmology and a naïve anthropology.

To the existential (and existentialist) interpretation of New Testament 'myth' which Bultmann considers so important I have referred only from time to time, as it does not seem to me, notwithstanding the place given to it in the demythologizing controversy, to be as fundamental to the problem and its solution as he insists. The reader who wishes to pursue the matter further had better turn to what Bultmann himself says together with the counter-arguments and replies of his critics.[1] It is clear that the Gospel has its 'existential' aspect, as any kind of thought is bound to have if it deals in any way with man's experience and with his actual situation in his world; but it is not primarily

[1] See also Ian Henderson, *Myth in the New Testament*, S.C.M. Press, 1952.

concerned with an ontology of existence. Further, the advocacy of a particular philosophical interpretation of the New Testament, even if it is the 'right' philosophy, as Bultmann considers existentialism to be,[1] has its perils, one of which is that it may be too academic for kerygmatic exposition. There are, moreover, several different kinds of existentialism: Heidegger's is the kind which Professor Bultmann happens to prefer, though others might be inclined to interpret New Testament thought in terms of (for example) Berdyaev, who also describes himself as an existentialist but who is very critical of Heidegger. It is not easy to reduce the type of thought which goes by this name to a neat system, though its contours are fairly clear and there is an attitude of mind common to its various representatives.

If, however, a philosophical interpretation is required, Bultmann is right in submitting that it shall be one which has to do with man's understanding of his own existence and which shall have something to say about the structure of the world into which he has been 'thrown', to use Heidegger's term. Bultmann himself, it should be pointed out in fairness, has drawn a distinction between the 'existential self-understanding' of the self and the 'existentialist' understanding of existence as expounded by philosophy, though this distinction came rather late in the controversy and not until there had been a good deal of by no means inexcusable confusion about Bultmann's point of view. Yet whatever the precise character of the approach to the problem, there should be agreement as to the main difficulty: namely, that of perceiving the relevance of much of the New Testament language and of many of its ideas to the knowledge and experience of the modern man, and, it should be added, to his spiritual requirements.

The problem confronting us, it is clear, is what is to be done with a religious terminology and a complex of ideas originating in an intellectual environment remote from the very world which the faith embodied in them helped to create and which has in many ways outgrown them. The problem becomes more acute when it is realized that many of the familiar ideas of the New Testament have close affinities with those of the Hellenistic

[1] *Kerygma and Myth* (E. trans.), p. 193.

world of the time, though the more recent tendency in theological studies has been to minimize their extent. Must they be abandoned, or can they be understood in such a way that their 'essence' remains undisturbed? Must they be retained simply because they occur in a sacred book? Is there a 'kernel' and is there a 'husk'? Today, in theological quarters, it is no longer the fashion to say so, as it was in Harnack's time; yet the task of theology is to distinguish between the kernel and the husk if New Testament thought, and particularly its 'mythological' constituent, is not to be considered irrelevant to contemporary needs and the moral experience, such as it is, of the man of the mid-twentieth century, inhibited as he is by emotional and intellectual prejudices against Christianity. Affirmations, for example, about the pre-existence of Jesus, his agency in creation, the Virgin Birth, cannot be proved or disproved, for they are not verifiable objects of knowledge. We may believe them if we wish, but theology has represented them as statements of fact which are beyond verification and are to be accepted in faith but may not be, and are not for many, necessary expressions of faith. If, in the last resort, they have meaning in so far as they mean something to me, though this meaning does not depend upon the precise form of the affirmation, little more is required than to say that Christianity is not a matter of intellectual statement but of my response, in my situation, to the Gospel.

The very term 'mythological' is, of course, question-begging. There are different kinds of mythology. It may be said that the New Testament contains 'mythological' thinking, though its subject is not myth but history, whereas mythology, or myth, does not deal with recognizable historical material. Myth has been described as

> a complex of stories—some no doubt fact, some fantasy—tales which, for various reasons, human beings regard as demonstrations of the inner meanings of the universe and of human life. Myth is quite different from philosophy in the sense of abstract concepts, for the form of myth is always concrete—consisting of vivid, sensually intelligible narratives, images, rites, ceremonies and symbols. A great deal of myth may be based on historical events. ... Myth itself is simply a numinous story.[1]

[1] Alan W. Watts, *Myth and Ritual in Christianity*, Thames and Hudson, 1953, pp. 7, 58.

Again:

> The imagery of myth is by no means allegory. It is nothing less than a carefully chosen cloak for abstract thought. The imagery is inseparable from the thought. It represents the form in which the experience has become conscious. Myth is to be taken seriously because it reveals a significant, if unverifiable, truth—we might say a metaphysical truth.[1]

Bultmann's description of myth is similar. It is

> the use of imagery to express the otherworldly in terms of this world and the divine in terms of human life, the other side in terms of this side.

He uses myth in the sense popularized by the 'History of Religions' school as

> an expression of man's conviction that the origin and purpose of the world in which he lives are to be found not within it but beyond it—that is, beyond the realm of known and tangible reality—and that this realm is perpetually dominated and menaced by those mysterious powers which are its source and limit. Myth is also an expression of man's awareness that he is not lord of his own being. . . . The real purpose of myth is to speak of a transcendent power which controls the world and man, but that purpose is impeded and obscured by the terms in which it is expressed. Hence the importance of the New Testament mythology lies not in its imagery but in the understanding of existence which it enshrines.[2]

The real purpose of myth is not to offer an objective picture of the world as it is but to express man's understanding of himself in his world.

It is clear from this definition of myth that Bultmann is insistent upon its interpretation in terms which shall conform to an existentialist ontology, for the 'myth' has to do with a perpetually 'menaced' realm: that is, one of such a character that the man who lives in it cannot escape from his sense of *Sein-zum-Tode*, 'living

---

[1] H. and H. A. Frankfort, *Before Philosophy*, Pelican Press, 1949, p. 15 (published first as *The Intellectual Adventure of Ancient Man*, University of Chicago Press, 1946).
[2] *Kerygma und Mythos* (E. trans. *Kerygma and Myth*, pp. 10, 11).

towards death', and the *Sorge* (anxiety) which is the most character-istic constituent of being.[1] Man's permanent tension, his existence between past and future, his need to decide, his continuing anxiety as a major characteristic of his existence, the inevitable-ness of death: these, Bultmann says, are what existentialism and the New Testament alike indicate as being implied in the under-standing of existence.

Now, though these factors cannot be omitted from an analysis of human existence, the point at issue is how far they are deter-minative for our understanding of what the New Testament, especially its 'mythology', has to say. In any case, to regard them as being that of which the myth primarily speaks is, in our view, severely to limit the scope of myth even as it is understood by Bultmann, and to select them with the emphasis usually accorded to them by Heidegger and Bultmann is to imply a somewhat one-sided view of existence and a biased view of the New Testament.

As for the 'existential' as distinguished from the 'existentialist' approach to the New Testament *kerygma* and its mythological expression, I have less to say against it. The Gospel proclaims eternal truths: what matters is how they help me to understand my existence, this situation in which I am living, though whether the *Geworfenheit* of which Heidegger speaks is more than a lugu-brious synonym for my being here at all I shall not argue. I am 'here', and that is sufficient. Any word uttered to be effective must be addressed to me in my situation and summon me to a decision and, if Christianity is a reality to me, to commitment. If the mythological language of the New Testament does this, then it does so 'existentially', though how each individual con-stituent of it does so I do not know, nor has Bultmann done more than offer an outline of this existential interpretation; and though he has on one occasion used the world 'analogy' in regard to mythological thinking, he does not admit that such thinking is merely symbolical or pictorial.

Although existentialism (however difficult to define) is doubt-less as good a philosophy as any for supplying terms for the reinterpretation of New Testament mythological thought, it is not my purpose to use theology in order to demythologize

[1] M. Heidegger, *Sein und Zeit*, 6th. ed., 1949, pp. 180 ff., 235 ff.

existentially, a task which I prefer to leave to an existentialist theologian or a theological existentialist. My purpose is rather to enquire how far New Testament concepts are mythological and into the nature and meaning of mythological thinking in so far as this applies to Christology. If much of what I have written is arranged round the central New Testament Christological idea of the Lordship of Christ, this is not because I consider the title *Kyrios* to be mythological, though there is a sense in which it is, but because it sums up the New Testament Christology including the mythological conceptions which form its background.

I should, moreover, express my gratitude to Dr. Bultmann as one of my former teachers for the incisive and exhilarating reminder with which he has confronted us of the need to revise our attitude towards the authority of the scriptural language and to come to grips with questions which faced the Liberals and Modernists of a previous theological generation. The need to restate in language compatible with twentieth-century thought what the New Testament writers stated in theirs is as urgent today as ever it was. Bultmann's achievement has been to force this upon the attention of a theology which, in reacting from the Liberal tradition, had grown complacent in seeking support in a recovered, and possibly excessive, biblical emphasis.

Although this investigation begins with Bultmann it is not an attempt to reinterpret the mythological material of the New Testament in the terms which he recommends. He is, so to speak, a spring-board, a starting-point. Nevertheless, it may be desirable to indicate briefly where I agree and where I disagree with Bultmann without attempting to comment in detail upon his thesis, which has already been done at considerable length by German and occasionally by British theologians. I agree with him that, as he describes it, the New Testament world-view is mythological; that the New Testament representation of Jesus as a pre-existent divine being taking human form is also mythological; that something has to be done about the mythological world-view: it should be either abandoned or retained or it should be reinterpreted in such a way that faith is not involved in it as an objective statement; that there are *some* points of contact between the existentialist philosophy and the New Testament interpretation of existence, and that the challenge to self-understanding is present, though not of decisive importance, in New Testament thought.

I do not agree that the reinterpretation of New Testament 'myth' must be only in existential/existentialist forms, for this would mean that only convinced existentialists should undertake the task; that the importance of the New Testament mythology does not lie in its imagery, for this would rule out an important alternative approach to the problem; that there is any need to distinguish as sharply and antithetically as Bultmann appears to do between the historical (*historisch*) and the historic (*geschichtlich*). Underlying his argument there seems to be the existentialist concern with the subject-object relationship which affects his conception of historicality and historicity. While what he says about the 'historical' as an object of knowledge may be true, it is important not to overlook its consequences for our assessment of the historical value of the Gospels.

Ultimately this problem of myth in the New Testament Christology is bound up with the place of poetic imagery and symbol in religion, with the question of how far what may have been believed as facts in the first century, and by those who hold certain beliefs about biblical inspiration, should be interpreted poetically by those who are reluctant to abandon them altogether but cannot accept them as they are; and in the last resort it is possible that, in seeking to accommodate the New Testament expression of the Lordship of Christ and the context in which this Christology emerged to what is considered acceptable to our so-called modern man, we are on the wrong track. However that may be, one cannot renounce one's freedom to conduct an enquiry into the tenability of the constituents of this expression and into their validity even if they are hallowed by their occurrence in Holy Scripture. And if the outlook and approach underlying this enquiry are judged to be those of an allegedly defunct Liberalism, I would reply that such an approach may be a much-needed counterbalance to certain tendencies in contemporary theology.

As the scope of this enquiry has to be limited, I have omitted any detailed consideration of the eschatology of the Gospels, which in its futuristic sense belongs to mythology and to the mythological world-view of the Apostolic age. It must suffice to observe that the modern interpretation of it as 'realized eschatology' is virtually equivalent to its demythologization, and Bultmann himself has remarked upon the demything of this form of the Christian hope.[1] The question of how far the eschatological material in the Gospels is genuine in the sense that it belongs to the spoken words of Jesus has been so extensively dealt with in commentaries and other books on the subject and with such varying results that no considerable reference to it by me is required. Jesus' interpretation of his eschatological mission and of the Messianic titles shows how far in his own mind these conceptions had been brought down, as it were, from the mythological level of apocalyptic futurism and ultra-historical expectation to that of historical reality. The mythology of Apocalyptic is a subject to itself as well as part of the larger subject of New Testament Christology.

I have therefore limited the scope of this investigation to the 'mythological' aspect of the Apostolic Christology, which I have subjected to a detailed examination within a framework wider than is usual in the study of Christology. Indeed, in view of the prevalence of the severely biblical approach to theology, I have considered it necessary to enquire analytically into what the New Testament terminology means. If the terms and concepts it contains are divinely inspired 'revelation', there is nothing to do but to accept them; there can be no argument about them.[2] But if they are believed to be intimately bound up with the Hellenistic-Hebraic world for which there can hardly be any indisputable divine sanction to make them sacrosanct, there is no reason why they should not be subjected to thorough critical examination, especially when there is involved in them the 'mythological' element which belongs to the cosmology and religion of antiquity. Bultmann's contribution to theology (or rather one of his many contributions) is in the stimulus which he

[1] *Die christliche Hoffnung und das Problem der Entmythologisierung*, Evangelisches Verlagswerk, Stuttgart, 1954.

[2] A point of view which is represented by Oskar Simmel, S.J., in his essay 'Myth and Gospel' (*Stimmen der Zeit*, April, 1952): 'As God is the author of Holy Scripture, so He is also the guarantor of tradition.' Fr. Simmel's argument is that the so-called mythological elements in the New Testament are there because God is responsible for them, though of course He made use of human writers. Otherwise his essay contains many justifiable criticisms of Bultmann though without giving his arguments full credit.

has given to the re-examination of what these categories mean. For one of the major problems confronting the interpreter of the New Testament is how far mythological conceptions should be retained by an age which no longer accepts their presuppositions. It is clear, however, that demythologizing is not synonymous with a theological bowdlerization of the New Testament which would eliminate concepts which are found to be questionable; for this would mean the radical elimination or excision of some of the most eloquent passages in the New Testament. What has been written has been written and cannot be unwritten. It can be either passed over or interpreted as a general idea against the total context, which is not necessarily to be understood by the modern reader as it was by the people of the Apostolic age and those who consider Apostolic conceptions to be valid in their own form for all time. Even the study of the Christology of the New Testament may show that the letter killeth, whereas the spirit giveth life; for its value may be less as formal statement than as a creative guide for further understanding of the Christian faith.

The hermeneutic principle underlying Bultmann's treatment of myth in the New Testament represents an approach which differs from that adopted in this book, the argument of which is that myth is the language of religion and should be taken seriously as such. As Prof. A. W. Watts says, the Western mind has run into difficulty with religious and mythological language because it mistakes 'symbolical expressions of the inexpressible' for statements of objective truth.[1] The modern mind, of which the philosophy of logical positivism is one symptomatic expression, asks for 'objective' facts and for literal intelligibility. What we are actually confronted with is the problem of the meaning of language, which is a problem not only for philosophy and religion but also for the understanding of poetry and indeed of all art. There is therefore a need to approach the question of mythological thinking (which is to be distinguished from pure mythology) from the standpoint of language and theological semantics, for until we know what the 'myth' is saying and what is the significance behind the formal language we cannot easily penetrate to its ultimate religious content and meaning. Regarding this matter of

[1] *The Supreme Identity*, p. 133 (Faber, 1949).

language, I should refer especially to two important books by Professor Wilbur M. Urban of Yale, *Language and Reality* and *Humanity and Deity*, which have contributed invaluably to the discussion of the significance of myth and symbol as forms of statement and represent a point of view completely opposed to that of logical positivism; to the collective work, originally published in the United States as *The Intellectual Adventure of Ancient Man*, by members of the Oriental Institute of Chicago University; and to the very different work of Prof. A. W. Watts, formerly of the North Western University and now of the American Academy of Asian Culture, San Francisco, whose *Myth and Ritual in Christianity* is a valuable reminder of the significance of symbols and archetypal images in the presentation of the Christian *Heilsgeschichte*. Ernst Cassirer's great work, *The Philosophy of Symbolic Forms*, the first volume of which is concerned with language as symbolism and the second (as yet untranslated into English) with mythological thinking, should also be mentioned as an indispensable contribution to the study of the nature and significance of symbolism and myth.

I have written this book because I feel the need for a full examination of the 'mythological' character of much of orthodox and biblical Christology and to reckon with the very important issues for Christian thinking with which Bultmann has confronted both the preacher and the theologian. Apart from the essays published in the two volumes of *Kerygma und Mythos* and a considerable number of other articles and smaller books in German, the most substantial treatment of Bultmann's theology as a whole and of the problem of demythologizing as raised by Bultmann known to me is *Le Message Chrétien et le Mythe*, by L. Malevez, S.J.,[1] which deals with his position from the standpoint of a critique of existentialism and also with the straightforward problem of demything. Written by a Jesuit, its aim is to show that Bultmann has not been able to shake the traditional theology of Incarnation. There have, further, appeared a number of brief treatments of the subject in English of which the following publications in Britain and the United States might be mentioned: Ian Henderson: ·

---

[1] *Le Message Chrétien et le Mythe: La Théologie de Rudolf Bultmann*, Desclée de Brouwer, Bruxelles-Bruges, 1954.

14

Myth in the New Testament (1952); 'Karl Jaspers and Demythologizing' (*Expository Times*, June, 1954); 'Christology and History' (*Expository Times*, Sept., 1954); J. S. Bezzant: 'Demythologizing the Gospel' (*Theology*, June, 1954); R.W. Hepburn: 'Demythologizing—the Problem of Validity' (*Theology*, Nov., 1954); Alan Barr: 'Bultmann's Estimate of Jesus' (*Scottish Journal of Theology*, Dec., 1954); R. Leaney: 'Mythology and Incarnation' (*Church Quarterly Review*, no. 318, 1955); A. N. Wilder: 'Mythology and the New Testament' (*Journal of Biblical Literature*, LXIX, 1950); Kendrick Grobel: 'Bultmann's Problem of New Testament Mythology' (ibid., LXX, 1951); Erich Dinkler: 'Existential Interpretation of the New Testament' (*Journal of Religion*, Chicago, April, 1952). Other references in English include Emil Brunner: *Dogmatics* II, Lutterworth Press, 1952, pp. 186 ff., 263 ff.; *The Mediator* (written long before the demything controversy but dealing with the subject of Christianity and Myth) pp. 377 ff.; and *Eternal Hope*, Lutterworth, 1954, p. 114 and elsewhere; Friedrich Gogarten, *Demythologizing and History* (S.C.M. Press, 1955, translation of *Entmythologisierung und Kirche* (Vorwerk-Verlag, Stuttgart, 1953).

The principal writings by Rudolf Bultmann to which reference is made below are: *Kerygma und Mythos* I and II (ed. H. W. Bartsch) (H. Reich, Evangelischer Verlag, Hamburg, 1948 and 1952); *Die Geschichte der Synoptischen Tradition* (Göttingen, 1931, 2nd ed.); *Theologie des Neuen Testaments*, (Tübingen, 1948–53; E. tr., *Theology of the New Testament*, S.C.M. Press, 1953); *Johannes Evangelium* (Göttingen, 1950); *Das Urchristentum* (Zürich, 1949); *Glauben und Verstehen* I (Tübingen, 1934, 2nd. ed., 1954) and II (ibid., 1952); *Jesus* (Berlin 1929); *Die christliche Hoffnung und das Problem der Entmythologisierung* (Stuttgart, 1954—discussion with G. Bornkamm and F. K. Schumann). In addition to the monographs by Prof. Ian Henderson and L. Malevez reference might be made to Prof. H. de Vos, *Nieuwe Testament en Mythe: Het Vraagstuk der Ontmythologisering* (Nijkerk, 1953) and to Dr. John Macquarrie's admirably lucid comparison of Heidegger and Bultmann, *An Existentialist Theology* (S.C.M. Press, 1955). A bibliography of chiefly German contributions to the discussion is given at the end of *Kerygma and Myth* (tr. R. H. Fuller, S.P.C.K., 1953).

In addition to monographs on various aspects of the subject of myth and mythology there are very adequate surveys of the subject as a whole in Hastings' *Encyclopædia of Religion and Ethics* (IX, pp. 117 ff., E. A. Gardner, art. 'Myth'); the *Encyclopedia Britannica* (Andrew Lang, art. 'Mythology'); *Die Religion in Geschichte und Gegenwart*[1] (1913), IV, 618-632 (Gressmann and Gunkel); *RGG*[2] (1930), IV, 364-394 (Tillich, Rühle, Gunkel, and Bultmann). G. Stählin, in his immensely erudite contribution to Kittel's *Theologisches Wörterbuch zum Neuen Testament* (1942), IV, pp. 769-803 (especially pp. 788 ff.), denies that the general conception of myth can be applied to New Testament thought, except perhaps analogically.

The origin and early history of the concept of myth and its application to biblical studies in the work of C. G. Heyne (1729–1812), J. G. Eichhorn (1752–1827), G. L. Bauer (1755–1806) and their Hegelian followers has been thoroughly investigated by Christian Hartlich and Walter Sachs, *Der Ursprung des Mythosbegriffes in der modernen Bibelwissenschaft* (Tübingen, 1952).

ACKNOWLEDGEMENTS

I am grateful to Professor Ian Henderson, D.D., and to Professor G. H. C. Macgregor, D.D., D.Litt., of the University of Glasgow, for their encouragement and for reading much of this book while it was being written; to my friend Mr. Idris W. Phillips, M.A., also of Glasgow University, for kindly relieving me of the onerous though necessary task of preparing the index; to Mr. G. F. Skinner for his assistance, and to the publishers' readers for their helpful suggestions.

Glasgow, January 1956

CONTENTS

B

PART ONE

PROLEGOMENA

SUMMARY OF ARGUMENT

One of the problems confronting theology is that of the validity of New Testament language and ideas and their relevance to modern ways of thinking. In Bultmann's view they are largely 'mythological'. Because of this they must be demythologized in terms of existentialism.

Our problem has not to do with the New Testament as a whole but with its Christology, the language of which, it will be seen, is mythological. Modern man, however, is not wholly reluctant to use symbolic modes of expression in art and literature, nor is he averse from pseudo-myths as expressions of ideologies. An example of the mythological element in Christology is the conception of pre-existence, which is assumed by Paul, John, and the author of Hebrews. Paul's cosmology is that of the Hellenistic world. What is to be done with these conceptions? Bultmann recommends not their elimination but their existentialist interpretation.

Bound up with Bultmann's attitude to the problem is his view of the 'historical' and the 'historic', the distinction between which, together with his analysis of existence, owes much to Heidegger. On Bultmann's premises no appeal can be made to the 'Jesus of history' from the 'mythical' Christology because of his rejection of the Gospels as a source of 'historical' knowledge, and in any case such knowledge does not possess existential value. It makes no continuing impact on man as does the 'historic' (*geschichtlich*). Bultmann does not share the Liberals' interest in the 'historical' Jesus. We do not accept this critical attitude as justified, and claim that the Synoptic Jesus may be appealed to as a corrective of the 'mythical' Christology of the Epistles.

CHAPTER ONE

MYTH AND GOSPEL

I

One of the problems with which theology is faced is that of the choice of satisfactory terms in which an adequate conception of the Person of Christ can be expressed, and in such a manner that it is acceptable to the modern man whose thinking is conditioned by science and who finds both the world of thought of the Bible and that of Patristic and orthodox Christology inconsistent with what he knows about man and his world. Contemporary man is not only remote from the world of Jewish eschatology and apocalyptic and the Hellenistic background of the New Testament with its unfamiliar presuppositions: he is completely outside it. Either the mythological material in the New Testament, he may argue, should be eliminated, though how this is to be done short of textual expurgation it is not easy to see; or it should be reinterpreted. If the latter alternative is preferred, how is the mythological thought-world of the New Testament to be understood? How much of it should be allowed to remain? What is to be the extent of the demything, and what principle is to guide it? What is the essential meaning of the New Testament language? What lies behind the myth? How far are we committed to accepting the New Testament world of ideas in its completeness as it stands?

These are questions which clamour for answers.

2

In his essay[1] entitled 'New Testament and Mythology' Professor Rudolf Bultmann, setting in motion a wide-ranging and profound

[1] The essay, written in 1941, was reprinted, together with criticisms of it, in *Kerygma und Mythos* (H. Reich, Evangelischer Verlag, Hamburg, 1948), and translated, with some of these criticisms and Bultmann's answers, in *Kerygma and Myth* (S.P.C.K., 1952). *Kerygma und Mythos*, II, followed in 1952. In my quotations from the essay I have sometimes made my own translation and sometimes used the English version.

controversy among continental theologians, stated the issue involved in the demything of the New Testament so trenchantly and penetratingly that theology cannot afford not to take account of the realism with which he stated his thesis. Although we are primarily concerned with Christology and Bultmann's essay deals with it only in passing, the issues raised are so wide that not only the whole of the *kerygma* but the greater part of the New Testament theological idiom is faced with the necessity of re-examination, and some realization of the broader implications of Bultmann's contention is required if the Christological problem is to be appreciated in its fullest perspective.

Although Bultmann approaches the question of demythologizing from the standpoint of the existentialist philosophy, this philosophy is not a necessary nor is it the sole instrument; indeed, so to interpret it is to tie the New Testament down to a philosophical idiom which may be superseded, and the assumption that 'modern man' thinks existentially is valid only in so far as it applies to those who are influenced by the thinking of Kierkegaard, Heidegger and their followers. Existentialism is a recent phase of modern thought, though it is not without its progenitors, and to accommodate the New Testament to it or to regard it as *the* interpretation of the New Testament and thereby to associate the latter with a particular philosophy is no more justifiable, though no less permissible, than was the close association of Christian theology with the Idealism of the nineteenth century which has so frequently been opposed by the dialectical theologians and by Bultmann himself. Indeed, one of the more questionable assertions in Bultmann's essay is that Heidegger's 'existentialist analysis of the structure of being appears to be no more than a secularized philosophical exposition of the New Testament conception of human life': and that the philosophers are saying the same thing as the New Testament and are doing so quite independently.[1]

---

[1] *Kerygma und Mythos*, I, p. 35 (E. trans. pp. 24–25). It is rather strange that many of Bultmann's critics, in their search for subtle and complicated criticisms of his thesis, appear to have overlooked the fact that demythologizing in terms of existentialism is virtually the abandonment of the mythology. Prof. Regin Prenter (*Kerygma und Mythos*, II, p. 70) is one of the few who have realized this. He states that Bultmann wishes to have the best of both worlds: he wishes to 'retain' the mythology, though if it contains a world-picture which is obsolete it is incredible to those who

The New Testament representations of the fact of salvation, in Bultmann's view, are inseparable from the mythical world-picture with its eschatology, apocalyptic, demonology, and three-decker universe, sacramentalism, Resurrection, and ideas of pre-existence: most of which are bound up with Jewish apocalyptic and, in Bultmann's judgment, with the Gnostic redemption myths. Such a mythical world-view, however, is not without value, for

it is quite possible that truth of which sight had been lost in a period of enlightenment can be rediscovered in an obsolete

do not share it. If the mythological representation of the world *is* outmoded, then it cannot be interpreted and in this case the mythology must be excluded. Or: it is to be interpreted, in which case it is not demythed, for, as Prenter points out, any interpretation implies the retention of the essential content of the mythology. See also Lohmeyer (*Kerygma und Mythos*, I) who makes a similar point. 'The literal meaning (of demythologization) . . . is the removal of the inappropriate mythical clothing with the false objectivity of its cosmic imagery—which means the abolition of the myth.' Elsewhere, Lohmeyer points out, the term has a somewhat different meaning: the *interpretation* of the myth, which means its retention. Prenter, too (ibid., p. 70), disagrees with Bultmann's statement that the interpretation of the mythology in terms of existentialist philosophy corresponds to the New Testament picture of God and man. Indeed, he continues, existentialist philosophies such as Jaspers' and Heidegger's are essentially 'secularizations', for human existence cannot be understood apart from the 'Christian event'. Hence to describe Heidegger's philosophy as a 'secularized version' of the New Testament is a self-contradiction, because the latter cannot be secularized. Further, Prenter is of the opinion that the choice is between a genuinely atheistic philosophy and a genuine Christian one; any compromise is neither one thing nor another. Fritz Bruin, however (ibid., pp. 85 ff.), is inclined to agree that the equation of existential *Seinsverständnis* with *Selbstverständnis* is a point of contact between the Christian faith and secular philosophy. Principal Vernon Lewis considers that existentialism is simply a means of escape for Bultmann from the New Testament mythology (*Diwinyddiaeth a Phregethu Heddiw* [*Contemporary Theology and Preaching*], 1954, p. 27). W. G. Kümmel, in a penetrating essay, holds that 'it is not the antique picture of the world but rather the *Heilsgeschichte* proclaimed in mythological language which constitutes the centre of the New Testament message, and this cannot be eliminated' (*Kerygma und Mythos*, II, p. 160). It is significant that the most outspoken defence of Bultmann comes not from an academic theologian but from a minister, Götz Harbsmeier, who is concerned with the practical task of preaching the Gospel in terms intelligible to a modern congregation. 'It is not so much that Bultmann demythologizes,' he says, 'as that we, as a matter of fact, and despite all pseudomyths and all attempts to bring them back to life, are living in a demythologizing age. . . . The modern man, if he is consistent, just *has* no access to the *kerygma* along the road of mythology' (*Kerygma und Mythos*, I, p. 62). It is strange that this essay in support of Bultmann should have been omitted from the English volume *Kerygma and Myth*, whereas the opponents of Bultmann are given full publicity.

The essays of Julius Schniewind and H. Thielicke are especially important, as are Bultmann's reply to the former and his final reply to the series. Thielicke, by the way, is right in saying that in adopting Heidegger's conception of understanding Bultmann is surrendering to the sovereignty of an intellectual world-view. Hermann Sauter (*Kerygma und Mythos*, I, p. 275) rightly points out that an existentialist interpretation is secondary to the problem of demything.

mythical view of the world, and it is the task of theology to examine this question in relation to the New Testament outlook. It is, however, impossible to rejuvenate an obsolete view of the world simply by desiring to do so, and it is above all impossible to revive it when all our thinking has been irreversibly formed by science.[1]

Only that kind of New Testament criticism can be relevant which grows naturally out of the situation of the man of today: the chief constituent of which Bultmann considers to be the existential factor of decision. Much of the object of the modern man's criticism was already disputed during the days of the liberal theology; indeed, to English liberal theologians there is little that is new in Bultmann's thesis if its existentialist context is excepted.[2] Where Bultmann would differ from Liberalism, it is said, is in his desire for the reinterpretation rather than the abandonment of the mythical categories, though this difference is by no means as great as he might be inclined to believe, for he agrees with the Liberals about their obsoleteness and inadequacy.[3] Bultmann considers, however, that earlier attempts to demyth, such as an allegorical interpretation, the liberal distinction between the 'kernel' and the 'husk' (Harnack), and the religious-historical method of finding a kind of 'essence' in mysticism, are inadequate because they fail to take account of the impact of myth on man's existential situation, for myth is not intended to provide an objectively accurate picture of the world but is something which evokes man's response to his situation in his own world. It also purports to show that the historical scene does not find its ground and purpose in itself but outside the known and the calculable.[4] The *form* of the *kerygma* is wholly mythical in its conception of the manner in which the historical is grounded in the supra-historical, for the redemptive act which gives meaning to history proceeds

---

[1] *Kerygma und Mythos*, I, p. 17.

[2] Cf. Nathaniel Micklem's essay in *Mysterium Christi*.

[3] J. Vernon Lewis, however, holds that Bultmann is a 'link between Liberalism and Orthodoxy', and that it is this paradox which often makes him so difficult to understand. On the one hand he is, as a form-critic, a thoroughgoing Liberal; on the other, as an interpreter of scripture he is, as an evangelical Lutheran, in the conservative tradition (op. cit., p. 16). Bultmann's separation of the faith from its foundation in the 'Jesus of History' is also a sign of his departure from liberalism.

[4] Ibid., p. 23.

from beyond history and is inevitably expressed in terms of myth.

As has been indicated, Bultmann is concerned with the problem as a whole rather than in the first place with the specific subject of Christology, though this is naturally included. The Christology of pre-existence and of the thought-world influenced by Jewish apocalyptic, he claims, is so 'mythical' as to have no apparent relevance to man's existential situation. But what of the starting-point of all Christology, the Resurrection? Is this myth or history? Bultmann considers that this is not a strictly 'historical' event, though it occurs on the historical plane. It is primarily eschatological and has acquired, or inherently possesses, a 'cosmic' significance which cannot be predicated of a 'historical' event. It is not, for Bultmann, an evidential miracle, for it is primarily 'mythological'. It is the object of faith rather than a historical attestation to it. Hence Bultmann's remarkable statement that the Christian Easter-faith is not interested in the historical question, and that the disciples' Easter-faith is not a *fact* in which we believe simply in so far as it relieves us of the element of hazard which belief in the Resurrection contains, for the belief itself is part of the eschatological event which is the object of faith.[1] The word of proclamation, the *kerygma* itself, belongs to the eschatological message of salvation, not to historical pronouncement.

Now whether it is agreed or not that the New Testament requires such radical demything as will make it intelligible or acceptable to the modern man, there is justice in Cullmann's statement that Bultmann's demand for the removal of the entire mythology would be more consistent than a demand for the removal of the eschatology.[2] It is, moreover, possible to speak of 'redemptive' history without introducing the mythological conceptions of the world of thought which lies behind the term 'eschatology' as it is generally understood. Bultmann may be

---

[1] 'Der christliche Osterglaube ist an der historischen Frage nicht interessiert . . . Der Osterglaube der ersten Jünger is also *nicht* ein Faktum, auf das wir glauben, in so fern es uns das Wagnis des Osterglaubens abnehmen könnte, sondern ihr Osterglaube gehört selbst zu dem eschatologischen Geschehen, das der Gegenstand des Glaubens ist' (ibid., p. 51).

[2] O. Cullmann, *Christ and Time* (E. trans.), p. 31. Actually, however, Bultmann does not demand the removal of the mythology but its reinterpretation.

right or wrong in maintaining that the mythical world-view cannot be patched up or dealt with by selecting what appears to be
credible, but must be accepted or rejected as a whole; it may well
be, also, that the Christian proclamation cannot be adequately
made without the use of myth. What is much more important
is to decide whether the concept of redemption can be understood without reference to its mythical-biblical antecedents,
and how far (as Bultmann suggests) it is the task of theology
to make this plain; for 'redemption' is a present experience,
indeed, an 'existential' one in that it involves the response
of the whole personality to the divine demand for decision, and
this without any association with an 'eschatological' conception
of fulfilment.

Stimulating though it is, Bultmann's argument for demything
is complicated and frequently touches matters such as the
concepts of sin, spirit, and sacraments, which would not usually
be considered as belonging to the sphere of mythological thinking:
possibly because he has not drawn a clear distinction between
myth, symbol, and metaphor, and in any case he is inclined to
regard as 'myth' anything belonging to a cultus. It may be claimed
for the sacraments that they are representational rather than
mythical, that they are signs and symbols rather than the expression of mythological thinking, though if conceived of in
certain ways they may become mythological; in any case myth
and symbol are not unrelated. Bultmann includes in his conception of mythological thinking whatever interprets the other-
worldly and the divine as this-worldly and human, that which
lies beyond this world as *of* it and translates divine transcendence
into terms of spatial distance. This covers a great deal, but in its
more limited application comprises such ideas as the God-Man,
the pre-existent Word, the demon-world as the temporal manifestation of a world peopled by invisible intelligences. It includes
miracle, Resurrection from the dead, and the Parousia; it is the
theological objectification of the conceptually abstract. Considered from this point of view myth is a quasi-historical representation of the ultra-historical, the translation of what is more
than human into humanly intelligible terms. It is the form of
the divine call making itself intelligible not to rational thinking

but through 'existential self-understanding'. Indeed, Bultmann tends to emphasize excessively this latter constituent of man's awareness of his situation, for the substance of the Gospel is not so much the summons to man's 'self-understanding' as the proclamation of the Lordship of Jesus Christ. The Gospel may have its 'existential' aspect, but it would be unwise to over-emphasize it, though there is truth in Bultmann's assertion that the words of Jesus 'confront us as questions about the way in which we understand our existence'.[1]

Bultmann's contention, however, is in the main just: 'modern' man does not, on the whole, think mythologically. That he is not unreluctant to accept certain kinds of 'mythical' ideologies does not mean that he welcomes myth as such, though the temporary popularity of the Führer-principle and the acceptance by large numbers of people of pseudo- or quasi-myths such as Rosenberg's Myth of the Twentieth Century and the myth of the Proletarian Man shows how far people will go in this direction. These, however, are not myths in the religious sense of the word or as primitive mythology is understood, but rather the pseudo-historical clothing or emotional objectification of political ideas. The 'myth' here results from the apotheosis of the nation or the Proletarian Man until it acquires a numinous aura which is developed in the interests of some particular doctrine. These so-called modern 'myths' are really the emotional representation of political or social ideas which without them would have been too abstract to obtain popular support. Although their purpose is similar to that of the religious myth—to propagate and maintain by pictorial symbolism notions which require for general acceptance something more forceful and memorable than mere propositional statement—they differ from it in that, whereas the religious myth so to speak works downward from the divine to the human, they begin with the human and invest it with a kind of religious authority. In the case of National Socialism the myth was given even more concrete representation by the elaboration of peculiar ritualistic ideas and the introduction of ritualistic symbolism, examples of which were the display of bloodstained swastika-flags at public parades and the almost ritualistic reverence paid

[1] *Jesus*, p. 15.

to the pseudo-martyr Horst Wessel. The starting-points, however, are different, and care should therefore be exercised in drawing comparisons between a political mythopoeia and the clothing of what might otherwise be abstract religious concepts in pictorial, spatial, or temporal form. Hermann Sasse has pointed out in his discussion of the Hellenistic attitude towards the Resurrection[1] that the objection was not to the resurrection of a *mythical* or cultic figure but to that of a historical person, and that myth as such was not disapproved of. It is not dissimilar with contemporary man, who will accept the mythological fictions of political emotionalism, but, like the Greeks in the Epistle to the Corinthians, considers the Cross, that is, belief in the resurrection of a historical person, to be foolishness.

While, then, it may be maintained that modern man does not think mythologically, it may be also contended that he cannot dispense with that kind of thought which can be covered by the terms symbol and myth. While these are by no means identical, they are both examples of the process of translating what cannot be stated precisely into proximate terms designed to express what is ultimate. The tension begins when it has to be decided how far an idea is to be understood symbolically and how far literally, for, as Prof. W. M. Urban has said, just what the literal *is* becomes one of the fundamental as it is also one of the most difficult of problems.[2] A mythical understanding of an alleged truth is useless without literal knowledge; but it may be questioned whether in religious affirmations with a historical content the 'historical' can be fully understood apart from the mythical method of indicating its significance. The story of Christ's Passion, for example, can be recounted more or less dispassionately as in John 18 or in a biography of Jesus which strives to be objective; but is the 'history', which is a religious history, really intelligible without the 'mythological' conception of the 'Word' becoming 'Flesh'? Certain it is that the mythological element in Christian theology can no more be transplanted into the language of science than can the artistic impulse, for it belongs to a different universe of discourse. If the conception of God cannot be given

[1] In *Mysterium Christi*, pp. 100–101.
[2] W. M. Urban, *Humanity and Deity*, 1951, p. 220.

meaning without the proximate analogy which is in the last resort symbolical, it may be that the whole complex of ideas which belongs to the realm of His dominion is equally incommunicable in any intelligible form without some degree of mythological representation. It is doubtful, for example, whether anyone actually believed that Jesus was literally seated at the right hand of God, though what is meant by the picture is clear enough.

It is not possible, moreover, to make statements about God which are literally wholly satisfactory. Any moral qualities predicated of God are conceivable only in terms of human experience, for what we mean when we say that 'God is love' is that we are imagining what God would be like if His relations with man were to be defined in terms of human affection, though 'love' may mean to God something very different from what it means to man. The 'wrath of God' may be analogous to human anger, but if it were the same, it would be human and not divine wrath. When we speak of God's 'infinite' goodness, whatever meaning the word 'infinite' may possess, it is different from what the mathematician means when he employs the term. But without some *analogia entis* the word 'God' has little meaning. As the Wholly Other, God can only be thought of, if at all, as the complete negative of all human concepts. The conclusion of apophatic theology that God cannot be named, meaning that He is a term which cannot be filled with intelligible content, is of no help to any religion. God as Absolute Being may, no doubt, exist in the purely noumenal sense, but He cannot be known; and any terms applied to Him are to some extent mythological or symbolical. 'Father' is an anthropomorphic symbol of a divine attribute; but the Fatherhood of God has little relation to the human notion of Fatherhood, with its implications of procreation, marital felicity, and the obligation to be a wage-earner. The symbol 'Father' has an anagogic function in that it points upward from the familiar to the unfamiliar, from the finite to the infinite, to a characteristic of God which is removed from its human analogy but which nevertheless can be understood only in terms with which man is already familiar. Myth and symbol are ultimately anthropomorphic ways of conceiving what is immeasurably greater than human knowledge can embrace, but which will remain purely conceptual apart from its reduction to some concrete form.

Indeed, the modern man's objection to myth as a vehicle of religious truth is due more often than not to what W. M. Urban, adapting a phrase of A. N. Whitehead's, calls the 'fallacy of misplaced literalism' which may in itself be a form of pedantry if what is demanded is exactitude in a sphere to which it does not belong. The problem for New Testament theology, however, begins at the point at which we enquire whether a certain mythical way of thinking is necessary or adequate, and here a distinction should be drawn between a legend-myth and a metaphysical myth. In the former category should be included the legends of the Tower of Babel and those of classical mythology: myths about either unreal people or fictitious events which are constructed as fictions to explain some natural phenomenon such as race or language. These are legend-myths in so far as they are narratives devised wholly by the imagination. The stories of the Voluspa or the Mabinogion, too, are in this sense mythological, and as narratives are satisfying without being understood in any aetio-logical sense. They are not designed with a view to providing some representation of ultimate truth, and do not set out to describe the structure of reality. Whether they are literally true or not is of no more account than whether *King Lear* or *Peer Gynt* is literally true. Literal truth does not enter into any considera-tion of them, and to dispute their historical accuracy would be pedantry.

By a metaphysical myth, on the other hand, I mean a supra-historical explanation in mythical terms of an event which is part of known history, the immediately relevant instance of which being the mythical form in which New Testament Christology is clothed. It belongs not to folklore transformed into literature nor to the conception of a fictitious pantheon but to the process of giving transcendent meaning to a historical occurrence of decisive significance. The Synoptic Gospels provide insufficient evidence for the belief that Jesus' contemporaries regarded him as the earthly manifestation of a divine being; and in any case the Gospel story is not a fictitious legend but a fragment of history.

Jesus was not thought of in the Synoptic Gospels as were Paul and Barnabas at Lystra.[1] The rest of the New Testament, however, including the Fourth Gospel, offers an explanation of the history in terms which are usually supra-historical; hence St. Paul's 'myth' of the pre-existent cosmic Son of God and the birth stories of Matthew and Luke, the most completely mythologized Christology being that of the Book of Revelation, for the picture presented there contains no suggestions of Jesus as a historical figure. He has become completely obscured by the symbol, and for St. John of Patmos the Jesus of history has dissolved into an apocalyptic myth.

Now, what is at issue is, on the one hand, whether a Christology arising out of mythological thinking is a necessary explanation of the history, or, on the other, whether this mythological way of thinking reflected what, for the thinker, was believed to be literally true, even though it was beyond verification; whether, for example, the great Christological passages in Ephesians, Colossians, and Philippians were intended as pictures or as statements about the pre-existent Christ, the agent of creation and the consummation of history; whether they were to be literally or symbolically understood. It is not known if Paul intended completely to apotheosize Jesus: all that can be said with certainty is that he used the highest conceivable categories consistent with monotheism in order to make clear what he believed about the status of Jesus in the universe as one who 'reigned' with God the Father. Nevertheless, it is apparent that St. Paul shared the contemporary world-view with its belief in angels, discarnate intelligences, hierarchies of Powers, the things 'above' and the things 'below': a world-view which was derived not only from Judaism of the late Hellenistic age but also from the curious complex of beliefs associated with various forms of Gnosticism and near-eastern angelology. It is not improbable that he regarded the exalted Christ as occupying an appropriate place in this strange cosmological picture; there is, however, no more obligation on the modern Christian to accept his Christology than the

---

[1] ' "The gods are come down to us in the likeness of men"; and they called Barnabas Jupiter and Paul Mercury because he was the chief speaker.' (Acts 14: 11. Cf. Acts 12: 22: 'And the people gave a shout, saying, "It is the voice of a god, and not of a man".')

cosmology to which it belonged. As Bultmann has said, we no longer require such a conception, though we need to retain Paul's 'Christological intention'.[1] Yet for the Apostle Jesus did not belong to the world of occult mythology: he was a historical person who had been crucified in circumstances to which there were contemporary witnesses, though what for Paul may have only been a speculation in mythological form as to the ultimate significance and nature of Jesus and his place in the providence of God came, through a particular view of biblical inspiration, to present literal truth. So, later, did the two-natures doctrine, in its classical form, become normative for subsequent theology. Yet however bold and far-ranging Paul's Christological speculation may be thought to be, such mythological thinking as it suggests is rooted in history. In so far as it represents an attempt to provide a rational interpretation of his own experience and of the presence and work of Christ in the church, it shows that St. Paul reasoned inductively from the empirical to the 'mythical' prolegomenon. He did not begin with the myth and deduce the 'historical' from it. The 'myth' was subsequent to the history.

Whether the Christological terms of the New Testament are to be understood as literally intended or figuratively, then, it is clear that they are foreign to a modern mode of thinking; for what is meant, apparently, in the relevant New Testament passages is the actual pre-existence of the Son of God (or Logos) who became man as Jesus Christ. The Johannine statements clearly imply, as do those of St. Paul, the direct continuity of the historical Jesus with the pre-existent Son and co-creator.

With such conceptions there are two ways of dealing: they can be rejected as incapable of verification and therefore as purely speculative and as not necessary presuppositions of faith, or, apart from their literal truth or untruth, they can be interpreted in such a way that they are seen to represent something of basic value, even though we are no more committed to them than we are, for example, to St. Paul's eschatology or his views about the place of women in the church. The problem, however, is part of a wider one: that of the modern relevance of the New Testament terminology as a whole, and whether it should be reinterpreted

---

[1] *Glauben und Verstehen*, I, p. 263.

merely because it is an inherited part of the Christian tradition, that is, whether something has to be done about it just because it is there. Most of the biblical terms have little place in the moral experience of the modern man who has not only broken away from the mythical archetypes of faith but also finds that the traditional biblical mode of thought is increasingly difficult to accept.

It would, however, be false to assume either that the world of myth or symbol is wholly alien to the modern man or that the symbolical and mythical manner of thinking can be dispensed with, for religious beliefs cannot effectively be expressed merely as bare concepts. As Berdyaev has said:

> myth is a reality immeasurably greater than concept . . . Myth is always concrete and expresses life better than can abstract thought . . . Myth presents to us the super-natural in the natural, the super-sensible in the sensible, the spiritual life in the life of the flesh . . . It is high time to cease being ashamed of Christian mythology and trying to free it from myth.[1]

Myths alone are able to explain life, which is always 'inexhaustible and unfathomable', and dogma

> symbolizes spiritual experiences and life by mythological re-presentations and not by concepts.[2]

Myth and symbol are closely allied and are necessary expressions of religious truth.

Religion, moreover, is not the only sphere to which symbol and myth are applicable. Poetry, for example, unless it is wholly descriptive or didactic, belongs essentially to the world of symbol; indeed, it is *modern* poetry, as exemplified in Mallarmé, Stefan George, R. M. Rilke, and others, to which the name 'symbolism' has been given; and the work of continental novelists such as Thomas Mann and Kafka is not fully intelligible apart from its symbolism.[3] Only the defunct naturalism of the turn of the century can be described as non-symbolical, if such a term can

[1] *Freedom and the Spirit*, pp. 70, 71.
[2] Ibid., p. 76. Berdyaev deals at length with this matter in the chapter entitled "Symbol, Myth, and Dogma".
[3] Cf. C. M. Bowra, *The Heritage of Symbolism*, 1943. Mann's world of fiction is very complex, especially as shown in *The Magic Mountain* and the *Joseph* tetralogy, where

at all be applied to art; and naturalism is in art what literalism is in religion.

Science, too, is accustomed to a certain kind of symbolic thought.[1] It cannot, for example, provide us with literal truth about infinity or the curvature of space or the principle of indeterminacy, for infinity is not a notion which can be intellectually grasped, and indeterminacy does not mean the same in the human world as in that of atomic physics. 'Waves' is an analogous term;[2] even such a term as 'libido' or 'subconscious' or *Gestalt* are symbols, for these are not empirically measurable. Formulae, too, are symbols, not literal representations. Science makes use of symbols, though they are necessarily different from the symbols of religion. Where they differ from them is in their reference to something measurable, whereas religious symbols, it is claimed by the non-religious, do not mean anything at all. Yet to those who believe in the validity of religious truth symbols or analogies have to be used if theological concepts are to be made intelligible, just as they are required for the purpose of interpreting scientific concepts to the lay mind. The question would appear to be less one of discarding symbol and myth than of deciding within which sphere they are relevant and to what extent, though it may be contended that they should be employed sparingly lest the historical should evaporate into a baroque world of sheer fantasy in which history is confused with myth, as in the mythological dogmas of the Roman Catholic Church which state as historical facts what are, to non-Catholics, manifestly mythological fictions. Here there is no clear idea of what history and mythology are; dogma is divorced from history and affirms as an object of faith what is often imaginary. Dogmas such as the Immaculate Conception and the Assumption of the Virgin are neither based on history nor are they necessary deductions from known facts. The Roman Church is the example *par excellence* of complete

---

there are two levels, one of formal narrative and the other of symbolism. In the Joseph tales Mann resorts to a subtle use of psychological myth and interior symbolism. See on this point Käthe Hamburger, *Thomas Manns Roman, Joseph und seine Brüder*, Stockholm, 1945; H. Hatfield, *Thomas Mann*, 1952, pp. 52 ff., H. Slochower, *No Voice is Wholly Lost*, 1946, pp. 190–303; H. Tauber, *Franz Kafka*, 1950.

[1] See W. M. Urban, op. cit., pp. 339 ff.; A. Eddington, *The Nature of the Physical World*.

[2] C. F. von Weiszäcker, *The World View of Science*, 1953.

freedom in conferring on mythological pictures what is intended to be literal truth. On the other hand, complete rejection of mythological and symbolical thinking may mean the rejection of the transcendental as such and with it belief in revelation, so that the repudiation of all but literalism may be so radical that what remains can hardly be recognizable as Christianity.

Symbolism, then, is inseparable from some forms of the working of the creative imagination. A work of art may be wholly symbolical on a deeper level though wholly satisfactory on the level of aesthetic appeal without reference to the truth or otherwise of the symbolism behind it. Yet though belonging to the same world as myth, in so far as it is representational and not to be understood 'literally', it differs from it, chiefly, as Brunner has pointed out, in being static, whereas the characteristic of myth is movement;[1] the symbol is 'myth without movement'. 'Symbolism in the conception of God makes Him visible in space; the myth makes Him visible in time.' The difference is not unimportant, though it should not be pressed too far. Myth is dynamic symbolism. Prometheus, a mythological figure, may also be the symbol of man's spiritual daring. Faust was not a mythological figure, but may be regarded as the symbol of Western man to whom Spengler gave the name 'Faustian'. The Cross is a symbol, but it is more than a symbol; and whereas for the Christian it represents the historical events of the Crucifixion and Resurrection of Jesus, to the rationalist who does not believe in the Christian history, or treats it merely as history, it may be no more than the symbol of the dying and the rising of a mythical son of an imaginary deity.

A symbol points to something beyond itself, to some event or principle; the myth is an enactment in time of an event or principle whose reality is actually beyond history but which, except when it is clearly legendary, has meaning only in relation to human destiny.

3

Bultmann's contention is that the New Testament world-picture is mythical, and, because it does not permit of '*Repristinierung*'

[1] *Revelation and Reason*, p. 400.

or rejuvenation, must be accepted as a whole or completely reinterpreted. But into his conception of the mythological there enter constituents whose character is wholly secondary to the biblical representation of the story of salvation. One of them is the New Testament cosmology, which can be detached from its theological framework without any serious loss to the latter. The three-decker picture of the world is not in any way indispensable to Christian doctrine; nor is the notion of heaven and hell any more dependent on 'up' or 'down' than on 'sideways'. Heaven and hell are moral, not spatial concepts, though they must be 'somewhere', though it makes no difference to the belief in judgment or in the world to come whether these are 'up' or 'down' or on some dimension of being to which spatial terminology does not apply. The New Testament cosmology, together with its belief in the baleful influence on human life of the planetary powers, can be jettisoned without in the least jeopardizing the redemptive history which is set forth.

The world, however, in the New Testament view, is not merely a geomorphic entity but the scene (in Bultmann's words) 'of the operation of supernatural powers, of God and His angels, Satan and his demons'. Man has no full power over himself, for he can be possessed by demons, and the whole world, this 'age', is under the dominion of the Evil One.

That these are 'mythological' conceptions is true enough; Satan and angelic and demonic powers belong to the world of myth. But is it true that they have *only* mythical significance? Demoniac possession is a phenomenon of which anthropology and psychiatry have to take account, and the belief in possession is not wholly confined to primitive peoples, for many who have been familiar with evil cults as well as with individual cases of possession in Africa and India say that they have been aware of some palpable, almost material quality of evil which is more than a morbid sensitiveness to the effect on the imagination of places associated with sinister cultic rites. Not only is demoniac possession well-attested but the 'evil' character of primitive art, as for example the Maya art of Mexico and the art of the South Pacific, points to some irresistible urge to objectify in some visible form a force whose invisible reality should not be summarily

dismissed as fantasy. Although 'Satan' is a convenient mythological and personalized symbol for the universal accumulation
of evil, to set aside the notion that there are no discarnate evil
intelligences because belief in them is a form of primitive superstition is too facile a dismissal of a universal phenomenon and fails
to do justice to experience. Yet to postulate a demon-ridden
world is to set a difficult problem for a theology which rejects
dualism, though it may mean that the universe is less rational
than we prefer to believe. The 'demons' represent a reality in
human life with which God and man wage continual warfare.[1]
Whether planetary bodies and astral influences affect man's
destiny as the Hellenistic age believed or not, only the excessively
optimistic can deny that evil exercises great power over life.
That the New Testament picture of the world is naïve is indisputable; yet there may be something behind its naïveté which calls for
more than a superficial explanation. There is always the possibility,
too, that the men of the ancient world were more aware of the
existence of occult forces than are their modern descendants.

The truth of Christianity, however, is in no way bound up
with the imagined character of the world in which it arose, and
the deliverance of the Christian from evil need not be described in
such terms as are found in the great and disturbing final chapter
of the Epistle to the Ephesians with its picture of man oppressed by
fear of evil cosmic intelligences, the 'cosmocrats' of the darkness.

Now, it can be contended that where mythological conceptions
are found as a background to New Testament Christology—
conceptions such as Son of Man, Messiah, Eschatology—these
are already on the way to being deprived of much of their
'mythical' content by the historical character of the mission of
Jesus, and that an allegedly 'mythical' event such as the Resurrection, despite the possibly legendary accretions of the Gospel
narrative, belongs not to the realm of the mythical but to that of
the historical because of its continuity with the 'historical' life of
Jesus. It is not a myth but a decisive historical factor; it is

---

[1] Even so lucid and unromantic a writer as Mr. Charles Morgan declines to dis-
miss the belief in Satan as superstition (Preface, 'On Power over Nature', *The
Burning Glass*, pp. vii–ix, 1953) and quotes with approval the views of Professor
Butterfield on this matter.

historisch as well as *geschichtlich* or eschatological. Moreover, if myth is what is essentially non-historical rather than merely pictorical, the mythical element in the New Testament is by no means as obtrusive as has been represented. Nevertheless, the New Testament world-picture differs radically from that which is described by the physical sciences, though there may be psychic depths in it which elude description in terms of observable law. The differences, however, are of secondary not primary importance, for it does not matter whether epilepsy is of demoniac or of physiological origin, whether Jesus 'ascended' or disappeared laterally or merely ceased to appear. These touch the heart neither of the Christian revelation nor of the Christological problem, nor do they in any way affect the 'existential' impact of Jesus upon the life of the individual.

Further, we have shown that modern man is not reluctant to retain symbolism as such, whether in science or in art, for it is the language of both, and even in order to make atomic or crystalline structure understandable to the lay mind it is necessary to transpose micro- or megalospatial relations into some pictorial form. And if symbol is but a static form of myth, the transition from the one to the other does not require an intellectual revolution. The obstacle in the way of the modern man's belief is not in the first place the allegedly 'mythical' expression of the Christian revelation (though he finds such expression difficult of acceptance), but the credibility of the revelation itself. There is no evidence that the Liberal's partial or the Modernist's almost complete abandonment of what is unacceptable to the 'modern mind' has been more fruitful of results than the orthodox insistence on what has been rejected. Indeed, non-credal, non-dogmatic, non-mythical forms of Christianity have not proved conspicuously successful in attracting the man of scientific temper to whom all claims made on behalf of a religion of revelation, or any faith which cannot be supported by purely empirical tests, are equally illusory. In his view the only permissible kind of demythologizing is the dissolution of both myth and substance.[1]

[1] Julian Huxley's *Religion Without Revelation* (1927) is an admirable example of this radical humanistic demything, which is virtually the dissolution of religion into a vague sense of sacredness without content or doctrinal substance. The symbols and the doctrine are reinterpreted and demythed out of existence.

It should be stated, too, that, while the purpose of demythologizing, in Bultmann's words, is to try 'to make comprehensible biblical truth which has become incomprehensible in mythological garments' and 'to make the Gospel comprehensible as a call addressed to us, and not for our rational thinking but for existential self-understanding',[1] Bultmann's conception of myth is somewhat sweeping, as is his opposition of 'self-understanding' and rational thinking; for the purpose of theology is to interpret and elucidate religion rationally. Is the statement that 'God so loved the world that He gave His only-begotten Son' an assertion in mythological form? The more succinct Johannine statement that 'God is Love' is a bare affirmation. That God 'gave His only-begotten Son' may, to Bultmann's way of thinking, be 'mythological', for it describes in human, this-wordly terms an action which is ultra-human, and the concepts of the 'Son' of God and the 'only-begotten,' Μονογενής, are familiar to the 'mythical' cults and religions of the Hellenistic age. Yet it is through the first statement that the second is understood: the love of God is made apprehensible, is seen to be operative in history, through the 'giving' of His 'only-begotten', for that is the meaning of the mission of Jesus and of his humiliation on the cross. Without the historical instance of what is 'mythologically' described the assertion that 'God is Love' is imperfectly understood. In other words, we cannot avoid asking what kind of demythologizing, if any, is necessary, in order to illuminate and elucidate this fundamental Christian affirmation.

[1] *The Listener*, Feb. 5th, 1953, p. 217.

CHAPTER TWO

HISTORY, *GESCHICHTE*, AND MYTH

I

So far Bultmann's contention for the demythologizing of the New Testament has been outlined, and there have been added some general considerations in support of it and in criticism of it. Underlying his approach to the problem there is a consistent philosophy and a clear theological and critical position. The philosophy is existentialist, the critical attitude, in so far as it concerns the historical reliability of the Gospels, negative and sceptical, and the theology kerygmatic and evangelical. That the combination appears curiously paradoxical does not affect the fact that Bultmann's work is influenced by these three attitudes.

It is apparent, further, that his attitude towards the 'mythology' of the New Testament is bound up with his conception of history and *Geschichte* and the *geschichtlich*, which might be rendered the 'historic' in order to distinguish between terms of which there is no adequately discriminating translation in English. By the *geschichtlich* Bultmann means that which, even though it is a past event, makes a continuous impact upon present experience, while the *historisch* refers to an object of scientific investigation. Bultmann's indebtedness to Heidegger's discussion of the structure of being has already been indicated, and he himself makes this indebtedness quite clear. It extends to his use of the terms *historisch* and *geschichtlich* and to his analysis of *Dasein* (Being) within the context of *Zeitlichkeit* (temporality) and *Geschichtlichkeit* ('historicality' not in the sense of historical authenticity but of the 'historic-significant'). Heidegger, too, employs the terms *Historie* and *historisch* when his reference is to history as an object of study.[1]

Heidegger distinguishes between four uses of the terms *Historie* and *Geschichte*, ruling out immediately the inappropriateness to

[1] *Sein und Zeit*, pp. 372–404.

his discussion of the notion of 'history' as an object of scientific study. History is in this sense *Gewesenheit* ('has-been-ness'), and the 'has been' should be regarded as possessing the attribute of *Vorhandenheit* rather than *Dasein*: it should be considered as an 'object' (for study) rather than as something with continuing existence, *Dasein*, which is the more inclusive, non-static, and continuously effective. *Geschichte*, in the broader sense, implies not only what is past or 'has been' but 'an interconnection of event and effect which persists through "past", "present", and "future". In this the past has no special precedence'. This conception of *Geschichte*, for Heidegger, is determinant in so far as it includes the others: the emphasis is on the *fortwirkende Geschehen*, the continuous happening, which is equivalent to contemporaneous historicality.

It is in this general conception of *Geschichte* (in which, Heidegger says, History is rooted), rather than in the detailed elaboration of its relation to time and being, that the point of contact with Bultmann's underlying attitude towards history and the importance of the historic, and ultimately towards myth, is to be seen, and not only in Heidegger's idea of *Sorge* (anxiety) as the essence of the temporal.[1] In Bultmann's adaptation of it it is not the 'past' which matters in the sense that the 'pastness' of the 'historical' Jesus is the object of academic study, but the continuously effective impact of the Crucified upon the present. The Resurrection is not an event of past history (presumably in the sense of Heidegger's *Vorhandenheit* and *Gewesenheit*) but as an ever-present reality with an existential reference to contemporary man.[2] 'If we are to perceive the real meaning of the Cross,' Bultmann asks, 'must we understand it as the cross of Jesus as a figure of past history? *Must we go back to the Jesus of History?*'[3] The Cross is not an object of historical study: it is 'historical' in the sense of being

---

[1] *Sein und Zeit*, pp. 323 ff.

[2] An illustration of this is Bultmann's attitude towards miracle and 'miracles'. The latter, as recorded in the Gospels, are mere past 'events' and are therefore worthless. The real 'miracle' is the continuing offer of forgiveness in Christ. There is always a temptation, he says, to make of God's word of forgiveness, of a present *Dasein*, a mere *Vorhandensein* which belongs to the past, for it is useless to apply the idea of revelation to a *historically* ascertainable personality (*Glauben und Verstehen*, I, pp. 227–228, 2nd ed., 1954).

[3] *Kerygma and Myth*, p. 38 (italics mine).

eschatological through compelling man to ask questions about his own existence. This is true enough, but Bultmann seems to isolate it (as far as we are concerned) from a series of historically attestable events, though these (that is, the facts of the Gospel story) led to the Cross just as the chain of events in Napoleon's life led to St. Helena. Ultimately the existential encounter between the ever-contemporary Cross and the Christian to the exclusion of the 'historical' Jesus must lead to a kind of mysticism without factual content.

It is this antithesis in Bultmann's mind which leads to his flight into existentialism rather than to the Jesus of history as the means of solving part of the problem of New Testament 'myth'. It is necessary, therefore, to examine his attitude towards the 'historicity' of the historical Jesus and the conclusion to which it leads.

2

In the introduction to his book *Jesus*, published in 1929, Bultmann stated quite clearly his attitude towards the 'historical' approach to the life of Jesus. His own intention, he said, was not to present the reader with a historical point of view, or to give him a glimpse of history, but to confront him with history.

> In the following expositions [he says] indications that Jesus might be regarded as the Great Man or Genius will be lacking; he appears neither as a 'demonic' nor 'fascinating' figure. His words will not be described as profound, nor his faith as mighty, nor his character childlike. Its subject is not the eternal value of his message, nor his discovery of the limitless depths of the human soul. Our attention will be directed to that which he *intended*, and which can, therefore, as the challenge of his historical existence, become a present reality.
>
> For this reason any concern with the 'personality' of Jesus is excluded, but not because I make a virtue of necessity; for I am naturally of the opinion that we know almost nothing about the life and personality of Jesus, as the Christian sources were not interested in them and are, further, fragmentary and overgrown with legend; and there are no other sources.[1]

[1] *Jesus*, Berlin, 1929, pp. 11, 12. Bultmann is careful to distinguish between history as 'chronologically ascertainable phenomena and happenings (that which has

Bultmann refers to the *Leben-Jesu* movement and asserts that Jesus did not regard himself as the Messiah. Had he done so there would have been no controversy as to whether he did or not. Consequently Bultmann does not deal with the question; not merely because there can be no certainty about it, but because in his view it is of secondary importance.[1] In any case, it is not the historical biography of a decisive personality that counts but his 'work': and 'work' is to be thought of not merely as what was done but as what was intended. Moreover, we do not seek in the words of Jesus an ideal system of thought with universal validity intelligible to all; on the contrary, they are to be understood in the sense of their meaning for a man who lived in the concrete situation of his time; they are to be understood 'existentially'. When we read Jesus' words they confront us not as a system but (we quote the phrase again) 'as questions as to how we understand the meaning of our existence'. The words, however, are not necessarily the actual words of Jesus; they are primarily the message of the church and are 'naturally' attributed for the most part to him. Even the exposure of the oldest layers of the tradition by form-criticism cannot guarantee that verbal authenticity of his teaching which is so desirable.

> That he was the originator of the historical movement of which the oldest Palestinian community represented the first tangible stage is perfectly clear. But how far the community preserved an objectively true picture of Jesus and his message is a different question. For those whose interest is in the personality of Jesus this state of things is depressing or annihilating; for our purpose it is not of any essential significance.[2]

I do not propose to outline further Bultmann's interpretation of the thought of Jesus which he expounds with a radicality and

---

"taken place")', 'occurrence in time' (cf. Heidegger), and the 'suprahistorical' which, so to speak, absorbs the 'zeitliches Geschehen' and gives it permanent relevance (Heidegger's idea again).

[1] In *Die Geschichte der Synoptischen Tradition*, 1931, pp. 275 ff., Bultmann analyses Mark 8: 27-30 and claims that the passage is too questionable to be regarded as providing evidence for Jesus' acceptance of the Messianic title which Peter is alleged to have ascribed to him. Cf. *Theology of the New Testament*, pp. 26 ff., where the problem is dealt with in greater detail.

[2] *Jesus*, pp. 16-17.

incisiveness with which we must reckon. It should be indicated, however, that for Bultmann its character is eschatological and 'existential' in that it forces one into a moment of decision, an either—or, confronting him with the absolute demands of the Kingdom of God. Indeed, the worth of a man consists not in any inherent human quality or in the content of his spiritual life, but is determined by the character of his decision 'in the here and now of his existence'. The main purpose of Jesus' message, or of the message ascribed to him, is to confront man with the necessity of decision (*Entscheidung*) in the light of the future eschatological Kingdom of God.

It is clear from this that Bultmann regards the 'Jesus of history' as of minor importance; that there was such a Jesus he does not doubt; but nothing can be known of him. It is therefore, according to Bultmann, impossible to turn to the Gospels in search of a standard by which the demything of New Testament Christology can be undertaken. For the Gospels are not 'historical' documents and should not be used as such. The message of Jesus is not concerned with ideals or with universal concrete questions of ethics; it is severely eschatological and a means of challenging man to act decisively in the situation of crisis in which God has placed him. Bultmann's Jesus is, in effect, the protagonist of the theology of crisis. As Dr. A. M. Hunter has commented, he 'might be said to be the reflection of a Barthian face. C'est dialectique, mais ce n'est pas histoire'.[1]

The implication of this is that it is useless to try to discover from the Gospel documents how Jesus' contemporaries reacted to him and what he may have thought about himself. All we are entitled to say is what the early church thought of him. We cannot say with any certainty whether his contemporaries regarded him as Lord, Teacher, or Messiah. We are confronted with a radical scepticism, a kind of historical agnosticism, with the negative results of the conclusions which Bultmann draws from his form-critical study of the Gospels.

It would seem, from an acquaintance with Bultmann's critical methods as they are applied to Christological problems, that his kinship is with the most radical of Liberal-Modernist critics of

---

[1] *Interpreting the New Testament*, 1900–1950, p. 54 (S.C.M. Press, 1951).

the Gospels,[1] while at the same time his emphasis is evangelical and his faith Christocentric. It is this being in two worlds that makes his position so difficult to define. Indeed, his attitude towards the New Testament itself is so ambiguous and so selective that it may be thought to be capricious. This is seen when comparing his evaluation of the Gospels, which are formally '*historisch*', with the Epistles, in which the 'Christ-event' is proclaimed, as *geschichtlich*. And as a study of his form-critical work shows, little historicity survives analysis, and in the extreme scepticism of his analysis his conclusions scarcely differ from those of Bousset and the religious-historical school of New Testament scholars or from those of such extreme Modernists as Kirsopp Lake. He will not admit that the Gospels are a source of knowledge about Jesus, yet without such knowledge as they provide the 'Christ-event' would be a revelation without ascertainable content. Yet with Bultmann's statement that 'the figure of Jesus cannot be understood simply from his context in human evolution or history', and that 'in mythological language this means that he stems from eternity, his origin transcends both history and nature'[2] there need be no disagreement, for it is not inconsistent with acceptance of the Gospel tradition as substantially reliable.

It is Bultmann's attitude towards the historicity of the Gospel which makes difficult any clear definition of his position in relation to either Liberalism or orthodoxy, for, unless I am misinterpreting him, he is willing to accept fully the apostolic witness as represented by St. Paul (subject, of course, to demythologizing), whereas the Synoptic Gospels are to be considered of such a character that their 'historical' witness to fact is negligible. Thus the miracles of healing, in his view, are 'mythological' because Jesus believed in demoniacal possession: a belief which can neither be demonstrated to be illusory nor shown to be founded on fact. What is important, however, is not that Jesus believed

---

[1] I am inclined to agree with Prof. de Vos (*Nieuwe Testament en Mythe*, p. 41) who says that Bultmann, despite his disclaimer, has more in common with the Liberal theology than he cares to admit, and that he gives an unfair picture of it, if not of its results at any rate of its intentions. Dr. de Vos states it as his view that the purposes of the Liberals was in complete agreement with Bultmann's, even to the point of *not* wishing to eliminate the mythological. The matter is discussed at length in pp. 40–51 of Dr. de Vos' book.

[2] *Kerygma and Myth*, p. 35.

in demoniacal possession (a belief which is today shared by Christian exorcists) but that the description of the symptoms as they occur in the Gospels are an accurate description of similar happenings in modern times.[1]

Now this does not prove that Jesus was the Messiah; but it is a class of incident of which the Gospel narrative is a faithful description, and shows that the likelihood that much of the Synoptic tradition originated in eye-witness reports or recollections is not to be dismissed as easily as Bultmann would dismiss it. Yet such historical objectivity, if it were obtainable, would not possess 'salvation value'. Indeed, Bultmann asks whether the Cross, 'understood as the event of salvation', is exclusively mythical, or whether it is able to retain its 'value for salvation' without forfeiting its historical character.[2] 'The Jesus who was crucified was the pre-existent, incarnate Son of God', that is, a mythological conception. This, however, if the Birth-stories are discounted as legendary, is *not* what the Synoptic Gospels say, for they do not affirm the 'pre-existence' of Jesus. This is a Pauline interpretation for which there cannot be factual proof and belongs (as Bultmann says) to mythological thinking, or at any rate to the mythopoetical manner of thought; but Bultmann gives far more prominence to it than he does to the less mythological Christology of the Gospels.

Again, we would agree with Bultmann when he says (concerning the Birth-stories) that

> the facts which historical criticism can verify cannot exhaust, indeed, they cannot adequately indicate, all that Jesus means to me. How he actually originated matters little. . . . Our interest in the events of his life, and above all in the cross, is more than an academic concern with the history of the past. We can see meaning in them only when we ask what God is trying to say to each one of us through them.[3]

But when we have indicated our agreement with Bultmann we have not agreed that the facts cannot be substantially recovered,

[1] See K. T. Oesterreich, *Possession, Demoniacal and Other* (Kegan Paul, 1930), chapter 1.
[2] *Kerygma and Myth*, p. 35.
[3] Ibid., p.35.

or that the Synoptic Gospels must be dismissed as factually un-reliable. Nor are we committed to the belief that the nexus of fact and meaning is applicable to the 'Christ-event' alone. Other events are not fully comprehensible if read about simply as chronicle; they can be fully understood only in the light of their impact on subsequent history.

How, then, does the 'Christ-event' differ from other events? The answer is that it differs in character, not in a special relationship between the 'historical' and the 'historic' or eschatological, for, in the sense of inaugurative finality, every decisive historical event which transcends its immediate field of reference is 'eschatological'. As Thielicke has observed, what Bultmann means by 'event' in this Christian-eschatological context is 'historical data elevated to cosmic dimensions by the acquisition of an understanding of human life which these data produce. Thus the event is not the Jesus of history, but Jesus valued as the Christ'.[1] With this interpretation of the term we have no quarrel, if the term is to be used at all. The facts (that is, the historical data) of the life of Jesus are not 'deducible from the Christian interpretation of life', nor, it could be added, are the facts of Julius Caesar's invasion of Britain deducible from the history of Britain in the twentieth century. But both sets of facts have produced a series of events or an experience which is inseparable from its historical foundation in them. But is the 'Christian interpretation of life' any more deducible from the Pauline commentary on the Gospel (on which Bultmann concentrates) than from the Gospels themselves? This is really the crux of the matter, and it is precisely here that the distinction between fact and meaning is erroneous. It is arbitrary to distinguish between various constituents of the 'story of salvation' as though one part were *historisch* and the other *geschichtlich*: as though the pre-Good Friday part of the narrative belonged to history or chronicle and the Resurrection and post-Resurrection part of it to the 'historic' or *geschichtlich*. Commenting on the passage just quoted from Bultmann's essay Thielicke says that its implication is such that it 'would be nearer the truth to say, "The Word did not become flesh".'[2] Even if this is an exaggeration, there is some truth in it; for what Bultmann seems

---

[1] *Kerygma and Myth*, p. 147.   [2] Ibid., p. 148.

to suggest is that, even if the Word did become flesh, what kind of flesh It became does not matter, and in any case we could not know anything about it 'historically', and even if we could that would not matter either, for what matters is not 'history' but Revelation.

That this is not an unjust criticism is shown by Bultmann's conception of the character and significance of the Resurrection. 'It was not,' he says, 'an event of past history with a self-evident meaning.' This is true enough, for it was not that for the Roman administration or for the Sanhedrin. (One might add that, in the time of Alexander Jannaeus (*c.* 75 B.C.) eight hundred men were crucified on one occasion,[1] but their deaths had no salvation-value. Their crucifixion did not possess cosmic meaning.) The Cross-and-Resurrection, however, forms a 'single indivisible cosmic event'. That is so; and in stating this Bultmann is actually affirming the continuity of the 'historical' as eschatological with the 'historical' as historical, though he says that the Cross is not an isolated event 'which needed the Resurrection subsequently to reverse it'.[2]

So far we are partly with Bultmann. But then he uses the same kind of argument as Matthew Arnold used against the evidential value of miracles: they do not prove the doctrine. The changing of my pen into a pen-wiper does not prove that what I write is true.

> The Resurrection cannot be a miraculous proof capable of demonstration and sufficient to convince the sceptic that the cross really has the cosmic and eschatological significance ascribed to it.[3]

But is not this just what it was for the disciples: the practical demonstration of this 'eschatological significance' of the Cross? That is at any rate the burden of the early kerygma in the Acts, which Bultmann ignores as though its testimony were valueless. Whatever else the miracles of the Gospels were they *were* evidential, and were so regarded by Jesus, as the Gospel references make quite clear, unless these are to be dismissed as evidence of the

---

[1] Josephus, *Antiquities*, XIV, 13.   [2] *Kerygma and Myth*, pp. 35 ff.
[3] Ibid., p. 39.

imagination of the early church working in retrospect.[1] It is, moreover, precisely the Resurrection which proves the Messianic character of the mission of Jesus. But we will attend to what Bultmann says about the Resurrection:

> The preaching of the cross as the event of redemption challenges all who hear it to appropriate this significance for themselves.
>
> But, it will be asked, is this significance to be discovered in the actual event of past history? Can it, so to speak, be read from that event? Or does the cross bear this significance because it is the cross of *Christ*? In other words, must we first be convinced of the significance of Christ and believe in him in order to perceive the real meaning of the cross? . . .
>
> An historical fact which involves a resurrection from the dead is utterly inconceivable!
>
> Yes, indeed: the resurrection of Jesus cannot be a miraculous proof by which the sceptic might be compelled to believe in Christ. The difficulty is not simply the incredibility of a mythical event like the resurrection of a corpse—for that is what the resurrection means, as is shown by the fact that the risen Lord is apprehended by the physical senses. Nor is it merely the difficulty of establishing the objective historicity of the resurrection no matter how many witnesses are cited, as though once it was established it might be believed beyond all question and faith might have its unimpeachable guarantee. No; the real difficulty is that the resurrection itself is an article of faith, and you cannot establish an article of faith by invoking another. You cannot prove the redemptive efficacy of the cross by invoking the resurrection. For the resurrection is an article of faith because it is far more than the resuscitation of a corpse—it is the eschatological event.[2]

Of course the Resurrection is an article of faith, but for the disciples it was also an object of belief. They believed because they had seen the Lord. It is precisely through 'invoking the resurrection' that we prove the 'redemptive efficacy of the cross'. The Resurrection *was* an 'eschatological' event; but it *was* an event, even though it was not scientifically verifiable by a panel of investigators because the Lord chose to appear only to believers

---

[1] Matthew 11: 2–5; Mark 2: 10, etc.
[2] *Kerygma and Myth*, pp. 37–38, 40–41.

and not to the general public. In any case, a historical event as an object of academic enquiry is in a wholly different category from material which is being examined in a laboratory. There is a sense in which a past event cannot be verified: the most that can be done is to make deductions from documents which are considered reliable. There can be no direct attestation to a remote historical event, for the event itself eludes direct investigation. All that remains of it is reference or a series of historical consequences. Whether the Resurrection 'occurred' on the mythological plane or not, the historian is obliged to take account of it because it is clear from the early chapters of the Acts that conversions to Christianity were due to the observation by non-Christians of the effects of the belief in the Resurrection on the Apostles. Indeed, Bultmann assures us that the Resurrection 'is not a mythological event adduced in order to prove the saving efficacy of the cross': it is an article of faith. But, on the other hand, Bultmann asks, 'is it not a mythical event pure and simple?' For obviously it is not a mere event of past history. It is not in the category of Heidegger's *Gewesenheit*; it is not a 'has-been', or shall we say that it is not merely 'has-been' but still *is*, and is able to make an 'existential' impact because of the existential interpretability of myth. Moreover, in his *Geschichte der Synoptischen Tradition* Bultmann has dealt negatively with the Resurrection-narratives; in this he conforms to the pattern set by other radical critics of the New Testament who are not more at home than Bultmann in the 'mythological' world which he desires to reinterpret.

Now, the arguments which Bultmann employs follow each other in a circle. Thus 'the saving efficacy of the cross of Christ is not derived from the fact that it is the cross of Christ: it is the cross of Christ because it has this saving efficacy. Without that efficacy it is the tragic end of a great man'.[1] But this particular cross *is* the cross of Christ. If it were not the cross would be someone else's and would not have this 'saving efficacy'. Indeed, because it was the cross of Christ it could not have been the mere 'tragic end of a great man', otherwise, by definition, it would not have been the cross of Christ. Yet the Resurrection was not that

[1] *Kerygma and Myth*, p. 41.

of a Word or a Logos but of a particular 'historical' man. That is the significant thing about it.

Reference to this historical man, however, is of little assistance in appreciating the truth of the Gospel apart from the Resurrection. In making this plain Bultmann is right. We do not reach the truth by historical methods alone. Yet when Bultmann says that 'to raise again the problem of how the preaching rose historically, as though that would vindicate its truth', would be 'wrong' in this part of his argument, for it would 'tie our faith in the word of God to the results of historical research', he appears to be saying that historicity is irrelevant to the Gospel. Indeed, A. N. Wilder has remarked, and with good reason, that Bultmann puts historical research 'out of court'.[1] Where, moreover, is the content of the 'word' to be found if not in the life and teaching of Jesus? In the Pauline kerygma, Bultmann would reply; but, we may ask, how can this be authenticated?

Now, here Bultmann makes a surprising statement, namely, that Jesus meets us not in the Gospels but 'in the world of preaching and nowhere else', that is to say, in human utterance. It is not the Jesus of the Gospels who is to be preached but the Christ of the Resurrection in his existential impact upon the hearer, though Bultmann does not explain how Christ meets us 'in the word of preaching' alone.

Although it has been stated more than once that, whereas the Liberals wished to eliminate the mythological element from the New Testament, Bultmann wishes to reinterpret it,[2] some points of contact and of difference between them may be mentioned. His historical scepticism, his dismissal of the miraculous as legendary, or mythical, and his conviction that the Gospel must be re-stated in terms consistent with the intellectual categories of the age, his belief that orthodox Christianity is mythological and difficult to accept (as it was for English Modernists and German Liberals), place Bultmann in the same class as the Liberals. The point of difference is that, whereas the Liberals and the Modernists were interested in the 'historical' Jesus, Bultmann is not. On the one

[1] 'Myth and the New Testament' in the Journal of Biblical Literature, LXIX, 1950, p. 126.
[2] The *Expository Times*, January, 1954, p. 98, and by Bultmann himself in *Kerygma and Myth*, p. 12.

hand he affirms the absoluteness of the Christian revelation in a positive and evangelical manner seldom encountered in Liberal theology, whose 'humanism' is abhorrent to the Barthian theologians. On the other hand, Bultmann is in agreement with the Liberals (at any rate with those of the British variety) in wishing to reinterpret the doctrines of sacrifice and atonement, for the notions of Jesus' bearing vicariously the sin of the world and enduring the consequences of sin on man's behalf in order to deliver him from 'death' are a 'mythological interpretation' and a 'hotch-potch of sacrificial and juridical analogies which have ceased to be tenable for us today'.[1] Yet Bultmann is animated by a profound concern that the evangelical character of the Gospel should not be lost sight of. In his reply to Schniewind he says:

> What I am concerned with is the permanent 'historic' significance of the unique event of past history, in virtue of which it possesses ultimate eschatological significance despite its character as a unique event of past history. That is how the New Testament interprets that event, and it is the task of the theologian to decide whether this is just mythology, or whether it is capable of an existentialist interpretation.[2]

Perhaps Bultmann defines too closely the task of the theologian; in any case the 'event' may be thought of mythologically as well as existentially, and the theologian is under no obligation to confine his interpretation to existentialist thinking. But whatever form of interpretation of this decisive event is offered, it should not be in terms of evolution or of any such type of thought as was popular with the Liberals of a generation ago.[3]

Bultmann's emphasis on the 'eschatological' character of revelation is conspicuously lacking in Liberal-Modernist theology; for the eschatological is one of the determining concepts in Bultmann's interpretation of New Testament theology and of such Christology as he is willing to concede to the Synoptic Gospels. Christologically Bultmann's emphasis is on the 'otherness' of

---

[1] *Kerygma and Myth*, p. 35. This was virtually the view of the older Liberals.
[2] Ibid., p. 110.
[3] For a fuller account of Bultmann's relation to Liberalism see my articles 'Bultmann and the Liberal Theology' in the *Expository Times*, June and July, 1956.

Jesus and of his message, which is very different from the Liberals' interest in his place in the human order, and the this-worldly content of his teaching. Whereas, further, the liberal tendency was to accord a subsidiary place to the Pauline witness and to give precedence to the teaching of Jesus, Bultmann does the opposite. He is concerned less with what Jesus proclaimed than with what the Apostolic writers proclaimed about him. The church is not a 'historical' but an 'eschatological' institution: it is the 'eschatological congregation' summoned into existence by the eschatological phenomenon of the Risen Christ through whom alone God's grace is offered to man and in the acceptance of whom grace is experienced.

This sufficiency of Christ as the only means of salvation and the only instrument of revelation is the theme of Bultmann's essay on 'The Question of Natural Revelation'[1] in which the evangelical faith is impressively affirmed. Knowledge of God, Bultmann says, is man's knowledge of himself and of his limitations, and it is God whose power 'breaks through these limitations', which happens not in nature or in history but in Christ. Indeed, according to Bultmann's interpretation of it, Christian faith asserts that God's omnipotence, as it is ascribed by man to God, is not encountered in the world, for nothing within the world is omnipotent, and in point of fact man cannot encounter the world as a *whole* but only fragmentarily. There is no meaning at all in speaking about the divine revelation in nature, 'for nature is precisely that which fails to show what God is essentially—omnipotence'.[2] Nature is not the revelation of God but merely a spectacle (*Schauspiel*).

Moreover, if human life is essentially a historical phenomenon, how far is it legitimate to speak of divine revelation in history? If by this is meant that God 'reveals' Himself in historical personalities, we shall not find such revelation, for, says Bultmann, all that is revealed is moral heroism, which may appeal to our will but does not cleanse us. And if we mean that God's rule is evident in the course of history and that all happens according to

---

[1] *Die Frage der natürlichen Offenbarung* in *Glauben und Verstehen*, II (vol. ii of the collected essays), pp. 79–104. It appeared first in *Offenbarung und Heilsgeschehen* (1941).
[2] Ibid., p. 88.

divine plan, this, too, is illusory, for history as a whole cannot be grasped, except, possibly, theoretically. The most that we can do is to contemplate it aesthetically. The only relation between history and ourselves consists in our being on the scene in which our future behaviour can be decided. History, for Bultmann, is therefore not a means of divine revelation but the scene of human decision. 'The word of history is obscure, and, if we listen to it, a gamble.' History is the history of man, and men are sinners; it cannot, therefore, reveal God.

No, says Bultmann, neither nature nor history is a revelation of God. Hence he implicitly dissociates himself from those who see in Jesus a culmination of human-historical qualities which are in different degrees discernible in other historical figures. Christian existence is not 'historical' but 'eschatological';[1] it is not in nature but in grace. Hence the Christian revelation is absolute and exclusive and is so because it is revelation in Jesus Christ.

> He who demands other forms of revelation together with Jesus Christ has not yet taken God seriously and has failed to understand the character of his own existence in its depths.[2]

Bultmann's theology is evangelically christocentric. Christianity is for him the proclamation of the Cross and Resurrection both as the unique instrument of revelation and as the revelation itself. It is in the manner of presentation and in the character of the emphasis that Bultmann is seen to be far removed from the Liberals.

In all this there is no acknowledgment of the Synoptic Gospels as a source of knowledge of the content of Christian belief. Neither in the essay on demythologizing nor in the one on natural revelation does Bultmann suggest that anything other than the Epistles is of any relevance to the understanding of the Gospel. With the exception of two incidental references to John and a casual allusion to Acts no citations are made except from the Epistles. As far as Bultmann is concerned the Synoptic Gospels might never have been written. There is no suggestion that

[1] Ibid., p. 96.   [2] Ibid., p. 100.

Jesus' own *kerygma*, with which, according to the Synoptics, his ministry began,[1] was of any significance, though he came 'preaching' the Kingdom. It is this attitude towards the Gospels above all which separates Bultmann from his predecessors the Liberals, even though liberal criticism did not ascribe unassailable historical reliability to them. The Jesus of history, as understood by liberal theologians and by Christian tradition as a whole, has disappeared in a mist of historical scepticism and in the Christ of an existential philosophy.

3

Such, then, is the tension between two conceptions of history: history as merely 'historical' and history as 'historic'. Myth is anti-historical but not necessarily anti-historic, for through its mythological form Christian doctrine, or the 'Christ-event', makes its enduring impact upon the believer. But this mythological form, whether in the theology of the Cross and Resurrection or of the pre-existent Word, has value, not as a factual or descriptive statement, but as a point of existential reference, confronting man with the necessity of asking questions about his own existence. Man is a being in time; in Heidegger's terminology he is *Dasein* in *Zeitlichkeit*, being in temporality, which means change within time, that is, in history. But a historical moment does not, so to speak, prolong itself from the past and through the present and future except in so far as it possesses the capacity for this 'existential' confrontation, which is not, according to Bultmann, possible with a merely 'historical' enquiry into the facts of the life of Jesus, even if this were practicable, which in his opinion it is not. The Christian story, which is a *Heilsgeschichte*, the story of salvation, must therefore be liberated from 'history' and be released, as it were, through becoming *geschichtlich* ('historic') in its importance; and this *geschichtlich*-historical is an

---

[1] The occurrence of forms of κηρύσσειν in the Synoptic Gospels is so frequent that the limitation of the term (and with it κήρυγμα) to the Apostolic preaching is hardly justifiable. It can be claimed that the greater part of what Jesus said was κήρυγμα of one sort or another as he himself began his ministry as the proclaimer or κῆρυξ of the Kingdom. The term κήρυγμα occurs eight times in the New Testament (four times only in definitely Pauline writings), and κηρύσσειν eighteen times in Paul as compared with a total of thirty-one in the Synoptics and eight in Acts.

existentialist and, in the New Testament context, an eschatological concept.[1]

It would appear, therefore, on Bultmann's premises, that any demythologizing would have to be made on an existentialist basis, and not in reference to the 'historical' picture of Jesus and through the attempt to understand Jesus' own conception of his person and mission. In other words, Christology according to Jesus is out of the question, and a comparison of the Synoptic Christology, even admitting its colouring by the theology of the early church (which in our view is considerably exaggerated), with the rest of the New Testament Christology and that of the orthodox tradition is not permissible. With such views about the unreliability of the Synoptic tradition (as exposed by form-criticism) Bultmann must seek some other refuge from the mythological, especially as, in his view, Jesus himself shared the mythological world-picture.[2] Bultmann has exposed himself to the criticism

---

[1] Although the existentialist conception of history occupies an important place in Bultmann's theology, its importance to the understanding of the problem of demythologizing has been exaggerated. Thus Gogarten, in his *Entmythologisierung und Kirche* (1953), regards as fundamental the appreciation of Bultmann's idea of history and attributes the lack of understanding displayed by many of his critics to their adherence to the Cartesian scheme of subject-object relationship and its implications for history, whereas the existentialist conception of such a relationship seriously affects one's understanding of the historical. Much of this discussion, it must be said, is extremely academic and does not really affect Bultmann's thesis in one way or another. The issue is made to appear far more complicated than is necessary by the peculiar character of German theological controversy (see pp. 68 ff.).

[2] That Bultmann is not alone in his distrust of the notion of the 'historical' Jesus and in his disparagement of the 'historical' (as differing from the *geschichtlich*) does not make his position any the more easy to accept. Brunner, for example, writes: 'The Christian faith has just as little to do with the influence of Jesus on the world as it has to do with his historical personality. It is not interested in the "Founder of Christianity" nor in His influence on history. . . . Whoever cleaves to Christ from the historical point of view does not cleave to Him personally, but in an aesthetic manner, as a spectator, not as a percipient' (*The Mediator*, p. 81). It is of the 'very essence of revelation and faith' that we should become Christians *not* through the historical picture of Jesus, but through the picture traced by the Gospels in the light of the Resurrection. 'The historian,' Brunner adds, 'lacks the knowledge of the Resurrection, the knowledge that was granted only to the Apostles and to those who believed through their word' (p. 159). The Jesus of history is known 'after the flesh'; the 'historical' picture can give rise to a perversion of faith. Brunner then makes the following surprising statement: 'If once the conviction is regained that the Christian faith does not arise out of the picture of the historical Jesus but out of the testimony to Christ as such—this includes the witness of the prophets as well as that of the Apostles—and that it is based upon this testimony, *then inevitably the preference for the Synoptic Gospels and for the actual words of Jesus, which was the position of the last generation*, will disappear' (ibid., p. 172). Brunner repeats the assertion which has been made so often that it has come to be regarded as true: that the aim of the

of confining himself to what has been called the 'Procrustean bed of Heidegger's existentialism'[1] and therefore of leaving himself no escape from the tension between the historical and the *geschichtlich*. His principle of demythologizing, though it has much to commend it, and is certainly *one* way of dealing with the mythological element in the New Testament, is not the only one. Indeed, it would be interesting to know how he proposes, in detail, to demythologize the New Testament, though indications have been given in his first essay and in his final reply to his critics. That the Gospel, whether mythologically or otherwise presented, must make an 'existential' impact is indisputable; what is disputable is what should be considered mythological, and on one's views about this depend the extent and character of the demything which is to be undertaken. In the last resort the impact of the Gospel is largely a question of communication. In spite of excellent intentions, 'demythologizing' in terms of evolutionary philosophy made little impression upon those for whom it was intended—the so-called 'modern men' of the first half of the present century. The fate of an existentialist demythologizing may not be different. Moreover, it is the Synoptic narrative, rather than the language of St. Paul, that has been most formative in the creation of Christian piety, despite the revolutionizing effect of the Epistle to the Romans on Augustine, Luther, John Wesley, and Karl Barth. It is the story of the Passion rather than its interpretation in theological terms which has been the more decisive, for the sayings of Jesus have been no less effective than the Apostolic proclamation of the Cross in confronting man with questions about his existence. It is a consideration such as this

---

Gospels 'is in no way historical'; they bear 'witness', as though a witness to the historical is to be ruled out as invalid. Again, 'faith presupposes, *a priori*, as a matter of course, that the Jesus of history is not the same as the Christ of Faith' (ibid., p. 184). Comment on this is perhaps unnecessary.

[1] In the *Expository Times*, January, 1954, p. 98, Bultmann, of course, was aware of this kind of criticism (*Kerygma and Myth*, p. 25). Whether because of lack of lucidity on his part, or of the unwillingness on the part of others, he seems to have been peculiarly open to misinterpretation. Thus Gogarten (op. cit., pp. 68 ff.) insists that the 'Lutheran theologians' have not only misunderstood his conception of history but have not taken the trouble to understand it; and Bornkamm (*Die Christliche Hoffnung und das Problem der Entmythologisierung*, p. 18) remarks that it is absurd to reproach Bultmann with having made the New Testament a sort of document of Heidegger's philosophy. But Bultmann's readers can hardly be blamed if they come to this conclusion.

that makes the distribution of treatment in Bultmann's *Theology of the New Testament* so heavily over-weighted, for the space devoted to the teaching of Jesus in this penetrating book is almost negligible, amounting only to some twenty-six pages. Presumably his teaching has too little theological value apart from its 'eschatological' character.

The following chapters are not primarily concerned to reinterpret the New Testament and its 'mythology' in existentialist terms but to examine the extent and character of the mythological element on the basis of Bultmann's definition of it, which, so far as the present purpose is concerned, is considered sufficiently adequate and comprehensive, though there may not be full agreement as to its application. It is nevertheless sufficiently broad to provide a basis for further investigation.

PART TWO

THE PROBLEM OF THE
MYTHOLOGICAL

SUMMARY OF ARGUMENT

With Bultmann's definition of Myth as a starting-point, we proceed to examine the mythological form of the Christology of the Epistles, and to enquire into its sources. The idea of the 'Logos' becoming man may prove to be 'mythological', and it has affinities with Gnostic and other extra-biblical conceptions. The most significant passages containing the 'mythological' picture are set forth: Jesus as the pre-existent co-creator of the universe. The religious-historical approach to the question is represented by Wilhelm Bousset, whose contentions are described and criticized. Notwithstanding possible affinities with Hellenistic thought, Paul is more likely to have been influenced by the Wisdom literature, the terminology of which was widely diffused. Another form of the mythological Christology is the kenotic interpretation of the Incarnation. The early *kerygma* of Acts, however, is free from this type of thought, and represents the beliefs of Jesus' immediate contemporaries.

If, then, the terminology is mythological, how is it to be interpreted? One element in the Pauline Christology suggests the needs to consider the *spatial* metaphors which his Christology contains. Modern philosophical categories may provide a means of interpretation, in which task Heim's are helpful. Paul's universe is a stratified one. Hence it can be thought of as consisting of ascending grades of reality, the highest being that of the Lordship of Jesus. The graded structure of the Pauline cosmology and anthropology examined in relation to Thornton's interpretation of the Incarnation in terms of Whitehead's terminology. This is one method of demythologizing.

CHAPTER ONE

THE SUBSTANCE OF THE MYTH

I

Although it may be necessary for every age to make the experiment of thinking out the meaning of the Christian faith in terms of the thought most appropriate to the intellectual climate of the time, it is essential that there should be fixed points, fixed centres of reference, from which the experiment shall spring. They provide the objective element in a world in which theological interpretation can never be final.

The great doctrine of the Word becoming Flesh is one of these. It is also a mythological description of what the Church has called the Incarnation. At the beginning of the Fourth Gospel and in the Christian Creeds the fundamental principle is affirmed: the Word became Flesh. This, however, is not exactly the substance of the earliest Christian *kerygma*, which spoke of the exaltation of him who fulfilled Messianic hopes: a proclamation which does not necessarily imply the Johannine doctrine, for it presupposes a different starting-point. This early *kerygma* knows nothing of an incarnational Christology, for the Messiah was not conceived of incarnationally. The *kerygma* was, if anything, vaguely Adoptionist; yet it was the Johannine doctrine which became normative for theology.

If, however, the Johannine pronouncement is examined it will be found to suggest mythological thinking as a means of adequately expressing the experience of the Church of the total impact of Jesus upon its life. John made use of the Logos-concept which was familiar both to Hellenistic and (as a term equivalent to 'Wisdom') to Jewish readers. The term itself can be described as mythological in so far as it implies that there existed 'with' God from the beginning a kind of hypostatized being, the Son or the Word, who 'became' man and lived an earthly life. The 'word' is actually an abstraction, however, for a 'word' cannot easily be conceived ontologically as a subordinate aspect of the Deity or as an independent entity existing in some ante-historical form. As a bare statement without further interpretation and elaboration with reference to a particular historical appearance the Johannine affirmation has little meaning; as a mythological assertion it is unsatisfactory because of the modern difficulty of imagining the existence of a 'Logos'. Yet within the context of the Christian story the meaning of the doctrine is clear: the divine appeared under conditions of humanity in Jesus, and somehow this Jesus, the Jesus of History and the Christ of Faith, was inseparable from the life of God and its visible manifestation in history.

There are two variants of this conviction in the New Testament: there is the Christology of the Prologues to Matthew and Luke in which the Incarnation is thought of as an act of divine generation by the Holy Spirit analogous with normal conception; and there is the pre-existence and 'kenotic' Christology of St. Paul. Each of these is a mythological version of the more philosophical and succinct affirmation of the Fourth Gospel. Yet whatever its form, a Christological statement belongs not wholly to the realm of fact but of hypothesis. As an affirmation of faith it cannot be proved or disproved, for metaphysical judgments about Jesus and his relation to God are incapable of precise verification. We do not know whether there was any objectively existent 'Word' of God in the sense in which it was represented by the 'Logos' philosophy and especially in the Christological speculations of the Fathers. 'Word' can be made intelligible only paraphrastically by translation into some other term such as 'creative will', 'mind', 'cosmic reason', 'intention', and the identification of it with the pre-existent Christ is a form of hypothetical thinking. If the 'Word' was only a 'part' of God, an aspect of His being, not God in His totality, or if it is regarded as an articulate extension of God (in which case the Logos in the Johannine sense would hardly be 'with' or 'pros' God), the Incarnation is a partial one, a fragmentary manifestation of God. If, however, God in His totality became Flesh, we are confronted, no matter how ingenious the explanations offered by theology, with a theophany in human form which it is impossible to conceive as in any way consonant with genuine human personality. To say, as Brunner says, that 'we are forced to state that Jesus Christ only assumed human nature but not human personality'[1] is to make a statement which is not only obscure but which, to one reader at least, has no meaning. As long as theologians speak of a being called Jesus Christ 'assuming human nature' as though it were something to be put on but did not really belong to him, they are using an idiom which means progressively less to the modern mind, and orthodoxy seems to be unable to liberate itself from this way of thinking. According to it Jesus is to be regarded as a supernatural, pre-existent divine being who somehow 'assumes human nature'. This is the essence of the Christological myth, and unless it is stated in some non-mythological form it is apt to be misleading; and as long as is stated in this mythological form it is likely to be understood literally.

Moreover, to interpret one mythological way of thinking in terms of another is likely so to confuse rather than clarify the issue that the problem remains further than ever from solution, though if the Christological statements of the New Testament were to be removed because they are thought to be mythological it would nevertheless be necessary to re-state them in some other form which, in turn, might be even more uncertain of reaching finality or of providing universal satisfaction. And once the process of elimination has begun it is impossible to foresee where it will end. Whatever problems are set by the statement that 'the Word became flesh and dwelt among us' this truth is fundamental to Christian thought and demands formulation in some such form. As it stands it embodies briefly the whole truth of the Christian revelation; but if it is enquired into closely it reveals a mode of thought which has affinities not only with philosophy but with mythology. Whether it can ever be matched in brevity, comprehensiveness, and profound theological insight is doubtful, though we are not committed to the literal acceptance of its 'pre-existence' presuppositions, even though it is admitted that it is not easy to see how otherwise the substance of what it says could be formulated. If the sayings attributed or ascribed to Jesus in the Fourth Gospel were his actual words this would be the logical

---

[1] *The Mediator*, p. 320.

deduction from them; but here we encounter the historical tension which makes of this Gospel an insoluble problem. Even the terminology of 'light', 'logos', 'life', with the implication of the 'heavenly man' which accompanies the Johannine presentation of the Gospel cannot be completely detached from its Hellenistic background with the Gnosticism which opens up vistas of further mythological ways of thinking. Whether the Prologue is, as Bultmann holds, a liturgical hymn of the Church incorporated into the Gospel and worked over by the Evangelist is not of primary importance, nor does it matter that the term 'logos' is not thereafter applied to Jesus. It is sufficient to observe that it sums up the theology of the Gospel and supplies the thematic overture of which the remainder is the symphonic development.

The overture, however, is conceived mythologically. Bultmann is of the opinion that in this context the term 'logos' has its origin neither in the Hebrew *memra* nor in the philosophical tradition of Greece, in neither of which is it regarded as a hypostasis existing, as it were, side by side with God. In his opinion it derives rather from the far more mythological realm of Gnosticism or even from pre-Gnostic speculation.[1] Whatever its origin may be, the 'Logos' has been given a soteriological as well as a cosmological function, and in the Johannine Prologue 'it' assumes a human form in order to exist in the 'lower' world[2] and thereby bring to men the gift of salvation. That this idea of the Saviour becoming flesh was prevalent in Gnostic systems there is abundant evidence, and it is thought that it was taken over by Christianity from Gnosticism rather than the reverse. Even though John may not have been as familiar as are modern scholars with the origin and background of the terms which he used, and doubtless understood them at their face value, the terms themselves have a complicated history, are remote from modern Western ways of thinking, and belong, generally speaking, to the world of myth. It is difficult not to conclude that the objectification of the 'logos' as the agent

---

[1] *Johannes Evangelium*, ed. 1950, pp. 5–18, where Bultmann seeks to draw a clear distinction between the Logos-character of Gnostic thought and that of the Greek and Hebrew terminology. The corresponding term in Hebrew thought was Wisdom rather than Word.

[2] Dr. C. H. Dodd, in his *Interpretation of the Fourth Gospel*, has emphasized the importance of this ἄνω-κάτω antithesis in the Johannine terminology.

of creation existing, somehow, not only as God but as πρὸς τὸν θεόν, 'with' God, is bound up with a religious-philosophical picture of the world which grows more remote as it is investigated. In this dual rôle of 'being God' and 'being with God' it can hardly be regarded as other than a kind of Gnostic 'emanation' of the Deity, the incarnation of which can only be conceived in mythological terms belonging to a completely different category from the earliest *kerygma* of the Acts.[1]

Nevertheless, the Christology of the Fourth Gospel is not Gnostic but anti-Gnostic and anti-Docetic in its emphasis on the historical appearance of Jesus and in its presentation of a very bodily Resurrection in contrast to the unreality of the Docetic Christ. But when this has been admitted, the mythological character of the setting of God's cosmic action should not be minimized. The 'glory' seen is that of the 'only-begotten' of the Father (even this term, μονογενής, derives from the same shadowy background), of the Divine, eternal Logos-Redeemer who was 'with God' before creation. Whether John 1: 1-5 can be detached from the following verses is doubtful, for as it stands the passage is a consistent unity as a philosophical statement about creation in which the philosophy and the myth merge into one another. Whatever may originally have been the constituent parts (if any) of the Johannine Prologue, they have been combined into a unity which can be neither dissected separately nor broken up into independent units. John 1: 1-18 should be read as a systematic whole.

Now, what the Prologue does is to state succinctly what could be stated only at considerable length as an abstract philosophical argument about the interaction of eternity and time, the irruption

---

[1] So also with the other constituents of the typically Johannine vocabulary such as the light-darkness antithesis and the associations of ζωή and φῶς, as well as other concepts which are drawn from the realm of mythological thinking (cf. C. H. Dodd, op. cit., ad loc., and the mass of material in Bultmann's monumental commentary on John). B. H. Streeter (*The Four Gospels*, pp. 436 ff.) discusses the hesitation of the Roman Church in the second half of the first century in accepting the Fourth Gospel, and mentions as possible reasons for this its popularity with the Gnostics and the inclusion of the Logos-doctrine. Streeter regards it as strange that 'the doctrine of the Logos would by some be regarded as a hazardous speculation savouring of that Gnostic theory of emanations which threatened to destroy the belief in the unity of God.' Yet, he adds, 'it cannot be said that the phrase δεύτερος θεός, a second God, used by Justin Martyr, the great champion of the Logos doctrine at Rome, was altogether reassuring.' The phrase was also Philo's.

of the Beyond into the present, and the redemption of man through divine intervention in history. It states clearly and briefly what formal philosophical theology would elaborate in a manner more academic than liturgical. Whether the early readers of the Gospel were aware of the allegedly Gnostic character of the background may be a matter for dispute. The question set for the non-mythological interpretation of the fundamental thought behind it is whether it can be formulated in any way to which the present mythological character of the passage is not integral. As, however, the presuppositions of the Johannine Christology should not be thought of in isolation from the rest of the New Testament, it is necessary to examine the Pauline and other parallels to it. Those passages which are most markedly 'mythological' will be selected.

2

The most significant passages in the New Testament Epistles which indicate a common 'mythological' background and content are the following.[1]

1. *Philippians* 2: 5–11

Have this mind among yourselves, which you have in Christ Jesus who, though he was in the form of God, did not count equality with God a thing to be grasped, but emptied himself, taking the form of a servant, being born in the likeness of men. And being found in human form he humbled himself and became obedient unto death, even death on a cross. Therefore God has highly exalted him and bestowed on him the name which is above every name, that in the name of Jesus every knee should bow, in heaven and on earth and under the earth, and every tongue confess that Jesus is Lord, to the glory of God the Father.[2]

---

[1] The version here quoted is the American Revised Standard Version.

[2] The question of authorship is not relevant to the character of the passage. O. Cullmann rejects the Pauline authorship, considering it to be a Christian psalm taken over by Paul from the early church (*The Earliest Christian Confessions*, p. 22). See also A. Seeberg, *Der Katechismus der Urchristenheit*, pp. 181–182, on this passage as a 'confession'. For a detailed analysis of the passage see E. Lohmeyer in *Die Briefe an die Philipper*, etc. (Meyers Handkommentar, 1930, pp. 90 ff.) Lohmeyer, who believes it to be pre-Pauline, convincingly demonstrates its liturgical character, though there is no inherent improbability in the supposition that the boldest and most poetic of the Apostolic writers should have been the author of a liturgical confession.

2. *Ephesians* 1: 9-23

For he has made known to us in all wisdom and insight the mystery of his will, according to his purpose which he set forth in Christ as a plan for the fulness of time, to unite all things in him, things in heaven and things in earth. In him, according to the counsel of his will, we who first hoped in Christ have been destined and appointed to live for the praise of his glory. . . .

For this reason, because I have heard of your faith in the Lord Jesus and your love toward all the saints, I do not cease to give thanks for you, remembering you in my prayers, that the God of our Lord Jesus Christ, the Father of glory, may give you a spirit of wisdom and of revelation in the knowledge of him . . . according to the working of his great might which he accomplished in Christ when he raised him from the dead, and made him sit at his right hand in the heavenly places, far above all rule and authority and power and dominion, and above every name that is named, not only in this age, but also in that which is to come; and he has put all things under his feet and has made him head over all things for the church, which is his body, the fulness of him who fills all in all.

3. *Colossians* 1: 15-19

He is the image of the invisible God, the first-born of all creation; for in him all things were created, in heaven and on earth, visible and invisible, whether thrones or dominions or principalities or authorities—all things were created through him and for him. He is before all things, and in him all things hold together. He is the head of the body, the church; he is the beginning, the first-born from the dead, that in everything he might be pre-eminent. For in him all the fulness of God was pleased to dwell, and through him to reconcile to himself all things, whether on earth or in heaven, making peace by the blood of his cross.[1]

4. *I Corinthians* 15: 45-50

Thus it is written, The first man Adam became a living being; the last Adam became a life-giving spirit. But it is not the spiritual

---

[1] E. Norden (*Agnostos Theos*, pp. 250 ff.) considers that this, too, is a liturgical passage incorporated by the author in his epistle. This is likely enough, and lends support to our contention that the content of such passages can be treated as mythopoetical. Even if, however, the passage is liturgical, it is not necessarily non-Pauline. For a further discussion of possibly pre-Pauline passages in the Epistles, see A. M. Hunter, *Paul and his Predecessors* (1940).

which is first but the physical, and then the spiritual. The first man was from the earth, a man of dust; the second man is from heaven. As was the man of dust, so are those who are of the dust; and as is the man of heaven, so are those who are of heaven. Just as we have borne the image of the man of dust, we shall also bear the image of the man of heaven.

5. I *Corinthians* 15: 26

The last enemy to be destroyed is death. 'For God has put all things in subjection under his feet.' . . . When all things are subjected to him, then the Son himself will be subjected to him who put all things under him, that God may be everything to everyone.

(Cf. Eph. 1: 22, where the words 'and he has put all things under his feet' refer to Jesus alone.)

6. I *Corinthians* 8: 6

There are indeed many 'gods' and many 'lords'— yet for us there is one God, from whom are all things and for whom we exist, and one Lord, Jesus Christ, through whom are all things and through whom we exist.

7. *Hebrews* 1: 2–3

But in these last days he has spoken to us by a son, whom he has appointed the heir of all things, through whom also he created the world. He reflects the glory of God and bears the very stamp of his nature, upholding the universe by his word of power. When he had made purification for sins he sat down at the right hand of the Majesty on high, having become as much superior to angels as the name he has obtained is more excellent than theirs.

In commenting on these passages the differences as well as the similarities between them and the Johannine Prologue should be noted. The latter is succinct and propositional, stating briefly the thought which the Evangelist considers basic to his Gospel. It is the Word, the Logos, whose nature is undefined, perhaps because the writer takes for granted that his readers know what is meant, who becomes flesh. Paul and Hebrews are more lyrical or at least more rhetorical, and the phraseology suggests terms which might have been drawn from Alexandrine neo-Platonism and contemporary Stoicism rather than from a background predominantly Hebraic. In both Paul and Hebrews is found the conception of the 'image' of God, 'likeness', 'reflection', the 'effulgence' of the Divine glory: a thought which is also prominent in St. John's Gospel—'we beheld his glory', though it would seem that the influence of the Wisdom Literature is more conspicuous in the language of Paul and Hebrews than in John.

Secondly, the cosmic function of the Son and Logos is emphasized by John, Paul, and Hebrews. In John it is through the Logos that 'all things' were made; without him there was no created thing. According to Colossians 'in him all things were created' and hold together, 'through him and for him'. In Hebrews 'through him He created the world'. Jesus the Son is not only the agent of creation but the principle of its cohesion. According to Ephesians all things are united 'in him', 'things in heaven and things in earth'. In I Corinthians it is Jesus 'through whom are all things and through whom we exist', and in Hebrews Jesus is represented as sustaining the universe 'by his word of power'. In Colossians he 'reconciles' all things to himself 'whether on earth or in heaven'.

From this it follows that Jesus the Son and Logos is to be thought of as pre-existent, which is also the implication of sayings in the Fourth Gospel.[1] The passages in the Pauline Epistles presuppose the pre-existence of him who 'came down', died, rose, and was exalted to the highest place of honour in the creation. In John Jesus 'came down from God' and returned to Him (combining 6: 38 and 13: 2). In Philippians Jesus 'emptied himself' and was found 'in human form'. Throughout the Johannine and Pauline writings, too, there is an explicit dualism: in John between light, darkness, truth and the evil cosmos, in Paul the dualism of flesh and spirit, the 'heavenly' and the 'earthly' man, the complementary dualism of the first and second Adam. Ephesians differs slightly from the other Epistles in that it almost lacks definite reference to Jesus as the agent of creation, and the emphasis is more on his elevation to a position of supreme authority than on his pre-existence. Yet here Jesus is he whom God 'chose before the foundation of the world': perhaps a

[1] e.g. 'Before Abraham was, I am' (8: 58); 'glorify me with thine own self with the glory I had with thee before the world was' (17: 5).

statement of divine intention rather than of the pre-existence of the Son. If Ephesians is Paulinist[1] rather than Pauline a further indication is provided of the diffusion of the Christology which is being examined, and we have thus four groups of writings in which Jesus is regarded as the manifestation of the divine, pre-existent Logos-Son—Paul, Ephesians, Hebrews, and John, which suggests that behind them all was a further and original form of this Christology. That the leading thinkers of the New Testament arrived at the same Christological conclusions, or started from the same basic assumptions, is significant, and would seem to be more than mere coincidence.

It may be accepted as certain, therefore, that there existed in Apostolic circles a conviction that Jesus was the manifestation of a pre-existent being, a Son of God, equal and yet somehow subordinate to God in status, through whom the 'worlds' were created, who was the principle by which creation coheres, and who, after a brief sojourn on earth and his exaltation, ascended to the 'heavenly places' whence he came, to rejoin the Creator in His pre-eminence over His creation.

The Fourth Gospel clearly witnesses to a belief in the pre-existence of the Word, though no utterance of Jesus in the Synoptic Gospels suggests it. How much of the Johannine Gospel represents either the thought of Jesus or his actual words is, of course, one of the insoluble problems of the New Testament, though it is, I believe, wiser not to err too much on the side of scepticism. There is also the further difficulty, peculiar to the Gospel, of distinguishing between the author's comments and the words ascribed to Jesus, as the style is similar, for where the latter are coloured by Johannine phraseology they often lead smoothly to the former.

An example of this is John 3: 11–21, the passage beginning with an anacoluthon resembling a commentary. In it is included the passage referring to pre-existence: 'And no man hath ascended into heaven but he that came down from heaven, even the Son of Man who is in heaven.' The same applies to vv. 31–36 which contain the words 'he that cometh from heaven is above all', though this does not necessarily mean pre-existence. John 8: 38—'For I came down from heaven'—purports to reproduce the words of Jesus, though it might be maintained that the 'coming down' need not be spatially but

---

[1] There is no need to discuss the complex questions of the authorship of Ephesians and its relation to Colossians. Despite the careful analysis of the two documents in Dr. Leslie Mitton's study of the Epistle (*The Epistle to the Ephesians*, 1952, especially appendix I, p. 283), I am not convinced that it is not of Pauline authorship, though I have allowed above for the possibility that it may not be.

theologically interpreted. Had the words actually been uttered, the reaction of the listeners would doubtless have been similar to what is described; but had Jesus been aware of his pre-existence it is unlikely that his references to it would have been confined to one Gospel only, and that Gospel the one most inclined to offer a philosophical Christology. John 8: 58 contains the statement 'Before Abraham was I am', and in 17: 5 Jesus is alleged to have referred to the glory which he enjoyed with God before the world was; so also 17: 24. How far these are Jesus' own thoughts and how far they reflect the Gnostic mythology of the Heavenly Man with which it may be assumed that the author of the Ephesian Gospel was familiar, it is not possible to say. It is strange, too, that whereas 'Son of Man' and 'Messiah' were terms fully intelligible only to Palestinian Judaism they should have been employed by St. John in what is believed to be a document emanating from a Gentile environment in which the terms, in their Hebraic sense, would have been unintelligible. However that may be, we are faced with the important passage in John 8 in which Jesus is represented as speaking of his pre-temporal existence with God. Assuming that the words were spoken in some form resembling that in which they are presented, they might be interpreted in two ways: literally or metaphorically. If the former, then Jesus (if the words were used by him) clearly believed in his own pre-existence; if the latter (which cannot be proved) the words might be understood as Dr. C. H. Dodd expounds them as a claim that Jesus stood in an order of being wholly different from that represented by Abraham: namely outside the prophetic line and outside temporal relations. 'The relation of Father to Son is an eternal relation, not attained in time, nor ceasing with this life or with the history of this world. The human career of Jesus is, as it were, a projection of this eternal relation (which is divine ἀγάπη) upon the field of time' (*The Interpretation of the Fourth Gospel*, p. 262). The whole paragraph on p. 262 suggests a kind of demythologizing, for any attempt to make the passage acceptable in a non-literal sense is inevitably a form of demything. The passage (8: 46–59) is different both in spirit and in form from the Synoptic controversies. Writing of the idea of pre-existence in the New Testament Hermann Sasse says: 'It is regarded as a philosophical speculation which is really foreign to the New Testament. The pre-existence of Christ, however, of which the New Testament speaks, has nothing to do with philosophy; and the expression "pre-existence" which has been derived from philosophy ought therefore generally to be avoided, and "eternal" or "supratemporal" existence substituted for it' (*Mysterium Christi*, p. 108). The word 'before', he says, as used in John 17: 24 and elsewhere in a similar sense, 'implies far more than the mere temporal difference between before and after. There is that in it which can never be expressed in human speech, the distinction between the eternity of God and the time of our world'. This is interpretation, for what it implies is that the notion of pre-existence as a pre-historical condition of the life of Christ has to be translated into other than literal terms if it is to be properly understood; and these terms do not involve the idea of existence on another plane before birth and then coming 'down' from heaven to participate in a short existence on earth.

71

The 'Logos' theology, though it implies a metaphysical endeavour to interpret the historical Jesus and his redemptive mission in terms of what lies beyond the historical and the temporal, can hardly be described as *wholly* mythological, for the term itself is an abstraction, a symbolic rather than a literal term, requiring, as Faust discovered when faced with the task of translating the Johannine Prologue, a paraphrastic rather than a precise literal understanding ('*Im Anfang war die Tat*,' *Faust* I, l. 1237). Two terms out of the three—'Word became Flesh'—are abstract rather than picturesquely mythical, and the third is used in a conceptual rather than in a concrete sense. The proposition takes on a mythical colouring only when the Logos is personally equated with him who 'became' the historical Jesus. There is, however, no such unambiguous identification in John 1: 1–5, and the crucial pronouncement 'the Word became Flesh and dwelt among us' is so phrased that no precise indication is given of *how* the Word became Flesh. Such is its greatness. It does not say that *Jesus* existed from the beginning, that he was 'with' God, or that he 'was' God, but that the Word was eternal and divine and entered history through Jesus the Son. Identity of Word, Son, and God is not stated; it is enough to say with Dr. Dodd that 'the ground of all real existence is that divine meaning or principle which is manifested in Jesus Christ'. The greatness of the Fourth Gospel is exemplified in the manner in which it can be understood without the threat of the 'fallacy of misplaced literalism': a literalism for which Jesus is represented as rebuking the disciples when they appeared to think that he was speaking in literal and not in symbolical terms (John 6: 60–63). 'It is the *spirit* that gives you life; the flesh is of no avail; the words that I have spoken to you are spirit *and* life.'

The Johannine problem is extremely complex, and not least in the passages containing references to pre-existence; and no matter what the method of approach to it, the tension between the historical and the theological cannot be resolved. For some the choice may be between Westcott on the one hand and Loisy on the other; but for others there may be no alternative but the unsatisfactory one of suspended judgment. Dr. Dodd is of the opinion that the discourses and dialogues of the Fourth Gospel are 'certainly an original creation of the evangelist'. If so, their Christological implications cannot be said to derive from the actual words of Jesus and are as open to question as any other theological judgments.

As for the concept of pre-existence in the thought of Paul, it is not one to which one is committed and belongs to the sphere of the unverifiable and of myth rather than to historical literal thinking. Whatever truth it may possess will have to be reduced to non-mythical terms. The difference between Paul and John, however, consists in the fact that whereas the words referring to pre-existence in the Fourth Gospel are usually attributed to Jesus himself, in the Pauline passages they take the form of the affirmation of the author's faith.

In these conceptions there are obviously mythological constituents: the personalized Logos, the divine being co-existent with

God since before the creation, descending, assuming human form, the 'likeness of sinful flesh', 'in the likeness of men', and living a kind of historical interlude between two cosmic existences outside time and beyond history. Whatever the term 'humanity' means in ordinary parlance, it is something radically different from this, despite the endeavours of Paul (Phil. 2) and the author of Hebrews to present the earthly life of Jesus as genuinely human. Such a conception of Jesus, although magnificent, is, to anyone accustomed to think in terms of human history and human personality as these are understood, either rhetorical metaphor or mythology. If it is the former it should be equated with poetry; if the latter, it should either be abandoned or made intelligible in historical-personal terms. Whether the writers who were responsible for the New Testament Christology actually believed in this mythological picture in any literal sense cannot be ascertained; but because of the factual method of its presentation it is most probable that they did. We know the result of their Christological speculations; we do not know enough about the interior workings of their minds as they came to formulate them.

3

Two main attempts have been made to account for or to interpret these impressive forms of Christological thought. The first is exemplified in the brilliant work of Wilhelm Bousset and the group of scholars such as Reitzenstein, Norden, Dieterich, and other students of the same 'school' whose fascinating researches have disclosed the strange world of Gnostic and pre-Gnostic and other forms of Hellenistic religion. The tendency of this religious-historical method of investigation has been so to over-emphasize the possible influence of the Hellenistic world on the New Testament that the result is somewhat one-sided, as British critics of this standpoint have been quick to indicate. Bousset, for example, is disinclined to believe that Paul, despite the citation of texts supposed to show familiarity with the 'facts' about the historical Jesus, was in the least influenced by them.

It should be definitely stated [Bousset writes] that what we call the ethical-historical picture of Jesus was of no significance what-

ever for the piety of Paul. It is futile to cite in contradiction of this
data from the life of Jesus which were known to him.

This means that, though for Paul Jesus was a 'figure of historical
magnitude',[1] what really counted for the Apostle was the
mythical figure of the 'heavenly man', the Gnostic Anthropos,
the antithesis of πνεῦμα and σάρξ, and the 'anthropological
pessimism' which was as Hellenistic as it was un-Hebraic, though
it should be admitted that Paul formally employed a terminology
to some extent dependent upon the Septuagint.[2] Even though
the antithesis of *pneuma* and *sarx* is not over-prominent in Gnostic
literature, it should not be regarded, in Bousset's view, as reflecting a distinction corresponding to the difference between *nephesh*
and *ruach*. What is held to be of importance is not the precise
phraseology employed but the actual context, which, according to
Bousset, is to be sought in Gnosticism and in the mystery religions.
The 'myth' of the dying and suffering god, it is alleged, plays a
decisive part in determining Paul's soteriology and his sacramentalism. So it is with the 'heavenly man' as the background
of the antithesis of the first and second Adam.[3] The appearance
of Jesus in this world should be interpreted as 'an almost contranatural combination of a pneumatic divine being with σάρξ
ἁμαρτίας',[4] and the introduction of this cosmic power, this
superhuman archetype, into the historical scene is 'an incredibly
bold action on the part of the Apostle'. The myth of the archetypal heavenly man is 'transplanted from the prehistoric into
the present and associated with history', thereby completely
ignoring the Jesus of the Gospels and elaborating him into a
myth,[5] with the consequent antithetical separation of redemption from the world of creation. Paul, Bousset's argument runs,
was familiar with oriental redemption myths, and it is the
Anthropos archetype, not Old Testament analogy, which should
be read into his Christological speculations, though Bousset
indicates the considerable differences between the Gnostic
Anthropos-myth and Paul's christianized version of it.

Bousset applies the same principle of derivation to other aspects

[1] *Kyrios Christos*, 2nd ed., p. 105. [3] Ibid., pp. 140 ff.
[2] Ibid., p. 134, footnote. [4] Ibid., p. 142.
[5] Ibid., pp. 144, 145.

of Christology. Paul, for example, has de-judaized the concept of the Son of God by completely transferring it to the Hellenistic *Kyrios*,[1] and in the Johannine writings the title 'Son of Man' has been liberated from its eschatological context and transplanted into an entirely different world of thought. The Fourth Gospel, in Bousset's view, represents the fundamental transformation of the Synoptic Jesus in a Docetic context. History is thereby dissolved into myth; for what the Fourth Gospel displays is the Son of God (or God Himself) appearing on earth as an epiphany in all His omnipotence and majesty; the homely miracles and exorcisms of the Synoptics have disappeared. The mythological has usurped the historical. It is not to be wondered at, therefore, Bousset continues, that Matthew 11: 26–27, words which have an unmistakably Hellenistic sound, should have been popular with the Gnostics. The parallels to it in Hellenistic writings are certainly striking,[2] and Dr. Rawlinson, after thoroughly discussing various critical interpretations of it, agrees that its 'Johannine' character is undeniable and confesses that he is not ashamed that he cannot make up his mind as to whether it is 'literally authentic' or not.[3] Perhaps it is no solution of the problem to say that if it is not, it ought to be.

According to this view, then, the presuppositions of the Fourth Gospel and of the great Christological passages in the Epistles are Hellenistic or Gnostic. Paul, it is contended, interpreted the appearance of Jesus on the historical scene in terms of the pre-existent, heavenly man of Gnostic myth, and the Fourth Gospel is said to be in great part a document of Gnostic origin. Bultmann[4] still adheres to this position, treating John as preponderantly 'Gnostic' and its opening statement as a Gnostic redemption-myth. The revelatory discourses (*Offenbarungsreden*) are, in his view, derived from a Gnostic source; indeed, on the basis provided by Bultmann this 'source' has been reconstructed as a continuous

---

[1] *Kyrios Christos*, 2nd ed., p. 152.
[2] E. Norden, *Agnostos Theos*, pp. 276 ff.
[3] The *New Testament Doctrine of the Christ*, p. 263. For a valuable account of various views of this passage see Note IV, pp. 251 ff.; cf. also W. Manson, *Jesus the Messiah*, pp. 71 ff., T. W. Manson, *The Teaching of Jesus*, pp. 171 ff.
[4] *Johannes Evangelium*, ed. 1950; see especially pp. 38, 102 ff., 188 and 462. Jesus is 'der vollkommene Gnostiker'.

document or set of documents.[1] Both Bultmann and Bousset have stated their theses with great brilliance supported by immense erudition.

Nevertheless, to consider Paul as completely hellenized as he is represented, or as a kind of christianizer of mystery-cults, is virtually equivalent to believing that his thinking is substantially derivative from an alien environment which he, as a Jew, would regard unsympathetically. Yet, on the other hand, we cannot avoid taking into account the Hellenistic factors, which are by no means negligible. If, intellectually, Paul was not inferior to the great Greeks (despite the difference in the quantity of literary output) it is improbable that he was unfamiliar with the many facets of religious thought in what was in many ways the melting-pot of civilization and the scene of religious syncretism. It is, however, difficult to believe that he was so indebted to the time-less forms of Anatolian-Syrian cultic sacramentalism and to the curious subtleties of Gnostic speculations as to be as dependent upon them as Bousset and others have maintained. And even if he was for seventeen years out of touch with the Jerusalem church —a fact which should not be ignored—it would be a mistake to accept as proved the supposition that his Kyrios-Christology, as well as other constituents of his religious beliefs, was taken over *in toto* from Hellenistic congregations rather than from the earliest pronouncements of the Apostolic *kerygma*. Indeed, as Anderson Scott has suggested,[2] the absence, with one exception (Phil. 3: 20, and if his authorship of Ephesians is admitted, Eph. 5: 23), of the term Saviour from his writings may well be attributable to a disinclination to be too closely involved in the cultic termino-logy of his time, thereby bringing Christ down to the level of the Sotēr of the mystery religions. While there may be affinities between the New Testament writings and the religious terminology of the age (and it would be strange if there were not), most of recent New Testament scholarship is inclined to react against the view that the former were as strongly influenced by Hellenistic thought and religion as they were thought to be. Thus Dr. C. H. Dodd, while noting some similarities between *Poimandres* and the

---

[1] B. S. Easton, *Journal of Biblical Literature*, 1946, pp. 143 ff.
[2] *Christianity According to Paul*, p. 277.

Fourth Gospel, sees no necessity to assume any interconnection, and while, he says, the 'creative theologians'—Paul, Hebrews, and John—show an acquaintance with diffused popular beliefs, partly Platonic and partly Stoic, this is because of the general intellectual climate of the age rather than attributable to a direct indebtedness;[1] and, as B. M. Metzger has observed, it is psychologically inconceivable that Judaizers would have acquiesced in Paul's 'contamination' of Judaic Christianity by introducing elements from the mysteries.[2] It has been observed, too, that the ordinary terminology of the mystery religions is absent from the New Testament.[3] Though there are similarities between the mystery cults and early Christianity, they are those of analogous rather than of genealogical parallels.[4] As long ago as 1910 E. Krebs[5] critically examined Reitzenstein's views on the relation between *Poimandres* and John, and concluded that the Johannine diction was explicable in terms of Old Testament influence. W. L. Knox, too, after subjecting the Q logion Matthew 11 : 25 to linguistic examination, concludes that, because of the use of the word ἐξομολογοῦμαι, which he considers to be a semitic term, there is no need to regard it as of Hellenistic origin, even though the passage shows a 'remarkable similarity to some Hellenistic utterances' which may have been borrowed from the semitic world.[6]

Moreover, even if linguistic study shows how closely the vocabulary of Apostolic writings and that of the extra-biblical world were related, the differences between the Hellenistic-Gnostic world and the climate of the mystery religions on the one hand and the thought of the New Testament on the other are profound.

---

[1] *The Bible and the Greeks*, p. 204. Cf. C. H. Dodd, *The Present Task in New Testament Studies*, 1936, pp. 15, 16, *The Interpretation of the Fourth Gospel*, 1954, Pt. 1, chaps. 2, 5, 6, and Dodd's conclusions on pp. 53, 113, etc., with regard to the relationship of John to the Hermetic, Gnostic, and Mandaic writings; also H. J. Cadbury in the *Journal of Religion*, October 1941; A. D. Nock, in *Essays on the Trinity and the Incarnation*; A. E. J. Rawlinson, op. cit.

[2] 'Considerations of Methodology in the Study of Mystery Religions and Christianity' (*Harvard Theological Review*, January 1955): a valuable bibliographical and critical survey of the subject.

[3] A. D. Nock, 'The Vocabulary of the New Testament' (*Journal of Biblical Literature*, LII, 1933, pp. 131 ff.).

[4] Metzger, op. cit.

[5] *Der Logos als Heiland im ersten Jahrhundert*, Freiburg, 1910, p. 161.

[6] *Some Hellenistic Elements in Early Christianity*, p. 6 (Oxford, 1944).

Bousset's own account of Gnosticism, for example, illustrates the depth of the difference,[1] and even if the Johannine presentation of Jesus and his discourses has points of contact with Mandaic and Gnostic literature, the priority of the latter has not been irrefutably demonstrated. The world of Barbelo-Gnosticism and of the Gnostic Anthropos-Saviour, together with the whole complex of ideas which Gnosticism brought to bear on the Incarnation, is a fantastic one, and the identification of Anthropos with Christos and the association of Sotēr with Sophia are equally peculiar. Even Sophia has no point of contact with the Wisdom of the Old Testament: she is a kind of emanation from one of the angels of the Μονογενής. Absolute certainty cannot be attained in either direction. Ultimately any judgment upon the indebtedness of Apostolic Christianity to the thought-world of the time is a matter of opinion and is dependent to a great extent on changes in theological mood; yet on such a judgment depends in turn the extent to which one believes the Christology of the New Testament to be mythologically conditioned.

Further: Paul's contemptuous references to the 'gods many and lords many' and to the 'weak and beggarly elemental spirits' (Gal. 4: 8, 9) and the 'elemental spirits of the universe' (Col. 2: 8) are not easily explicable if he was consciously indebted to the world of ideas of which they were constituents. There is a difference between addressing people in terms which they understand and accepting the validity of those terms oneself. If any explanation of the mythical element in Paul's writings is required, it should be sought not only in the more esoteric religious systems of the time but also in the somewhat fantastic speculations of late Judaism, where the myth of the pre-existent Messiah and man from heaven was already available for him to draw upon.[2] Bousset inclines to the view that there was a combination of the Messiah-con-

---

[1] W. Bousset, *Hauptprobleme der Gnosis*, chap. vi, 'Die Gestalt des gnostischen Erlösers' (Göttingen, 1907). See also F. C. Burkitt, *The Church and Gnosis* (1932), S. Angus, *Religious Quests of the Greco-Roman World*, pp. 376–413, 1929, R. Liechtenhahn in *RGG*, II, 1478. In the light of Bultmann's views on John perhaps a second-century attribution of the authorship of the Gospel to the Gnostic Cerinthus was not altogether nonsensical.

[2] *Religion des Judentums*, p. 307 and passim. H. A. Fischel, 'Jewish Gnosticism in the Fourth Gospel' (*Journal of Biblical Literature*, 1946, 173), in a discussion of the influence of Rabbinic Gnosticism on the Johannine idea of the prophet, observes that the myth of the primal man occurred in Jerusalem Tannaitic teaching.

ception with that of a pre-existent being whose heavenly origin was obscure.

While bearing in mind, therefore, the possibility of the effects of syncretistic influences upon some aspects of the thought of St. Paul, the immediate source of the mythical element in his Christology lies nearer at hand: namely in the Hebraic tradition of the Wisdom literature, with which it may be assumed that the author of Hebrews was also familiar; for it is clear that one component of the idea of the pre-existence of the Christ and of his being the principle of cosmic cohesion was the identification in Paul's mind of Jesus with the Wisdom of God. In the Wisdom literature Sophia is described as the 'reflection of the glory of God', that through which all things exist, the agent of creation, and although the references are not numerous, they are typical and their content is plain.[1] If the passage Colossians 1: 15–18 were to be taken out of its context it might easily be read as a eulogy of Wisdom, which is not merely a commendable quality to be sought and acquired by the ambitious and the discreet (as in Ecclus. 6: 13) but also the creative word of God, the equivalent of the Logos. In the Wisdom of Solomon Wisdom is described as follows:

> She penetrates and pervades all things by reason of her purity.
> For she is as a breath of the power of God,
> A clear effluence of the Glory of the Almighty. . . .
> She is an effulgence from everlasting light,
> And an unspotted mirror of the working of God
> And image of His goodness.
>
> (Wisdom 7: 24–26)

The parallels to the Christological passages are plain. The 'Son' also 'reflects the glory of God and bears the very stamp of His nature' (Heb. 1: 2).[2] He is 'the image of the invisible God' (Col. 1: 15).

---

[1] But see below, pp. 176 ff.

[2] The words ἀπαύγασμα and εἰκών, used in this passage, also occur in Hebrews 1: 3 and Colossians 1: 15 respectively. The Philonic terminology is similar. The Logos is the εἰκών of God and His seal (σφραγίς), which may be compared with the 'stamp' (χαρακτήρ) of Hebrews 1: 3. Philo's word πρωτόγονος υἱός corresponds to πρωτότοκος in Colossians 1: 15. Cf. Dodd (*The Interpretation of the Fourth Gospel*, pp. 71–72, 275 ff. where close resemblances between Philo, Wisdom literature, and John, are set out and pp. 50–51 for parallels between the Hermetica and the Johannine writings. H. A. Wolfson, in his massive study of Philo, shares the view that Philo equates Wisdom with Logos (*Philo*, vol. i, pp. 253 ff., Harvard, 1948).

Wisdom, again, is pre-existent to creation:

> All wisdom comes from the Lord,
> And is with him for ever. . . .
> Wisdom has been created before all things.
>
> > (Ecclus. 1: 1, 4)

> The Lord possessed me in the beginning of His way,
> Before His works of old.
> I was set up from everlasting,
> Or ever the earth was.
>
> > (Prov. 8: 22–24)

Wisdom is the agent of creation:

> O God of the fathers, and the Lord who keepest thy mercy,
> Who madest all things by thy word,
> And by thy wisdom thou formedst man
> I came forth from the mouth of the Most High,
> And covered the earth as a mist.
>
> > (Ecclus. 24: 2 ff.)

Then follows a picture of her pre-eminence in creation.

In II Enoch God is represented as having ordered Wisdom to create man on the sixth day, and in I Baruch 3: 4–4: 4 there occurs a poem in praise of Wisdom.

Wisdom, it appears, is a hypostatization of the Creative Word of God, eternally present with Him and through whom all things subsist. She is the law-giving divine reason, God's assistant, the governess of man. So valued was she that she inspired some of the finest poetical passages in the Old Testament and the Apocrypha; it may be doubted, even, if Wisdom is there thought of in any terms but those of poetical symbolism. For it is not easy to distinguish here between what is literally believed and what is metaphorically or poetically expressed: the truth probably lies in a combination of the two. However that may be, in the Wisdom literature Sophia is not only a quality desirable in man, consisting of insight, common sense, shrewdness, 'wisdom' as generally understood, nor merely as an enlargement of this quality as an attribute of God, though she is the source of human wisdom.

It (or she) is at the same time a kind of functional hypostatization of an aspect of God. In the late apocalyptic writings she has become a concrete, independent figure existing side by side with God, the instrument of the creation of man (II Enoch 30: 8). The conception of Wisdom leaving her heavenly home, coming into the world and returning thither because she found no suitable home on earth, is also incidentally in evidence in the Enochic writings.[1]

Alexandrian Judaism was also familiar with the 'Wisdom' speculation. In Philo the Logos takes precedence over Sophia, though the latter term is by no means absent. Here again Wisdom is pre-existent as the creator of the world. Indeed, the Hebraic inclination to hypostatize the Divine creativeness seems to have been fairly general, for it occurs in other extra-biblical writings such as the Onkelos and Jonathan Targums[2] as well as in the formal Wisdom literature. Wisdom, Glory, Spirit are more or less interchangeable hypostases of various facets of the divine activity, magnificence, and power. Indeed, a comparison of the terminology of the Hermetica, Philo, John, Paul, Hebrews, and the Wisdom literature testifies to the existence of a kind of theological *lingua franca* of interchangeable terms applicable to the Hermetic God,[3] the Philonic Logos, the Creative Wisdom of the Old Testament and Apocrypha and to Jesus in the Christology of Paul, John, and Hebrews. This terminology was, it appears, taken over and appropriated to Christian requirements without any fine sense of discrimination. What is predicated of Thoth, Sophia, or Logos is easily transferred to Jesus. So it is with the conception of the Heavenly Man. In the Pauline context it is clear who is meant; there is no ambiguity in the use of the term.

---

[1] 'As Wisdom came down to make her dwelling-place among men and found none, she returned to her own place and resumed her seat among the angels' (II Enoch 42: 1–2). The similarity to John 1: 11—'he came to his own home and his own people received him not'(R.S.V.)—is obvious.

[2] e.g. the Onkelos Targum, 9, 15, 49 on Genesis and 26 on Leviticus, Jonathan Targum 17, 22 on Genesis, etc.

[3] Cf. the Poimandres hymn v. 31: 'Holy art Thou, who holdest all things together by the Word; Holy art Thou of whom every creaturely image hath been born; Holy art Thou whom the creaturely did not shape." Cf. Philo, *On the Creation (de Opif. Mundi)* 25, *On Dreams (de Somniis)* 2: 45, *De Plantatione* 8: 19, 20, where the same set of ideas recurs: the Logos as χαρακτήρ, the ἀρχέτυπος σφραγίς, the stamp, the archetypal seal and primordial image.

But further investigation shows that the contrast between the earthly man and the heavenly man also occurs in the work of Philo,[1] and in Dr. Dodd's opinion the 'Son of Man' of the Fourth Gospel has more affinity with the Anthrópos of *Poimandres* (which is manifestly mythological) than with Jewish apocalyptic.[2] We move in and out of the philosophical and mythological worlds almost without being aware of the transition. Nevertheless, St. Paul's 'heavenly man' is identifiable without any reference to Philo or to the shadowy background of the Hermetic and Gnostic writings, the precise date of whose composition is not known, which makes any attribution of indebtedness difficult.[3] Wisdom as Logos (in Philo) is a philosophic conception; Dr. Dodd points out that in the Philonic context the notion is identifiable with the Platonic world of ideas. Only in the Fourth Gospel does the Logos become incarnate, and it is precisely this conception of the Incarnation of the Logos which brings us into the world of mythology which is not sharply demarcated from philosophy.

It is this general uncertainty about direct relationships between the similar terms of the religious thought of the age which should put us on our guard against explaining Paul in terms of some archetypal redemption-myth or John and Hebrews in terms of Alexandrine philosophy or Hermetic combination of Platonism and Stoicism. In any case, it was easy enough for the Apostolic writers to make a series of cross-identifications and, in the light of their religious experience, to associate the Christ, the *Kyrios*, with the creative Logos, the Wisdom, and also with the apocalyptic archetype of the super-human Messiah.

Where, then, alternative explanations are available the wiser course is to accept that which is closer at hand and begs fewer questions, even though one has to conclude in the last resort that the problems of origins and indebtedness do not permit of solution.

---

[1] 'There are two types of man: the one a heavenly, the other an earthly. The heavenly man, being made after the image of God, is altogether without part or lot in corruptible and terrestrial substance; but the earthly one was compacted out of matter scattered here and there' (*Allegorical Interpretation of Genesis*, 1: 31–32—*Leg. Alleg.*). The heavenly man is here not a primordial archetypal being, as in the Anthropos myth, but the Platonic heavenly counterpart of the earthly man.

[2] *The Interpretation of the Fourth Gospel*, p. 44.

[3] Dr. Dodd (ibid., p. 52) believes that biblical influence is to be detected in some of the Hermetic writings, especially on *Poimandres*.

One can do little but hold opinions. The Wisdom-theology is clearly that which is most likely to have been uppermost in the minds of biblical writers, and Colossians 1 : 15 ff. is pure Wisdom-theology, as is Hebrews 1 : 2–3. 'Image', 'reflection of glory', the creation of the world by a divine agency, the subsistence of all things through Wisdom: these are typical terms of the Wisdom literature, and it is through their adoption and elaboration no less than through the assimilation of parallel Hellenistic terms that we are most likely to possess the key to the mythological character of the more eloquent examples of New Testament Christology.

It might be mentioned in passing that the hypostatizing (or mythologizing) of Sophia is prominent in Russian Orthodox theology, whose developments have been different from those of Western Christian thinking and have at times been so elaborately speculative as to recall the speculations of Gnosticism. The formative influence in Russian sophiological thinking was Vladimir Solovyev, who believed that he had a mystical experience of Sophia: an experience which gave its direction to the first period of his writings. In his *Lectures on God-Manhood* the hypostatization of Sophia occupies a prominent place, as does his interpretation of the Logos as the rational expression of the Deity in creation. The perfect man is the supreme expression of Sophia, the divine Wisdom; the God-Man in Jesus Christ is a combination of Logos and Sophia. In his divine being the generative forces are the Logos and Wisdom (chaps. vii–viii). Sophia is also the soul of the world, and as the church she is the Bride of the Divine Word. Pavel Florovsky (1882–1946) elaborated still further this kind of sophiological theology. For him the cosmic reality as a whole is Sophia, who is a kind of 'fourth hypostasis' and 'the great root of the created world in all its wholeness and unity'. The Divine Wisdom is the guardian of the created world, its ideal substance, its reason and that which provides its truth and meaning, and is somehow related to the Logos who also assumes the substance of the created world. Sergius Bulgakov (b. 1871) in his *The Unfading Light* and *The Bride of the Lamb* became so speculative that the Metropolitan of Moscow criticized his ideas as 'alien' to the orthodox tradition. Bulgakov, like Florensky, regarded Sophia as a fourth hypostasis providing the organic unity of the Ideas of all living creatures, 'the divine Archetype and basis of man's being', a living entity though not a personal one; her hypostasis is the Logos who reveals the Father as demiurge. The Logos is the Eternal Man, the Heavenly Man, the Son of God and the Son of Man. There are even two Sophias: the divine and the created. The former is 'the divine all-qualitative all-unity' of God in His self-revelation, which is called in the Scriptures the 'Wisdom' of God. Nikolai Lossky (b. 1870) also accepts this Russian sophiology, and considers Sophia, who is the 'head of the world' or the 'world-spirit', to be the closest worker with

Jesus, though this thought is but incidental to his large output of philosophical writings (see N. O. Lossky, *The History of Russian Philosophy*, Allen and Unwin, 1952).

I have referred to the sophiology of Russian Christian philosophers in order to show that the hypostatization of an aspect of divine Being is not merely a poetical metaphor practised by Hebrew Wisdom writers but occupies a prominent place in modern and even contemporary Russian Orthodox thought. Whether this ascription of cosmic pre-eminence to Wisdom, and the objectification of it in the 'person' of Sophia, who cannot be considered to exist ontologically, have any real meaning is arguable; but if such hypostatization is a form of mythological thinking it shows that modern theologians of the Orthodox tradition regard it as quite as justifiable as did St. Paul. Their procedure is, in fact, similar to his own. They hypostatize the creative aspect of the divine energy as the ground and sustaining power of creation and, though possibly in a more questionable and speculative manner, transfer it to Jesus. The affinities of this type of theology are with the Alexandrine-Byzantine rather than with the Western-Reformed traditions; and the Orthodox Church not only mythologized the Divine Wisdom but canonized her as St. Sophia.

4

If it can be maintained, then, that St. Paul, while still making use of a mythological way of thinking, and while doubtless aware of the religious mythology of the contemporary world, found the stimulus to his Christological affirmations not mainly in Hellenistic but in Hebraic sources, it can with some justification be submitted that his Christology was a stage removed from, rather than nearer to, the mythological thought-forms and archetypal concepts of his age. 'Wisdom', whether thought of metaphorically or onto-logically, was identified in some way by St. Paul with the historical Jesus and through his Resurrection and exaltation to the status of *Kyrios* was given cosmic redemptive significance. On the one hand Jesus was for him to be identified with the divine Wisdom, thereby sharing in divine pre-eminence over the cosmos. On the other, the Wisdom of God is personalised in the historical agent of redemption, and the latter is raised to the position of an aspect of the divine energy and a participator in the divine sovereignty. We are, however, still left with the idea of the pre-existence of the Son which is logically implicit in St. Paul's identification of Jesus with the eternal wisdom of God pre-existent to creation. We have seen, moreover, that the form in which this pre-existence is described is formally mythological in its representation of the descent of the Son of God into the world. By this method of identification and equation St. Paul has committed himself to the doctrine that it is not only the divine energy but the Son, the present *Kyrios*, who is the instrument of creation and the medium of its consubsistence. The implications of this will be examined later; it is necessary, however, to enquire more closely into the meaning of the concept of pre-existence and into its necessity or otherwise as a 'mythical' presupposition of what the Apostle was endeavouring to express.

Though it is a category foreign to the modern mind it was not foreign to Paul. Both the Alexandrine philosophy of hellenized Judaism and the Messiology of contemporary Palestinian Judaism provided the intellectual framework within which his Christology took shape. The Logos-Son and the Messiah-Son of Man groups of religious personifications were conceived of as existing independently of history and as belonging to a realm beyond time, though the latter figure was thought of as appearing in the future on the historical scene at the end of the age. The mental climate of St. Paul's world, as regards both its Hellenistic and Hebraic components, provides a ready-to-hand metaphysical interpretation of the redemptive mission of Jesus and of his eternal co-existence with God as the present *Kyrios* of the Church, and with complete confidence he expresses his belief in the pre-existent Christ Jesus as one who, as it were, had lived elsewhere before his historical existence. As H. R. Mackintosh has rightly said,[1] the only pre-existence in which the Apostolic writers were interested was not ideal but real and personal. It should be assumed that Paul would have no difficulty in concluding that he whom he had encountered on the road to Damascus with such cataclysmic consequences, and whom in his own experience he acknowledged as Saviour and Lord, existed not only after his death but in some manner prior to his earthly life. If, however, we assume, from the standpoint of a modern interpretation, that the doctrine (if it may be so called) of pre-existence is, as H. R. Mackintosh has expressed it, 'an imperfect means of representing eternity in the forms of time', it should be frankly admitted that

---

[1] *The Person of Jesus Christ*, p. 447.

there is no indication that Paul conceived it in this philosophical and demythologized manner. He clearly believed, as the Philippians passage shows, in the self-emptying and voluntary humiliation in history of one whose appropriate sphere was not history but eternity.

Lest it should be thought that more than justifiable meaning is being read into the term ἐκένωσεν, it should be stated that on the four other occasions on which forms of κενόω occur in the New Testament (Rom. 4: 14; I Cor. 1: 17; 9: 15; II Cor. 9: 3) the word implies the notion of 'empty' or an extension of it. It may be that the A.V. 'made himself of no reputation' is closer to Paul's intention than the literal translation 'emptied himself'. Bishop Morgan, in his 1588 translation of the Bible into Welsh, rendered it as 'disbrisiodd' (depreciated), while Luther translated it more literally as 'entäusserte'. If the Kenotic Christology really means that Jesus divested himself of his divine attributes in their fulness, and if this is what St. Paul meant by the term in Philippians 2: 7, the comment of so conservative a theologian as William Temple should not pass unnoticed. 'I confess,' he wrote (*Christus Veritas*, p. 141), 'to an uneasy feeling that when this vigorous expression of a great spiritual truth is taken as a precise and scientific theology, we are involved in something dangerously close to mythology. To say that God the Eternal Son at a moment of time divested Himself of Omniscience and Omnipotence in order to live a human life, reassuming these attributes at the Ascension, seems to me just the kind of thing that no event occurring on this planet could ever justify.' D. M. Baillie (*God was in Christ*, pp. 94 ff.) has made a similar criticism of the Kenotic Christology, though in his view it can 'hardly claim the direct support of that lyrical Pauline passage or mistake its poetry for theological theory'. While Dr. Baillie's criticisms of this Christology are unanswerable, it is nevertheless the case, in my view, that the Kenotic Christology is a not illogical deduction from Philippians 2 and from the general trend of the traditional Christology of the Church. It has been at any rate so understood by many writers of hymns from which popular Christology is derived. Cf.

'Lo! within a manger lies
He who built the starry skies' (Edward Caswall).

'Who is this, so weak and helpless,
Child of lowly Hebrew maid. . . .
'Tis the Lord of all creation . . .' (W. W. How).

'Lord of Life and King of Glory,
Who didst deign a child to be' (Christian Burke).

'He came down to earth from heaven,
Who is God and Lord of all' (C. F. Alexander).

Examples of this kind of hymn-Christology could be multiplied. So much of what is understood as orthodox Christology seems, as Dr. Baillie says, 'more like a pagan story of metamorphosis than like the Christian doctrine of Incarnation, which has always found in the life of Jesus on earth God and man in simultaneous union—the Godhead "veiled in flesh" but not *changed into* humanity' (ibid., p. 97). But it is difficult to see how this interpretation is to be avoided as long as theology retains a term such as 'God the Eternal Son', which makes some kind of belief in pre-existence, and with it a Kenotic Christology, inevitable, though post-apostolic Christology has on the whole been more guilty of this kind of thinking than (taken as a whole) the Apostolic writers themselves. H. R. Mackintosh makes a valiant attempt to re-interpret the basis of the Kenotic Christology and to retain what he believes to be the substance of the idea of pre-existence while unable at the same time fully to avoid its logical consequences. He admits that it was not the historic Jesus 'exactly as he was known in the Gospels' who pre-existed and that we cannot 'simply' equate the pre-temporal one with the exalted Lord (*The Person of Jesus Christ*, p. 457). Indeed, this is the official teaching of the Roman Catholic Church. (See, for example, the *Catechism of Christian Doctrine*, art. 39, 40: *Was Jesus Christ always Man?*—Jesus Christ was not always man. He has been man only from the time of His Incarnation. *What do you mean by Incarnation?* I mean by the Incarnation that God the Son took to Himself the nature of man.) But if continuity and identity have any ascertainable meaning when applied to Christology, to say that it was not Jesus who pre-existed but the Word, or the Son, is illogical. If the Son pre-existed, and Jesus was the Son, then by a simple equation Jesus must have pre-existed. I am not disputing Dr. Baillie's phrase 'God and man in simultaneous union', and this is doubtless what is meant by the Definition of Chalcedon. But the 'mythological' understanding of the Incarnation together with the implicates of pre-existence is the popular one, and it is not without justification in the Philippians passage, even if this has been misunderstood, or at any rate literally interpreted. Hastings Rashdall (in a series of articles entitled 'Plain Words to Bishop Gore') once accused the bishop of heresy for believing that the Incarnate Son was continuous with the pre-existent Logos, to which Gore replied: 'I cannot think that Dr. Rashdall holds that the person who appeared as Jesus Christ was really an Eternal Person in the Blessed Trinity who at a certain date took flesh and became man, remaining always the same. I feel sure that for Dr. Rashdall the Person of Jesus began to exist when He was born of human parentage. And yet the former of these theories is the theory which Catholic terminology is quite deliberately fashioned to express, and so to express as to exclude the second' (*Modern Churchman*, vol. IX, p. 478).

Nevertheless, the substance of St. Paul's Christological thought is not obscure, and to take exception to its precise form may be an instance of the 'fallacy of misplaced literalism' which has already been mentioned as equivalent to the rejection of symbolical thinking as such. If we could be certain that St. Paul's thought was symbolical the problem of re-interpretation would be less difficult of solution. Moreover, it is not simplified but complicated by the fact that its presuppositions were shared by the authors of Hebrews and the Fourth Gospel.

The problem, however, is not merely one of unanimity of use but of the validity of the terms employed, for within the context of their age their unanimity is not difficult to account for. The New Testament writers drew upon a common store of Old Testament thought and of contemporary religious philosophy. It is therefore not superfluous to enquire into the basic meaning of that on which they were in agreement and to ask whether this, when reduced to its essential content, requires the support of mythological thought-forms, whether the mythological clothing cannot be discarded while the body which it conceals remains, and whether a distinction should not be made between the kernel and husk, between the content and the form. The content is the heart of the Christian kerygma; the husk is the contingent form of its expression. For if it is not necessary to believe that Jesus literally sat down at the right hand of God it is reasonable to contend that it is no more necessary to accept the other mythological or symbolical constituents of the 'husk' to which this metaphor belongs. The first stage in the non-mythological interpretation of the great New Testament proclamations is to approach them as boldly imaginative metaphors, whether they were originally so intended or not.

Now, it should be apparent that the consequences of this treatment of the Christological passages which are being discussed will be considerable; for if the orthodox doctrine of the Incarnation as the becoming-flesh of a divine being derives from a literal acceptance of what are mythological conceptions, it may with justice be asked what remains of it. For the Incarnation, according to orthodox definition, means the becoming-flesh of one who, in a previous state of being, was not in the flesh, though this is not a logical inference from the Messianic self-consciousness of the Son of Man in the Synoptic Gospels; nor, so far as can be ascertained, is it implied in the earliest Christian kerygma, which was the affirmation that the Jesus of history, through his Cross and Resurrection, had been elevated to the status of the Lord of Life. The Petrine 'sermons', for example, show how little a 'mythological' Christology had been evolved in the early days of the faith by those who had been daily in contact with Jesus. Their interpretation of his mission was historical, not, if the terms are not inappropriate, mythological or cosmological. The things 'which God foretold, by the mouth of all the prophets that His Christ should suffer, he thus fulfilled'.[1] Peter refers to the promise of Deuteronomy 18: 15–16, according to which Moses predicted that 'the Lord God will raise up for you a prophet from your brethren as He raised me up . . . God, having raised up his servant, sent him to you first';[2] 'Jesus of Nazareth, a man attested/ accredited to you by God with mighty works and wonder and signs which God did through him in your midst',[3] who was genealogically 'of the seed of David'.[4] Jesus is the 'Holy and Righteous One', the 'Prince of Life'. There is no suggestion here that the companions of Jesus ever thought of him as the pre-existent Son or Word as one who had 'descended': he was born of the line of David, and chosen in God's predetermining wisdom; he was the historical-eschatological fulfilment of the prophetic hope. This, whether we agree with the Apostolic exegesis or not, was the substance of the early kerygma, and its genuineness is attested by the fact that, even if as late a date as A.D. 80 is accepted for the composition of Acts, the Christology is virtually unaffected by Pauline and Johannine elaborations. It is succinctly expressed in Acts 10: 35–38.[5] Following the Resurrection, God has 'made' Jesus 'Lord and Christ'; Jesus is exalted to the place of supreme honour at the right hand of God. It is through this divine seal set on his mission that he becomes the *Kyrios*: the one who is worthy of reverence and faith and is now one with God the Father, Judge, and Creator. The emphasis is throughout on the exaltation of the 'prophet' who was of the line of David: that is, one whose descent according to the flesh is understood in terms

---

[1] Acts 3: 18.
[2] Acts 3: 22, 26.
[3] Acts 2: 22.
[4] Acts 2: 10–11.
[5] See Torrey's reconstruction in C. H. Dodd, *The Apostolic Preaching and its Developments*, pp. 54–55.

of human paternity. As fulfilment, as 'realized eschatology', Jesus' mission is understood in terms of historical reference to divine promises made within the framework of recorded history. On the one side the answer to the historical hope is given from within history. To that extent the primitive kerygma shows that a full appreciation of the 'salvation-event' did not depend upon its transcendent-mythological interpretation.

Moreover, if (despite Brunner and Bultmann) we return to the Synoptic tradition, assuming that it represents early traditions and not the theology of the early church, there is no evidence that Jesus thought of himself as the enfleshment of a divine pre-existent being; nor did he make any claim to creative pre-eminence over the cosmos. His conception of Sonship was that of complete spiritual intimacy between himself and God:[1] an intimacy which is often implied and affirmed but into the character of which we can enter, perhaps, only conjecturally. In the light of the Lukan story of the visit of the boy Jesus to the Temple, which bears the marks of authenticity, it is improbable that this awareness of Sonship began with the experience accompanying Baptism; otherwise as to the nature of the hidden years we can do no more than indulge in guesswork. We can only assume that from the beginning their character was conditioned by divine intention and that it was the purpose of God to reveal Himself to Jesus so intimately that no other term but 'Son' was adequate to describe their relationship. Of the later belief that Jesus was God Himself in the flesh there is no trace in the Synoptic Gospels, and the foundation for it in the rest of the New Testament is slender. It was certainly no part of the acceptance of belief in Jesus as Messiah, who, in the words of the early kerygma, was 'a man accredited by God'. If this is considered to be, in Sanday's phrase, a 'reduced' Christology,[2] it may be legitimately asked what higher Christology is there than that which is consistent with the teaching of Jesus about himself? There can be no more profound or comprehensive term describing Jesus' complete unity with God than the word 'Son', which the early preachers

---

[1] e.g. the Q saying Matthew 11 : 27.
[2] William Sanday used this term in a paper read at Oxford in 1901 in which he dealt with Harnack's *Das Wesen des Christentums*, which had recently appeared.

interpreted through the picture of the Suffering Servant of God, and which reached its richest expression in the Fourth Gospel. It is an error to regard this Christology of 'Sonship' by the intention of God as any more 'reduced' than the mythological Christology of church orthodoxy.[1]

On the other hand, we should be careful, as Dr. C. H. Dodd has said, not to select from the New Testament passages which seem to have a ' "modern" ring', and to declare that these represent the 'permanent element' in it; to do this is not necessarily to preach the Gospel, for it is easy to be mistaken, on a superficial reading, about the true meaning of passages which strike us as congenial. The 'crude early formulation of the Gospel' should not be suggested as an exclusive standard.[2] Yet it does not follow that late formulations are necessarily to be preferred to earlier ones. The early preaching has no 'modern ring', though its simplicity and directness are such that its meaning is more easily accessible to the modern Christian. It is freer from intellectualism and from the more mythological idiom of a more developed theology, and shows that earlier formulations may still be an adequate instrument for the expression of the 'existential' experience of the early church.

In the last resort no precise definition of what the Incarnation means can have final validity, though it is necessary to have a fixed point of reference (even if this has to be re-interpreted or demythologized) to which all Christological thinking can be referred. If this sounds paradoxical it must be admitted that such paradox is inevitable, for we are dealing not with logic but with faith, and the paradox of divine exaltation through humiliation

---

[1] I am not ignoring the value of the increasing richness of Christological apprehension in the New Testament but contending that their mythological formulation is not necessary to an adequate Christology. Dr. Vincent Taylor has shown that even short periods within the Apostolic age were characterized by different groups of Christological ideas which replaced earlier ones. During the first period, that is of the historical ministry, the titles in use were those such as Jesus, Son of Joseph, Teacher, Son of Man, 'he that cometh', Son of God—nineteen in all, of which eight continued to be used. In the second period, A.D. 30–65, the titles Jesus Christ, Son of God, the Son, were dominant. The third period, A.D. 65–100, was characterized by the use of metaphors rather than by titles indicative of status or function. Of the forty-two principal names and titles (with the exception of three soteriological ones) twenty-five are metaphorical and of a dozen descriptive of status or function only four survived generally (*The Names of Jesus*, 1954, pp. 66 ff., 169 ff.).

[2] *The Apostolic Preaching and its Developments*, p. 187.

is no greater than that of asserting the need for mythological symbols and archetypes which gain their depth of meaning through being non-mythologically interpreted. The 'myth' of the self-emptying of the Son of Man is a paradox, for in his self-abnegation, in his self-limitation, is to be found his glory, his victory in his defeat, his triumph through his self-effacement, his Lordship through his being in 'the form of a Servant'. Jesus confronted his contemporaries with the paradox of the suffering Son of Man which was overcome through its resolution by the Apostolic acknowledgment of his Lordship, and his liberation through the restrictive consequence of his unconditional obedience 'even to the death of the Cross'.

The doctrine of the Incarnation does not necessarily imply the mythological notion of a miraculous birth, the 'descending' and 'ascending' pre-existent Son of God, nor the temporary abdication of the Son from his cosmic jurisdiction. It does, however, mean that 'God was in Christ reconciling the world to Himself', that in a non-mythological sense the 'Word became flesh' and that in him was seen the glory 'as of the only-begotten of the Father'. It does mean that 'he who has seen me has seen the Father', and that, in terms of perfect intimacy, 'I and the Father are one'. If Incarnation describes the relation of the Son to the Father as a personal experience within history, rather than a process of becoming, then the term means all these great and fundamental affirmations of fact and faith, of fact interpreted by faith, and of faith given historical foundation by the fact. For what matters is less the supposed manner of the process of the Incarnation than the affirmation of God in Christ.

CHAPTER TWO

THE INTERPRETATION OF THE MYTH

I

Implicit in the 'mythological' type of Christology which is being examined is the concept of time; for existence, whether pre-historical or historical, is inseparable from the notion of time. The very term pre-existence involves 'time'-thinking, the relation of time to eternity, of history to what is beyond history, and a dimension in which the Incarnation, so to speak, happens. Space, however, is also a dimension of existence, for what happens must happen somewhere, that is to say, in space; even the pre-eminence of Jesus is described not only in temporal but also in spatial terms and relationships, such as 'ascended into Heaven' and 'on the right hand of God' (expressions which are metaphorical as well as mythological) and phrases in which the exalted Lord is described as exercising the attributes of one who is supreme 'over' the order of creation. Whereas, however, the theme of Christ and Time has received some attention in recent theological writing,[1] the subject of Christ and Space has been overlooked. Yet it may be said that, without introducing by force notions foreign to New Testament thought, space-time is also a Christological category in so far as Apostolic conceptions of the mode of Jesus' being involve some consideration of the space-time factor. The two concepts, space and time, are, moreover, inseparable, for he who is thought of as existing, or having existed 'outside' time, that is, eternally in the bosom of the Father as well as 'in' historical time, is thought of also as being in a kind of structural-spatial relationship with the rest of creation. As in the Fourth Gospel ἄνω and κάτω, which are spatial concepts, are inseparable from the notion of pre-existence, so there

---

[1] e.g. O. Cullmann, *Christ and Time* (1951), John Marsh, *The Fulness of Time* (1952), Karl Barth, *Kirchliche Dogmatik*, III, 2, pp. 574–780, and earlier F. H. Brabant, *Time and Eternity in Christian Thought* (1936) and the essay 'God and Time' in *Essays on the Trinity and the Incarnation*.

appears to be in the mind of St. Paul a close association of pre-existence with extension in the cosmos.

For what is revealed in the great Christological passages which have been quoted is the conviction that, somehow, the Lord not only exists independently of a human conception of him, but also that his exalted status can be adequately described only in terms of transcendence 'over' the rest of the cosmic series. This transcendence takes the form of occupying the highest place in an ascending order including creation, man, and angelic-demonic beings, and also a qualitative transcendence by virtue of the Lordship which has been conferred upon him or which he enjoys by nature.[1] As anteriority of being is one side of the Christological dimension, so superiority of status, hierarchically conceived, represents the spatial category of New Testament thought. Jesus has been 'exalted' so that God has bestowed upon him a 'name' (*Kyrios*) which is 'above' every name (Phil. 2: 9, 10); he 'unites' all things in heaven and earth and is 'far above all rule and authority and power and dominion' (Eph. 1: 10, 20–22); 'in' him all things were created, 'through' him and for him, and 'in him all things hold together' (Col. 1: 16 ff.); 'through whom are all things and through whom we exist' (I Cor. 8: 6); he is the upholder of the universe (Heb. 1: 2).

In these passages there is implied a pre-eminence not only of spiritual quality but of cosmological status, for it is questionable whether Paul was using metaphorical terms only: his cosmology was such that a spatial pre-eminence seems also to be implied. In any case, Jesus' pre-eminence can be described diagrammatically as the highest of ascending levels of reality.[2] That the attributes of the Christ are those of Hebrew 'Wisdom' makes no difference to the dimensionality of the Pauline type of Christology. Wisdom was conceived both temporally as being with God from the beginning and spatially as an omnipresent creative activity. As a kind of subordinate hypostasis of the Deity Wisdom was thought

---

[1] It is not improbable that the word πρωτότοκος in Colossians 1: 15 implies rank or pre-eminence as well as, or rather than, a cosmic anteriority, 'born first before all creation'. The question is briefly discussed by Dr. H. G. Meecham, *Expository Times*, Jan. 1955, p. 124.

[2] W. Temple, *Christus Veritas*.

of in terms of pretemporality and panspatiality: attributes which, as we have seen, Paul transfers to Jesus, the identification of whom with the Spirit (pneuma) implies some kind of ubiquity or omnipresence and independence of 'objective' space.

The New Testament conception of a universe ('all things') cohering in space through Jesus is, it must be admitted, foreign to modern ways of thinking if what is meant is that Jesus is the agent of creation and the force which holds all together so that without him it would fall apart. It is not a necessary deduction from any known data, least of all from anything that Jesus is reported to have said in the Synoptic Gospels. Paul is clearly thinking in mythological terms in transforming the *Kyrios* into a principle of cosmic cohesion, the 'suprapolar space' of which Karl Heim writes as the *locus* of all objects and the invisible dimension of all-embracing spirit.[1] Like Bultmann, Heim understands the thought underlying the grandiloquent Christological utterances in terms of its existential impact upon the person. He sees in the 'suprapolar space' the conception of the unifying, sustaining principle mythologized by St. Paul (though he does not exactly express himself in this way), that which invests the whole cosmos with meaning and gives to it a religious rather than a kind of gravitational coinherence.

> All these tremendous universal pronouncements [he says] rest upon the certainty that He who has come among us in the name of God speaks in terms of the cosmic whole. He sees into the depths of the cosmos. . . . Here then for a start the aim of relativism is achieved, that all-embracing breadth which comprises the whole wealth of the immense plenitude of reality. But if there is a suprapolar space, then this breadth of horizon does not have to be paid for, as was the case with relativism, by a corresponding loss of that unity and coherence in the directing of my life. . . . The accent of eternity rests upon one quite definite point where there is revealed

[1] See *Christian Faith and Natural Science*, S.C.M. Press, 1953, in which Heim uses the concept of suprapolar space in order to interpret theism in terms consistent with modern mathematical physics. Heim's suprapolar space, the absolute dimension, which includes all relative polarities and is the 'eternal counterpoise to the totality of all polar spaces' (p. 177), is synonymous with the 'all-presence of God' transcending three-dimensional space. Heim works out his thesis with the problem of space in modern physics as his starting-point. His line of thought is continued in *The Transformation of the Scientific World View*, S.C.M. Press (1953).

to me the direction in which now, in the name of God, I must go forward. . . . That which was from the beginning and in which was potentially the whole intrinsic meaning of the world that was still to come into being, is here revealed in an individual figure in which the whole abundance of light of the cosmos is concentrated as though in a focus. . . .[1]

In so far as Paul's thought can be considered to have meaning for today it might be translated into such terms as these, which doubtless interpret the faith behind the metaphor, or the reality behind the myth. Perhaps the real question is whether the notion of the Christ 'in' and 'through' whom 'all things' exist should be abandoned forthwith, for any attempt to make it intelligible in language which means anything to contemporary man suggests the process of intellectual gymnastics for the purpose of making at all costs remotely intelligible what may not, after all, be capable of precise interpretation. It may be that the great Pauline conception may be too deeply involved in what Heim calls the 'mythical space-picture of the primitives' to bear the interpretation which he puts upon it; for the universe is held together by something quite different, namely, a gravitational system so involved and complicated that it cannot be visualized by the mind but only, if at all, in terms of mathematical symbols. The theist, no doubt, believes that such a universe consisting of mutually supporting systems exists by the will of its Creator; but to identify the Creator as He in whom all things hold together (συνέστηκεν) with the glorified, exalted Jesus of Nazareth is to perform an intellectual leap which is strange to him who does not share St. Paul's world-view and is unable to make a factual assertion in such mythological terms.

From this it becomes apparent that St. Paul was thinking of Jesus in terms, inapplicable to a historical personality as he is conceived today, which point to the question: 'What is the character of Christ's dimension of existence now?'—a question which can be answered, perhaps, only through the use of a term such as is suggested by Heim, namely the dimension of supra-polar space to which the limitations of chronological time and

[1] *Christian Faith and Natural Science*, pp. 189–190.

three-dimensional space do not apply. Indeed, it is clear from the Gospel accounts of the Resurrection that the Risen Lord had already transcended this Euclidean-temporal world. It was natural that after his Resurrection Jesus should be freed from the limitations of this-worldly space-time in order to be able to appear and disappear at will independently of material and spatial restrictions. It was probably because of this release from the conditions imposed by what Heim calls 'non-objective' space that Paul identified the Lord with the Spirit through which he became extended in space and able to operate in the universal church. Although Paul's doctrine of the Spirit is complicated (and in Bultmann's view mythological), one interpretation of it might be that it is the dimension of the activity of Jesus in the world, and Jesus is to that extent identifiable with the Creator Spirit in whom all things exist.

Moreover, according to the popular cosmology of the ancient world space was not 'empty' but peopled by invisible beings. It was the strange world of which there are suggestions in Colossians, Ephesians, and late Jewish angelology. This world-space was essentially mythological space, for it was represented as a cosmos ruled by the Seven Deathless Cosmocrats, the 'world-rulers' of Ephesians 6: 12. In it planets became elements (Gal. 4: 3, 9) and the elements were equated with demons. Here there was no real freedom but only necessity and fate. The stars were thought of as real gods and as invisible divinites; moving in the world above, which was a truly divine world, and ordering human destiny, they were objects of veneration. Dr. Gilbert Murray has described this strange cosmocracy as follows:

> Here on earth we are the sport of fate; nay, on earth we are worse still. We are beneath the moon, and beneath the moon there is not only Fate but something more malignant: Chance. Above the moon there is no Chance, only Necessity; there is the will of the six other kosmokratores, Rulers of the universe. But above them there is an eighth region—the home of the Ultimate God, whatever he was named, who was before the Kosmos. In this is true being and freedom. Though the kosmokratores cast us to and fro like their slaves or dead chattels in soul at least we are of equal birth to them. The Mithraic votary, when their wrathful

and tremendous forces break in upon his vision, answers them unterrified; I am your fellow-wanderer, your fellow-star.[1]

That Paul was familiar with this world-picture is shown by the eloquent passage in Ephesians 6 and in the passage in the Epistle to the Galatians where he uses the expression 'in bondage under the elements of the world' (ὑπὸ τὰ στοιχεῖα τοῦ κόσμου ἤμεθα δεδουλωμένοι) which accurately describes this astral fatalism.[2] For it he substituted his own conception of freedom resulting from the supersession of the rule of cosmic spirits by that of the Lord Christ who rendered them impotent and asserted his sovereignty over the 'things under the earth', 'the earth', and the 'things above the earth' and the ascending grades in which the various cosmocratic hierarchies were situated. The 'all things' of Colossians 1: 16 and I Corinthians 15: 27, 28 as well as the spiritual beings of Ephesians 6: 12 belong to the same kind of mythological thought-world as the cosmocrats and discarnate inhabitants of the Gnostic universe. Exactly how Paul regarded them can only be conjectured. He may, as Dr. G. H. C. Macgregor has assumed, have admitted their existence while denying their divinity.[3] In the letter to the Colossians, in particular, he deals with the Hellenistic-Gnostic environment of the Church, and the recipients are warned against the corrupting effects of 'philosophy' and of belief in the 'elements' which, he points out, are no real receptacles or manifestations of Divinity. Jesus has spoiled the principalities and powers by virtue of his crucifixion and Resurrection. These 'powers' are no imaginary figments but actual spiritual realities and potencies striving to subdue

---

[1] *Five Stages of Greek Religion*, pp. 179–180. Cf. W. Bousset, *Kyrios Christos*, 2nd ed., pp. 185 ff.

[2] Bousset, in the chapter on angelology in *Die Religion des Judentums im neutestament-lichen Zeitalter* (pp. 368 ff.), states that belief in 'demons' and the stars was a characteristic of late Judaism—*vide*, also the chapter on Dualism and Demonology, pp. 381 ff. Ernst Percy, *Die Probleme der Kolosser und Epheserbriefe* (Lund, 1946), gives some account of the background of the *stoicheia*, which figure in Jewish as well as in other late-antique religions. The term stands for the elements of the material world, the alphabet, the Platonic world-substance. They were not objects of worship in Palestine. Galatians 4: 3, 9 Percy considers to refer to the Jewish Law and calendar (pp. 156 ff.). Cf. R. Reitzenstein, *Das Iranische Erlösungsmysterium*, p. 237; E. Meyer, *Ursprung und Anfänge des Christentums*, II, pp. 330 ff., especially pp. 95 ff.

[3] 'Principalities and Powers' in *New Testament Studies*, p. 22, September 1954. Cf. also Macgregor and Purdy, *Jew and Greek: Tutors unto Christ*, p. 297; R. Bultmann, *Das Urchristentum*, p. 211.

man to their rule; indeed, we wrestle with them as with creatures of flesh and blood, only now there is no need for fear of defeat, for Jesus is supreme, he is pre-eminent in the cosmocracy of unseen intelligences. Whether the *ktisis*, *ta panta*, and the *kosmos* are thought of as a unitary system or as consisting of the material universe together with its invisible inhabitants, the pre-eminence of Jesus in both spheres is a necessary affirmation of faith so long as the correct belief of the Hellenistic Christians is in danger. In order to be able to make this affirmation intelligible it had to be made within the context of the terminology with which Paul's readers were familiar. This defeat of the 'powers' was most easily thought of in terms of the actual historical *Kyrios*, who, on behalf of God, superseded the rule of the cosmocrats and provided a new principle of universal coherence. With the supersession of the astral powers it was necessary to offer an alternative principle through which 'all things' could 'hold together'. It is against this kind of background that the Pauline ideas as expressed in Corinthians, Galatians, and Colossians should be understood. They take a mythological form because Paul's argument was on the plane of mythology and would be more easily grasped by those who had to be weaned from the pagan-mythological cosmology. Translated into non-mythological terms, Jesus is represented as the focus and consummation of all things historical and suprahistorical and associated with the power and principle by which the universe is made to cohere.

We are not, however, committed to the biblical terminology, which, in its spatial thinking, is as obsolete as the Ptolemaic cosmology; yet it may preserve a fundamental value which may be lost sight of if the terminology is completely abandoned. What is rejected as cosmology may be retained as metaphor, and it may not be wholly meaningless to suppose that there may be a dimension in which modes of being different from those of three-dimensional space and chronological time are conceivable. The terms employed, even though descriptive of a world which is not known to have objective reality, stand for an existential experience in which man finds himself compelled to decide between the powers of darkness and the Lord of Light. He who has been in conflict with anti-Christ in the form of the modern pagan state knows that the Principalities and Powers and the World Rulers of this darkness are too palpable to be dismissed as fictions, and that the final chapter of Ephesians is more than mythology supported by rhetoric.

2

One thing which emerges clearly from the study of St. Paul's epistles is that his thinking cannot be easily epitomized and crystallized into brief formulations. It is clear, too, that for him speculation was secondary to personal experience and was the result not of intellectual restlessness or curiosity but of an existential encounter with the Risen Lord which had cataclysmic consequences. His writings, moreover, reveal a coherent body of thought which can be described as a whole, for they disclose a theology expressed in terms of which his experience, his conception of community, and his cosmology can be understood. The basic presupposition of his thought is to be found in the affirmation of the supreme Lordship of Jesus Christ over all life and his preeminence over nature both human and cosmic. This Lordship is not to be described as a theoretical deduction from general experience but from his own immediate personal awareness of the activity of the Spirit in his own life and in that of the New Creation of the Christian community.

Moreover, just as the cosmic-spatial pre-eminence of the Lord is conceived in terms of ascending grades of reality, so does Paul's conception of his pre-eminence over the human order conform to a similar scheme of ascending levels or structures, and in this, it will be seen, he was anticipating modern conceptions of structure and not merely indulging in mythological idiom.

For Paul the human organism is thought of as consisting of ascending levels of being. The lowest grade, the biological, is that of σάρξ (flesh), the element which man possesses in common with creation. It is his 'natural' constituent; from it he derives the complex of impulses, desires, and activities which belong to the 'lower' order. It is polaristic in relation to πνεῦμα (spirit) and throughout the whole of Paul's writings the antithesis of the two concepts is maintained. Σάρξ is the material counterpart of φύσις ('nature'): the 'fleshly' man whose element is

100

'natural'; the term σωματικός (bodily) or σαρκικός (carnal) refers not to the whole of man but to his physical, instinctual nature; the words φύσις, φυσικός, occur only infrequently: the 'natural' (as distinguished from the innate) is the sarkic, the somatic.

Next in the series comes the 'psychic', which for St. Paul denotes the lower level of the immaterial; it is part of the somatic complex in a way in which πνεῦμα is not, and is opposed (as in I Cor. 2: 14) to the 'spiritual', the *pneumatikos*. The ψυχικός ἄνθρωπος is the unspiritual man rather than the merely σαρκικός or σωματικός: he who lacks the insight to discern the things of the 'Spirit', though he may not be lacking in intellectual perception and controlled instinctual responses. That Paul's terminology is not obsolete is shown by the fact that it has been adopted by modern psychology and psychotherapy. The term 'psychosomatic', for example, preserves the Pauline gradation and the differentiation between ψυχικός and σωματικός.

Man, however, is not merely somatic and psychic: he is 'pneumatic'. Part of his nature, the uppermost of the ascending series, is lived on the level of the spiritual, though there is some ambiguity, or at least uncertainty, in Paul's conception of *pneuma* as a natural attribute of human nature. The term is certainly more complex than either σῶμα or ψυχή, and is thought of usually as an inrush from the divine world rather than as a mode of being characteristically human. The body, however, can be 'dwelt in' by the Spirit of God; the 'fruits' of the Spirit are exhibited in the practice of the basic Christian virtues (Gal. 5: 22); the Christian is exhorted to 'walk by the Spirit', and though it is 'by the Spirit of God' (the Spirit which is given to him, I Cor. 12: 3) that he confesses that 'Jesus is Lord' and that the Church becomes an organism and not a mere assembly of like-minded people, man is capable of receiving the gift of the Spirit and thereby ceases to be merely somatic and psychic. The phrase 'spiritual man' implies that spirituality is a mode of being which is achieved through 'rising' to a higher grade than that which is inherent in man as such. Yet it would be inconsistent with Paul's anthropology as a whole to assume that man is compounded only of *sarx* and *psyche*; that he can be, and is, the 'temple of God' clearly means that he is 'naturally' or potentially a vessel fitted for the immanent indwelling of the Divine Spirit. That Spirit is primarily an attribute of God, the mode of the divine activity, requires no emphasis; this is apparent both from the Pauline and the Johannine writings; but it is also something which, when received by man, is as much a part of his nature as are *soma* and *psyche*, and infuses his whole life as the life infuses the organism and becomes its principle of unity. As in the organism there is a biological urge towards wholeness which rectifies physical injury, so man, the psychosomatic organism, is given completion through the immanent *pneuma* which is the downward reach of the divine world.

Man, then, should be regarded as an organism consisting of ascending levels: body, psyche, and spirit, the higher absorbing the lower and infusing it with its own quality. *Soma* is given unity through the *psyche*, otherwise it would be merely a congeries of conflicting and destructive impulses; but without *psyche* the psychosomatic organism would be incomplete because psycho-somatic man by himself is unable to realize his destiny as a 'son' of God.

Now, it may be asserted that while spatial categories are not implied (except diagrammatically) in this picture of the structure of man, it is spatial in the sense that psychology uses spatial terms in speaking of the 'subconscious' or 'depth' or *Gestalt* (for there cannot be form—'*Gestalt*'—without space. The term is meta-phorical, but no more so than any interpretation of the spatial category is compelled to be. The emergence of body, mind, and spirit is, in the evolutionary sense, temporal; the relation of the one to the other can be described only in terms such as 'higher' or 'lower' which involve, at any rate as metaphors, some notion of spatial relationship as a description of qualitative or functional differences. Man, further, exists in space, endures in time, and his structure not only exists 'in' space-time but is most easily visualized in terms of relationship, of an ascending series, and of emergent qualities which, if only diagrammatically, have to be represented spatially.

It is through the reception of the Spirit, then, that man emerges on to a new structural level and becomes a 'new man' in Christ. The Church is the new community and becomes a new kind of social organism sharply differentiated from other societies. 'Old things are passed away: they are become new.' Through the double action of the 'downward' infusion of the spirit (represented mythologically in the Pentecost narrative) and the 'upward' movement of the new community under its influence the Church reaches a level at which the decisive ingredient of its life is more than human, just as Christ, who was once regarded from the human standpoint, is to be so regarded no longer (II Cor. 5: 16). The 'new' quality of life becomes normative; as Christ after his Resurrection became a 'pneumatic' being, so the new man, the new creation which is the Church, shares in this life of the Spirit. Christ has ascended from the human series characterized by *soma* and *psyche*, into the realm of *pneuma*, and his elevation is shared by the 'Body' of which he is the principle of organic unity as well as the 'Head', just as the *nisus* towards wholeness, on the biological level, constitutes the principle of unity in the organism. As the *soma* is 'in' the psyche, which is its organizing principle, and the lower is absorbed by the higher, so, through being 'in' Christ, the lower levels of the human structure are absorbed into the higher pneumatic existence. In this way the natural structure of man is seen to be parallel to the ascent from the human to the spiritual in Christ, who is seen to be the crown of humanity. He is the one who is raised to a position 'above' the human level in which he once shared. The Lord is by nature 'above' the disciple, as the Lord, the Kyrios, or owner, is 'above' the slave, for though he may inevitably live in a relationship of closeness to the slave, the 'lord' is separated from him by distance. All levels of human and cosmic existence are subordinate to Jesus, for it is he who throws light on the meaning of the totality of things. From him these levels reach downwards in a descending series of strata to the material level of creation represented by *soma* or *sarx*, which is redeemed by his Spirit. The mythology is the symbol of universal redemption.

The Lord, then, acts through the Spirit, which is the dimension of his activity. Through it the transcendent Lord is immanent in the Church which is his visibly spatial body, his extension in the world. Whether St. Paul had any thought-out notion of the ubiquity or omnipresence of Jesus is not known; but the problem of his presence 'in' the Church cannot be separated from that of the mode of his manifestation. 'The Lord is the Spirit.' In the early *kerygma* (Acts 2: 33) the Spirit is regarded as having been 'poured out' by Jesus on the day of Pentecost. The author of the Fourth Gospel represents him as the giver of the Holy Spirit (John 20: 22), as though this were a semi-physical exhalation communicated by breathing. Jesus will 'send' the Spirit of truth, 'who proceeds from the Father' (John 15: 26; 16: 7 ff.). Though there is no warrant for this association of Jesus and the Spirit in the Synoptic Gospels, it was in the minds of other Apostolic writers and was later embodied in the doctrine of the Trinity.

The Spirit is the dimension in which Christ performs his work in the world. But in so far as it is thought of as the medium of his present activity in the believer personally and in the Church as a community, it is also the extension or intrusion of the past into the present. Through it the 'historical' Jesus continues his work in the present and the future and becomes *geschichtlich*; for the New Testament does not allow it to be forgotten that the Risen and Exalted Lord is the Jesus of history active in a new dimension of space-time in which historical space and time are transcended. Jesus is 'with' the Church in all ages and in all places. The meaning of his words 'Where two or three are gathered together in my name, there I am in the midst' (Matt. 18: 20) may elude precise elucidation; but as they stand they seem to be a promise of his actual presence in a mode which is independent of mathematical time and geometrical space; and the words of Ignatius, 'wherever Jesus is, there is the Catholic Church',[1] imply that the existence of the Church is dependent upon the universal presence of Jesus. St. Paul's famous words 'The Lord is the Spirit, and where the Spirit of the Lord is, there is liberty' (II Cor. 3: 17) also imply the identification of the Lord with the Spirit and the realization of a certain condition of being through his presence. Luke, too, in his interpretation of the reason for the obstruction to the preaching of the Gospel in Bithynia, suggests that Jesus was in some way ubiquitous, for the barrier was the 'spirit of Jesus'. The life of the Church in the New

---

[1] ὅπου ἄν ᾖ Ἰησοῦς, ἐκεῖ ἡ καθολικὴ ἐκκλησία (*ad Smyr.* 8: 2).

Testament is represented throughout as a fellowship not with a memory but with a present Person: present, it may be presumed, in the sense that he is believed to be 'there' in space, not imagination.

It is not improbable, however, that this interpretation will be regarded as importing into the New Testament notions which are extraneous to it and which would not have occurred to the men of the Apostolic age. Such procedure is, of course, inevitable if what is required is not exposition but interpretation in terms consistent with the thought of a subsequent age. Yet if the argument is carefully examined it will be seen that Paul does make use of spatial metaphors and that his cosmology necessitates some form of belief that Jesus occupies a position 'above' the heavenly hierarchy. While such a mode of thought may be metaphorical, the metaphor *is* spatial, and it is difficult to see how there can be any experience of the 'presence' of Jesus 'in' the Church or anywhere else (though expressions such as this require more careful examination than they have usually received) which does not involve some kind of existence in space, whether 'objective' or 'non-objective', to use Heim's terms.

The problem with which we are confronted, further, takes this form: Granted that the dimension of 'mythological' space is inseparable from the Wisdom-Christology of the Epistles, how is it to be so interpreted that it can lose its mythological content without sacrificing its essential meaning? The Wisdom-Christology is mythological in so far as it presupposes the transference of hypostatized attributes to a historical person. Yet what is implied in this kind of imagery is that Eternity has somehow entered into time, that is to say, that the divine mode of being has been incorporated into the cosmic series (to resort in anticipation to the terminology employed by Dr. Lionel Thornton), and also that the cosmic series has been 'taken up' into the divine mode of being. Paul clearly thought of Jesus the Lord as the one in whom these two processes meet. As the Lord exalted to cosmic pre-eminence he belonged to the cosmic series, and by virtue of his being the one in whom God 'dwelt', the point in time and space at which the world could be reconciled to God, he belonged to the transcendent world. The dimensional aspect of the problem has already been touched upon with reference to Karl Heim; the other aspect, namely the translation into non-mythological terms of the fundamental problem of Christology and of theology as a whole, has still to be examined. This involves the consideration of what kinds of categories should be employed if the problem of the relation of God to creation, of the Eternal to the temporal order, as it is focused in the Incarnation, is to be clarified.

3

One of the difficulties, indeed, the chief difficulty, inherent in the reinterpretation of the thought of the New Testament is that of discovering the appropriate terms into which it can be translated; for the danger which lurks behind any such enterprise is that the result of the reinterpretation may be very different from that which is to be reinterpreted. If mythological terms are not to be accepted literally, what is to be done with them? When they are reinterpreted do they so change their meaning that they become what they were not before? If, for example, the Pauline cosmology is translated into terms considered to be congenial to the non-mythologically-minded person of the mid-twentieth century, what remains of the material so closely associated with it? May it not be that what remains is not the cosmology, except as a metaphor or symbol, but something quite different—not what the New Testament said but what we might have said had we set out to say it? Myth, again, tends to be concrete and picturesque; it is expressed in action and, usually, in some kind of narrative, as in the primordial myths of Adam and Prometheus. The tendency of demythologizing or reinterpretation in general terms, however, leads to abstraction; the residue of meaning is abstracted and becomes a pale distillation of the original potent liquor; the picture becomes a diagram, the poem a proposition. The product of the synthetizing imagination becomes a piece of philosophical analysis.

So it is with the reduction of the Christological myth to the level of rational acceptability or with its adaptation to what is theologically congenial or scientifically credible at any time. We no longer think of the Risen Lord as spatially occupying a position of pre-eminence above the astral circuits or, as the Logos, as having existed in some form before creation, which has been approximately dated (if it can be thought of as beginning at a point in 'time') at about three thousand five hundred million years ago. The best that can be done is to regard such conceptions as metaphor; but metaphor of what? Both Bultmann, who advocates demythologizing, and Brunner, who does not, agree that, in the form in which it exists, the Christian kerygma cannot be separated from myth. But Brunner is surely going too far in suggesting that, because the mythical is related to the question of the historicity of the divine revelation and has to do with the nature and action of God, it is something quite apart from the question of a world-view, which is a 'truth of natural science'.[1] For the manner in which God is conceived as acting and the setting in which the action takes place are determined by the world-view prevailing at that time; and if the world-view of the New Testament is mythical, as Bultmann asserts, that is, if it is non-scientific, either it must be abstracted from the essence of the theology associated with it, or some other kind of terminology must be substituted for what is no longer tenable.

We have been considering one aspect of St. Paul's mythological thought in relation to Christology and to cosmology: the conception of cosmological structure as envisaged in terms of ascending grades, which we have seen to apply, in a different manner, to the structure of man in relation to the 'pneumatic' pre-eminence of Jesus. Bultmann considers the term 'Spirit' to belong to the realm of mythology, and that Paul himself has begun its demythologization through moralizing and spiritualizing what was originally considered to be a kind of substance.[2] Any attempt, therefore, to discover non-mythological terms has a precedent in the New Testament.

One of the most considerable and ambitious products of modern British Christological thinking is Dr. Lionel Thornton's *The Incarnate Lord*, which is primarily an interpretation of theism and the Incarnation in terms of organic conceptions and is indebted, both in substance and in terminology, to the philosophy

[1] *Dogmatics*, II: *The Christian Doctrine of Creation and Redemption*, 1953, p. 265.
[2] *Kerygma und Mythos*, I, pp. 32–33.

of A. N. Whitehead. It also shows affinities with the philosophy of emergent evolution as exemplified in the work of Samuel Alexander and Conwy Lloyd Morgan. Dr. Thornton's book claims rightly to take cognizance of modern scientific and philosophical thinking and is a valiant endeavour to apply some, at any rate, of the idioms of a particular philosophy to a restatement of a picture of the structure of reality in terms of philosophical theology and to see in it a vehicle for the expression of Christological conceptions which the classical Christian theology had expressed in the terminology of its time: one which was, of course, associated with the mythological or primitive world-picture.[1]

To begin with, Dr. Thornton states, it is necessary to take note of the 'organic' conception of the universe which implies the knowledge of a hierarchy of grades and the recognition that all knowledge has an objective reference.

> The universe as it is known today presents the appearance of an ascending series like the steps of a ladder or the storeys of a building. Corresponding to each grade in the series there is a typical unit of structure which determines the characteristics of that grade.[2]

Two points, he says, are of special importance: the mode in which the series is built up and the conception of the organism which pervades the whole series. The series is knit together in a 'vast interrelated system' containing higher and lower grades. Secondly, an organism has not only this 'graded' characteristic: it is a whole which pervades the parts and expresses its own law of unity through them. The whole is a highly complicated

---

[1] Space does not permit of any detailed account of Dr. Thornton's debt to Whitehead. In an appended note (pp. 456–469) he gives some account of the latter's conception of objects and events and indicates the character of his indebtedness to Whitehead which is, however, easily perceptible to anyone who is familiar with Whitehead's thought. An exponent of the latter, Dorothy M. Emmet, suggests that Dr. Thornton's use of Whitehead's philosophy of organism does not support his Christological contentions. 'He can indeed claim Whitehead's support,' she says, 'for the view that our apprehension of the eternal order depends on the fact of a developing incorporation of that order into the succession of events in space-time through an ascending cosmic series,' but this, she says, has no bearing on the part of the book dealing with the Incarnation, since Thornton claims that Christ is not a product of the organic series (*Whitehead's Philosophy of Organism*, Macmillan, 1932, p. 255) but an irruption of the Logos-Creator; a criticism which is justifiable.

[2] *The Incarnate Lord*, 1928, p. 36.

hierarchy including many grades of being. This organic concept is not merely biological: it is extended 'downwards' into the realm of physical science and 'upwards' into that of mind and spirit, thus covering the cosmic series as a whole. A third characteristic of this organic series is described as 'transcendence'. Enduring objects, for example, transcend the flow of events by existing in the dimension of space-time; the objects themselves and our perception of them transcend their temporal duration; living objects, however, that is organisms, are to be understood not only as transcending temporal flux but also in the mode of their persistence through time, namely in terms of their life-history.

Having stated his conception of the organic interrelatedness of the cosmic series emerging on to a level of spirit,[1] Dr. Thornton proceeds to examine the character of spiritual organisms and the question of the relation of theism to his structural analysis, which he believes to consist in man's awareness of the eternal order which transcends him and which is, so to speak, on the next of the ascending levels of the cosmic series.

In considering man as a spiritual organism Dr. Thornton states that, though incomplete, he is the summation of the organic series.

> All levels [he says] of the series are gathered up in him. But this organic summation of the series in man does not make him the true summation of creation. It is through the revelations which come from the eternal order that the *nexus* between man and that order is established, [and it is in religion that we] discern revelation descending directly from Absolute Actuality into the concrete activity of human experience.[2]

This takes the form of the break-through of the transcendent in such a way that it becomes immanent in the this-world of the organic series. This occurs in the New Creation, both social and individual, achieved through the Spirit. Christ is himself the

[1] It should be said in passing that Dr. Thornton's conception of the philosophy of organism is much less abstract than Whitehead's as developed in *Process and Reality*, which had not appeared when *The Incarnate Lord* was written. Dr. Thornton, though using some of Whitehead's terminology, is not committed to its highly specialized and idiomatic character, even in the form in which it had appeared up to the publication of *Science and the Modern World*.

[2] *The Incarnate Lord*, p. 150.

'actuality of God embodied and incorporated into history. Thus He is also the goal of the organic universe, of man, and of history, and sums them up in Himself'.[1]

In the second part of his book Dr. Thornton relates the Incarnation to the organic conceptions elucidated in the first part by declaring that 'Jesus Christ is Absolute Activity incorporated into history in the form of concrete individuality'. As the organic universe is 'an adequate organ of the eternal order' some other principle must be found to provide the adequacy. It is at this point that the philosophical notion of the organic conception of the universe can provide assistance; for the humanity of Christ, a spiritual organism, shares in the transcendent order and reaches downwards into the order of creation. Christ has his own principle of unity; he does not belong to the organic series: rather does it belong to him. The Incarnate Lord is organic to the universe, but is not himself an organism.

> The Eternal Word, who is one with the eternal order, became incorporated into the organic series at its highest point. He is, therefore, both incarnate in a human organism and yet transcendent over that human organism.

The antithesis between transcendence and immanence is thereby overcome, as in Heim's reinterpretation it is transcended by suprapolar space—a term for which in Dr. Thornton's book 'superorganic' is an approximate equivalent, for that, too, is a dimension of the Holy Spirit.

Although Dr. Thornton was not concerned in *The Incarnate Lord* with the question of demythologization, his essay is a skilful attempt (though not free from the temptation to be Apollinarian) to work out a Christology in modern philosophical terms which may be employed to clarify and to a certain extent to make tenable St. Paul's bold Christological speculations in which he sees in Christ the summation of creation and the principle of its coherence. 'What we want,' said Professor Samuel Alexander in an address to the University Science Federation at Manchester University in 1932 in which he pleaded for a closer association

[1] *The Incarnate Lord*, p. 213.

of science and religion, 'is a religious mythology that does not contain flat inconsistencies with our ordinary experience'. Dr. Thornton himself recognized that the language of religion in its beginnings is symbolical and mythical, and referred to a stage 'in which scientific observation and rational reflexion develop and abstract terminology of their own which has a different genealogical descent from that of religious terminology proper'.[1] In *The Incarnate Lord* an abstract terminology has been substituted for the mythological, but in so far as scientific thought requires to some extent its own symbolism, the philosophy of organism may perhaps approach sufficiently near to the point of consistency with scientific knowledge of which Samuel Alexander spoke. It is at any rate an important contribution to the translation of religious into philosophical and non-mythological terms, though not on the level of ordinary experience in which the myth as a story of redemption confronts man existentially as Bultmann employs the term.

For evangelical purposes a philosophical demythologization of the Gospel is not what is required but rather a kind of demythologization which commends itself in terms generally comprehensible. As our present investigation, however, is concerned not with evangelical homiletics but with theology, a restatement such as Dr. Thornton's is valuable in that it shows a non-mythological interpretation, or at least a philosophical paraphrase, of New Testament categories to be possible within the framework of orthodox Christology, and that St. Paul's spatial metaphors, closely allied with mythological thinking, are capable of reinterpretation in the language of a particular philosophy which can be regarded, as mythological thinking cannot, as an attempt to state a non-mythical structural ontology in contemporary terms.

[1] Op. cit., p. 12.

III

PART THREE

KYRIOS CHRISTOS

SUMMARY OF ARGUMENT

The title most frequently applied to Jesus in the New Testament is Lord, κύριος, which Bousset regards as mythical in origins and association. But even though his thesis is questionable, Kyrios, in the Pauline Epistles, is associated with mythological ideas such as pre-existence, the heavenly being who is co-creator with God. The term, however, does not necessarily indicate mythological thinking; nevertheless, the connotation of the title should be enquired into within this context and an interpretation of it in non-mythological terms should be sought. Illumination is looked for in the notion of emergent evolution on the one hand and in historical-religious culmination on the other. Neither of these is found wholly satisfactory because it does not allow sufficiently for the transcendent element in Jesus and for the belief in his finality as personal revelation; nor is it consistent with orthodox ideas of the Incarnation as katagogic, though an anagogic interpretation may be as valid as the katagogic. Lordship, within the New Testament context, can be thought of as perfect Sonship.

As the Pauline Christology implies the relation of Jesus to creation, we proceed to examine the two questions of Jesus' transcendence over the created order and his position within the created series. The former is bound up with the idea of cosmic salvation, the meaning of which is enquired into.

Further, the New Testament belief involved the notion of Jesus' immanence in creation as well as his transcendence over it. The mythological Christology, however, makes difficult a full understanding of his belonging to the human series. Analogies drawn from science and art suggest that continuity and discontinuity are not necessarily incompatible. The 'new' can emerge from the human series and does not need to be injected into it.

H

Finally, in Bultmann's view the New Testament presentation of the fact of evil is wholly mythological in its belief in a demon-world. This is an over-simplification, for the problem of evil is intractable and complex, and the 'mythological' picture corresponds to human experience. Investigation of psychological phenomena may provide grounds for belief in an objective world of evil. But the conception of Jesus' triumph over evil is mythological in form and respect for truth should warn us against accepting it as it stands.

CHAPTER ONE

KYRIOS CHRISTOS

I

The title most frequently applied to Jesus in the New Testament is 'Lord';[1] it is also the most easily interpretable and the closest to the historical in that it is a term applied to a person actually known in history. The title raises fewer controversial issues and insoluble problems than did the endeavours of the theologians of the first five centuries or so to work out a philosophical Christ-ology.

Indeed, as we leave the New Testament and attempt to follow the Christological controversies and speculations of the Patristic age, we are conscious of moving into a world very different from the 'historical' world of the Apostolic writers, for Jesus has almost ceased to be a historical human figure and has become the 'mythological' subject of metaphysical speculation. For despite its mythological thinking the New Testament, with the exception of the Apocalypse, never completely lost sight of the humanity of Jesus or ceased to think of him as one who had lived a genuinely 'historical' life. The pronouncements of the early *kerygma* are simple. Their substance is that Jesus of Nazareth, in whom the 'Scriptures' are fulfilled, is exalted by virtue of his Resurrection to be Lord and Saviour. The proclaimers of this *kerygma* were concerned more with the fact of the experience than with specu-lations about 'natures' and the manner, which is destined to remain a veiled mystery, of the Incarnation. It does not appear that the condition of baptism into the Church in the Apostolic age was any more complicated than a simple profession of faith

---

[1] The phrase 'Lord Jesus Christ' occurs forty-two times in Romans and Corin-thians, apart from the term *Kyrios* alone which may sometimes refer to God but usually to Jesus. 'Son of God' occurs only three times in these Epistles, whereas 'Lord' occurs seventy-seven times, and phrases including or resembling 'Lord Jesus Christ' are found some one hundred and forty times in the Pauline literature (ex-cluding the Pastoral Epistles).

in the Lord Jesus. Christians were described as those 'who in every place call on the name of the Lord Jesus Christ' (I Cor. 1: 2). 'Whosoever shall call upon the name of the Lord Jesus Christ shall be saved' (Rom. 10: 13). The fact that the word *Kyrios* occurs twenty-six times in the Acts shows (assuming that its usage indicates the Christology of the early *kerygma*) with what alacrity it was seized upon in the early days of the Church.[1]

I am assuming, then, that the title *Kyrios* should be regarded as originating in the Jerusalem community very soon after Pentecost, and also that, despite the arguments of Bousset, Bultmann and others who have ascribed great importance to the religious-historical approach to New Testament studies (though it should not be disregarded), there is no need to attribute its prominence in the early Church to the existence of other Kyrios-cults, about the precise time of whose existence, as well as the scope of whose influence, there is so much conjecture and so little certainty.

Kyrios is not a Christological title in the earliest Synoptic documents; where it occurs it is often little more than a form of polite address to a superior. In Mark 11: 3, 'the Lord has need of him', the word is, at first sight, somewhat ambiguous; for according to one interpreter ὁ κύριος αὐτοῦ may mean the 'owner' of the colt. Dr. Vincent Taylor (*The Gospel According to Mark*, pp. 454–455) suggests this interpretation, though there is no indication of who the owner was. In Luke 19: 33, however, it is the owners (ὁι κύριοι αὐτοῦ) who are told that the Lord has need of him, which may indicate an embellishment on the part of Luke (the only Synoptist to apply the term *Kyrios* to Jesus in the sense which we have in mind) or that the Markan tradition was uncertain as to how *Kyrios* should be understood. ὁ κύριος αὐτοῦ should not be translated 'the' Lord, but 'his' lord (or owner), for the animal can hardly be regarded as having a 'Lord'. This is the only occasion on which, in Mark, there is any probability of Jesus using the term of himself, and the manner in which the word is used makes it doubtful if he did so. In Mark 2: 28 ('the Son of Man is Lord also of the Sabbath') *Kyrios* is used not as a title but as a synonym for 'master', 'he who has disposal of'. Elsewhere in the Synoptics *Kyrios* is used in contradistinction to δοῦλος (Matt. 10: 24, Luke 14: 21, etc.).

In Matthew and Luke there are some occasions when the term might be interpreted either as Master or Lord (Luke 6: 46—'Why call ye me Lord, Lord?'); Matth. 14: 28 (Peter in the lake: 'Lord, save me'), and Matthew 20:

[1] The question of where this term *Kyrios* originated is disputable. Bousset's theory of its Hellenistic origin, repeated by Bultmann, is not generally accepted. Bousset neglects the simplest and most obvious explanation for one which is not only complicated but dubious. W. Foerster assumes a Palestinian origin (Kittel, *ThWB*, III, pp. 1094 ff., where the title is fully discussed; see especially pp. 1038 ff.)

31 which alters Mark 10: 27—'Jesus'—to 'Lord'. Luke alone of the Synoptists unambiguously uses *Kyrios* as a Christological title with any frequency (Luke 7: 13–15; 10: 1, 39–40; 11: 39, etc.) but curiously retains the Markan title in Mark 9: 5, whereas Matthew alters it. In view, however, of what has been said of Jesus as a numinous personality, it is probable that κύριε means more than 'Sir', e.g., 'Depart from me, for I am a sinful man, O Lord', where the vocative form is unlikely to be the equivalent of Sir or Teacher, for the term implies a recognition of Jesus' spiritual superiority and power.

It is after the Resurrection that ὁ κύριος becomes the regular Christological title, for Jesus is now the exalted Lord. God has made him 'Lord and Christ' (Acts 2: 36); people are baptized into the 'name of the Lord Jesus' (2: 38). Yet in the early 'sermons' there is no suggestion that the Lord is any other than Jesus of Nazareth exalted to a more than human status: Lordship does not seem to mean the return of a pre-existent being to his more appropriate sphere. It is clear, however, from the last words of Stephen—'Lord Jesus, receive my spirit' —that the title was in use at a very early date, and that it implied an attitude of faith and trust on the part of the believer and not only the affirmation of historical existence. Ananias receives instructions from the 'Lord' in a vision (Acts 9: 10); Peter (10: 36) proclaims Jesus 'Lord of all', and after the conversion of Paul the title is used with greater frequency. If its occurrence in the first days of the Church is attributed to a more fully developed Christology of later times, it may reasonably be asked, What did the apostles preach about? What, if not this, *was* the earliest kerygma? What could it have been? Baptism was given 'in the name of the Lord'. Paul speaks of 'faith in the Lord Jesus Christ', of 'the words of our Lord Jesus Christ'; and even though the time-span of Acts appears to be foreshortened (no precise date can be given for St. Paul's conversion, and the whole narrative reads like a rapid series of events occurring within a short period) it would seem obvious that the title 'Lord' was the universal term for the Risen Jesus at an early stage. It is not used in any 'mythological' sense, but as the title of one who had been contemporary with those who employ it.

The Fourth Gospel is sparing in its use of ὁ κύριος, as the emphasis throughout the Gospel is on the Sonship rather than the Lordship of Jesus; yet in ch. 11 there are no fewer than eight instances of the use of the term. Here it means considerably more than 'Teacher' or 'Sir', for where the former is implied διδάσκαλε occurs as well as κύριε. If it is here a term of address, it is certainly more significant than the usual vocative case, though in John 13: 6, 9 it may be used in this sense. In John 13: 13, 14 Jesus says that the disciples refer to him both as 'Teacher' and 'Lord', 'for so I am'. Something more than respect is implied here, namely reverence and obedience in the presence of numinous holiness. How far these instances of the use of the word in John represent a genuine tradition it is impossible to say. The infrequency of the word in the Fourth Gospel is worthy of mention, especially in view of its infrequent occurrence in the Synoptics. The surprising thing, however, is the occasional use of *Kyrios* at a late date when this title was accepted generally in Apostolic circles.

On the whole the title *Kyrios* is not used in the New Testament in a conspicuously 'mythological' sense, for whereas the pagan religions possessed their 'gods many and lords many'—that is, gods and lords who should be considered as belonging to myth, not to history—*this* term *Kyrios* referred to a historical personage. That Paul, in his endeavour to find terms appropriate to the magnitude of Jesus' significance, used terminology which can be called mythological has already been stated, for affirmations of pre-existence belong to the sphere of mythological thinking, though the precise character of this pre-existence is not indicated. It is, however, possible to interpret a passage such as the 'kenosis' passage in Philippians in mythopoetical terms which do not give undue weight to the myth; for that Paul did not intend his words to be understood literally on every occasion is clear from the words in the Epistle to the Ephesians 'made us sit with him in the heavenly places' (Eph. 2: 4–6), which are obviously metaphorical.

While, however, his conception of the Lordship of Jesus was rooted in the latter's historical mission and in the Resurrection of him who had been historically known, Paul ascribed to Jesus, the Lord, a position sometimes almost indistinguishable from God's. The Apostolic greeting shows that he regarded Jesus as the source of grace together with God the Father; he uses the phrase 'through Jesus Christ and God the Father'. Jesus is the 'Son of God', by which Paul doubtless meant a divine being as John conceived him to be. In Ephesians and Philippians Jesus is referred to as 'Saviour'; yet nowhere is the Lord actually equated with God, even though ὁ κύριος was the Septuagint word for God. In Ephesians 3: 14 Paul writes 'I bow my knees unto the Father of our Lord Jesus Christ', though in Philippians 2: 10 it is stated that 'at the name of Jesus every knee should bow', which seems, in view of the distinction in verse 14 between Jesus and God the Father, to whose glory confession of the Lordship of Jesus is made, to suggest reverential faith rather than the actual worship which is due to God alone. In Jesus the fulness of the Godhead— τὸ πλήρωμα τῆς θεότητης —dwells 'bodily' (Col. 2: 9—in Col. 1: 19 only 'the fulness' occurs).[1] Jesus

---

[1] πλήρωμα (also Eph. 1: 23) was also a technical term in Gnosticism representing the totality of cosmocratic beings who come between man and the Absolute.

possesses the name 'that is above every name'. He is the Lord of
the Church and to him 'all things' are subjected. In Thessalonians,
presumed to be the earliest of the Epistles,[1] there are frequent
indications that Paul was thinking in eschatological terms (I Thess.
4: 15–16, 5: 2; II Thess. 2: 1–2), and though these play no
conspicuous part in the other Pauline writings, it is possible that
Paul was identifying Jesus with the 'heavenly man' of apocalyptic.
Here there may be some justification for the view of Bousset that
Paul may have been familiar with non-Jewish Gnostic speculation,
but it is not necessary to seek affinities with the 'heavenly man'
outside Judaism. Though it would be strange if Paul were not
indebted to contemporary traditional religious ideas and archetypes, what is more strange is that these play such a relatively
minor part in his Christology. The reference to 'the Son of God
who loved me and gave himself for me' hardly suggests a Gnostic
redemption myth.

In the Pastoral Epistles, further, there is reference to one
Mediator, 'the man Christ Jesus' (I Tim. 2: 5—a somewhat
un-Pauline phrase). 'Saviour' is sometimes a predicate of God
(I Tim. 2: 3; Titus 3: 4), though God 'poured out his Holy
Spirit in Jesus Christ our Saviour' (Titus 3: 6). Similar terminology is employed in the Petrine Epistles, the second of which
speaks of 'our God and (the) Saviour Jesus Christ', of the 'Lord
and Saviour Jesus Christ' (II Pet. 1: 11; 2: 20; 3: 2—'the Lord
and Saviour', 3: 18). How much of these letters is of Petrine
authorship cannot be established, though the apparently auto-
biographical references (II Pet. 1: 17 ff.) may indicate a Petrine
substance. In Hebrews the term 'Lord' is presupposed rather
than overtly used. The Johannine letters, like the Gospel,
emphasize divine Sonship rather than Lordship, though the
two are scarcely distinguishable from one another.

Because of the frequency of its use, it is important that lines
of investigation of the meaning of the term *Kyrios* should be
indicated. In the first place it should be asked whether the word
is synonymous with 'divine', that is to say, whether it is a title

---

[1] Dr. V. Taylor (*The Names of Jesus*, p. 47) concludes that the frequent employment of the term in Thessalonians implies its general use in the decade 40–50 and
probably even in the preceding decade.

borne by a divine being after his translation from historical existence. That the *Kyrios* is the Risen Jesus raised to a position of pre-eminence over the whole cosmos has already been indicated at some length, and the possibly mythical ingredients of the term have been indicated. Yet although it is used for God in the Septuagint and also in the New Testament, the latter does not imply its synonymity with God. That this is so is shown by the employment by Paul of ὁ θεός when he means 'God' and ὁ κύριος when he means Jesus; and that the latter title does not exclusively mean a divine being is proved by its secular usage. In the Epistles the word means, generally, not a supernatural God-like being, but Jesus Risen and exalted as the one to whom the reverence of the Christian is accorded and towards whom his faith is directed. Whether Jesus was actually the object of worship in the early church is difficult to establish; too little is known of liturgical practice in the Apostolic age. Certainly there is no cultic Jesus-worship in the Acts. Stephen's final words are words of committal. That the *kyrioi* of the pagan religions were the centres of cultic worship (which Bultmann does not believe to have existed in the very early church)[1] and were worshipped as gods does not mean that Jesus occupied precisely the same status.[2] To 'call upon' a name that is 'above every name' means the invocation of one who is in a different category from man, but not that he was actually addressed as God. Jesus' function in the New Testament is mediatorial, and as the Lord-Mediator he was 'with' God, reigning with Him, seated at His 'right hand', the consummation of the human series; but he is not stated to be θεός. Thomas' words in the Fourth Gospel are the solitary exception. Otherwise the terminological distinction between *Christos Kyrios* and *Theos* would be meaningless. The identification of the two was the achievement of post-apostolic thought, which developed in a very different climate and at a time remoter from historical experience of Jesus than was the Apostolic age.

---

[1] *Theologie des neuen Testaments*, p. 51 (E. trans.).

[2] It should be noted, however, that W. W. von Baudissin, in a criticism of Bousset in his exhaustive enquiry into the use of *Kyrios* as a divine name in Judaism and other religions, says that he knows of no instance of the employment of the term as a designation of a god in his position as the centre of a community-cult (*Kyrios*, II, p. 283, 1929).

Bousset is of the opinion that for Paul the term 'Son of God' was not understood in any metaphorical sense but as a supernatural being standing in close
metaphysical relationship to God. 'There is no question of any thought of
election on the basis of moral worth, and the question of identity of will does
not arise. In the term "Son" two things are realized: on the one hand the
heavenly nature of Christ is brought as near as possible to God the Father, and
on the other it is at the same time definitely differentiated from Him' (*Kyrios
Christos*, p. 151). That God sent His Son in the 'likeness' of sinful flesh means
that Jesus was a divine being appearing as man, which in Bousset's view points
the way to Docetism, though Paul did not think out how the divine, supernatural being actually became a historical man. Although Paul did not
identify Jesus with God, Bousset continues, 'nevertheless the dogma of the Godhead of Christ is on the march'. It should not be forgotten for a moment that
behind Paul's personal piety and theology the 'cultic worship of the *Kyrios* by
the Church stands as a real power and a living reality' (ibid., p. 154). This, we
have observed, is the basic thesis which Bousset allows to determine his estimate
of Paul's Christology and which should not be considered as having been proved.

What is clear, however, is that the distinction between θεός and κύριος in
time becomes blurred and then vanishes precisely in the Hellenistic environment on which Bousset places such emphasis. Although in the Ignatian Epistles
the term θεός is frequently applied to Jesus, the distinction between it and
κύριος is still maintained. Whatever may have been the origin of the term, it
is quite probable, as Bousset believed, that the subsequent development of its
history was wholly affected by the practice of the post-apostolic Hellenistic
churches. In the apocryphal Acts of Peter the phrase 'O God, Jesus Christ'
occurs. With eucharistic developments comes the idea of the bodily-spiritual
presence of the *Kyrios* as the object of worship. According to the apocryphal
Acts, for example, prayer is offered to Jesus, which would seem to be normative
for popular cultic practice. Here it is more or less the rule, though it is rejected
by Origen. The Kyrios-cult, in Bousset's view, was influenced by the Imperial
Ruler-cult of the Roman-Hellenistic world. Whatever the precise contacts
between the Church and that world, it does seem clear that the cultic worship
of the *Kyrios* leads in primitive Christianity to the deification of Jesus, and that
out of the *Kyrios* grows the θεὸς Ἰησοῦς Χριστός. Thomas' confession in the
Fourth Gospel reflects this development. In some examples of liturgical
practice, as indicated in II Clement and the Epistle of Barnabas, the difference
between Christ and God has virtually disappeared, though in the light of this
the surprising thing is the comparative infrequency of the full divine title as
ascribed to Jesus, which may, as Bousset suggests, be explained by the still
potent influence of Paul and John.[1]

---

[1] Despite, however, the occurrence of phrases such as 'For our God Jesus Christ'
(*Ephesians, Trallians*), 'Jesus Christ our God' (*Romans*); also 'Our God Jesus Christ',
with a similar example in the letter to the Smyrnaeans, the ascription of Godhead
to Jesus in the Ignatian Epistles occurs less often than the title 'Lord Jesus Christ'.
A phrase such as Δοξάζω Ἰησοῦν Χριστὸν τὸν θεόν is nevertheless significant (vide *Trall.*
7: 1; *Smyrn.* 1: 1; 10: 1; *Eph.* 15: 3; 18: 2).

It is in the Ignatian writings that the absolute Godhead of Jesus, mentioned without any kind of reservation, first appears in any conspicuous degree: 'our God Jesus Christ', for example. Deacons are the servants of 'God Christ'. Also in Justin Martyr the same tendency is evident. Primitive hymnology implies the denial of any real difference between Father and Son: Christ is God become visible. He *is* God. 'There is no way of modernizing this,' Bousset observes, for there is no question of 'the realization of the moral-religious picture of Jesus of Nazareth'; what happens now is that Jesus as God is worshipped in the church services. In the apocryphal Acts there is evidence of this. In the sacramental prayer ('O God Jesus Christ') the identification is complete. Bousset is quite definite in explaining the source of this identification. 'The primitive Christian belief in the Godhead of Jesus grew wholly out of the cultic worship of the *Kyrios*' (ibid., p. 257). It was Christianity's tribute to Hellenistic piety, for the resemblance is neither accidental nor superficial. In the Kyrios-cult the *Kyrios* has become the ἕτερος θεὸς προσκυνητός. Christ has become the new God of the cultic community, and Paulinism has been left behind. The mythology is now complete.

Now, even though the exaggerated emphasis of Bousset's thesis is taken into account, the difference between the Christology of the post-apostolic Age and that of the New Testament cannot be ignored, for the deeper we go into this period—the period when Catholic orthodoxy was being formed in a non-Hebraic world—the more foreign does it appear to the modern mind. The man Jesus of the Synoptic Gospels, the Risen Saviour who was known as man, has become God. The historical sense has completely disappeared. With the identification by the Apologists, and even more so by Irenaeus, of Jesus with the Divine Logos, Christianity was on the verge of ceasing to be a monotheistic religion. It is apparent that in this early period of the Church dogmas were being shaped to an increasing extent by conditions and beliefs which belonged to a world very different from that of the Hebraic tradition and of the historical scene of the Gospels. The idea of a divine supernatural being becoming a man was not foreign to the Hellenistic world, and the intellectual atmosphere of second-century Antioch was hardly that which a modern Christian would regard as essential to the formation of his Christological beliefs.

In what way, then, is Jesus 'Kyrios', if the term, as used in the New Testament, is not synonymous with Godhead? At its lowest level, that is on the rare occasions on which it is used in the Synoptic Gospels, it means something more than 'Sir'. 'Lord, I believe: help thou mine unbelief' (Mark 9: 24). Here more than Rabbi or *didaskalos* is indicated, and it is likely that it was used in this way in the Fourth Gospel. But whether it was used in that sense or not in the Synoptic Gospels, the picture there presented is that of a numinous personality who, in his contacts with his contemporaries, was regarded as something more than *didaskalos* and as deserving more than the respect due to a superior person.[1] Even when demythed as far as justice to the records permits, what is left is much more than a supremely good man, namely, one to whom the title 'Lord' would have been eminently appropriate had it been regularly ascribed to him. The acceptance of the Messianic title would have justified the ascription of Lordship to Jesus, especially in view of the *logion* Matthew 11 : 25 Q, for in the sewords was expressed a relationship between Jesus and God which in comparison with ordinary human status was different in kind rather than in degree. The awareness of a much deeper and more intimate personal *filial* relationship with the Father showed that what was involved was something profounder than is indicated in mystical experience.

So, too, with the miracles, which demonstrated a power far removed from that which is present in ordinary human nature; and if it is argued that the miracles of healing are in some measure paralleled in modern divine healing, it should be stated that these are usually performed in the 'name' of the Lord Jesus Christ and belong to the class of Apostolic healings rather than to that of Jesus' own miracles. Whatever else it may signify, the term implies a principle of differentiation from 'ordinary' humanity.

Is Jesus, therefore, to be regarded as 'Lord' because of some extraordinary intensification of a human quality, because in some way he shares in the divine life in a manner which cannot be predicated of any other person, or because he virtually does not belong to the human order in any sense in which that term is usually understood? And does mythological thinking about the 'Lordship' of Jesus remove him from the category of manhood?

2

There are several possible avenues of approach to these questions. One of them is the supposition that the quality describable as 'Lordship' is an emergent, the 'next' highest quality in a graded organic series as the result or culmination of an evolutionary movement or *nisus*. The difficulty here is that this quality

---

[1] e.g. the incident, variously reported, of the anointing at Bethany.

is not noticeably emergent in human nature as such, for mere spirituality is of a lower order than the 'Lordship' of Jesus. Although *pneuma* is the highest level in the series creation-life-body-mind, the pneumatic character of the *Kyrios*, as understood by Paul, was of a different order from the human; rather was its affinity with the divine *pneuma* which confers on man such spiritual nature as he possesses (cf. I Cor. 2: 10 ff.).

Moreover, the concept of emergence belongs to a certain type of evolutionary thinking whereas Christian theology has always considered Christology from the standpoint of revelation, though it might be argued that 'emergence' by divine intention could be considered a form of revelation. It is, however, difficult to avoid the conclusion that, in any form, the concept of revelation implies (in terms of spatial metaphor) a movement 'down', a katagogic movement from 'above', not an anagogic or rising movement from within the process. If it has any definite meaning, it is that this order mediates what is 'beyond' it and impregnates it or is immanent or 'ingressive' in it (to use Whitehead's term). In this sense the concept of deity as emergent, as expounded, for example, by Samuel Alexander, cannot be said to have much relevance to the actualization of a more-than-human quality, for its character is essentially that of the 'next' in the series, and ceases to be deity once it has been realized.

The discussion of Deity in Book IV of Alexander's Gifford Lectures (*Space, Time, and Deity*, vol. II, pp. 341 ff.) is, as is to be expected, on the metaphysical-philosophical rather than on the religious-theological level. Hence what is in religious terms to be thought of as 'deity' is the next higher empirical quality to mind. 'Within the all-embracing stuff of Space-Time, the universe exhibits an emergence in Time of successive levels of finite existence, each with its characteristic empirical quality. The highest of these empirical qualities known to us is mind or consciousness. Deity is the next higher empirical quality to the highest level we know' (p. 345). 'We cannot tell what is the nature of deity, of our deity, but we can be certain that it is not mind, or if we use the term spirit as equivalent to mind or any quality of the order of mind, deity is not spirit, but something different from it in kind' (p. 349). Deity is not an enlargement of mind or spirit; such things as spirit, personality, mind, are human or mental qualities which 'belong to God but not to his deity', not to His deity but to His 'body'. Deity is to be distinguished as a 'quality in the hierarchy of values' from the idea of value itself. 'Even God himself does not as actual God possess deity attained, but only the *nisus* towards it. Men of transcendent gifts of perfection are thus in their degree exemplars of this *nisus*. The description is false if it means that they in any sense possess the divine quality or even adumbrate it. Deity on such conception would be no more than the perfection of manhood, whereas it is something which transcends in kind the most transcendent manhood. The ordinary theism, therefore, when it postulates a human intermediary between us and God who is conceived as endowed with deity actually attained, acts consistently in believing the intermediator to be more than man, human and divine at once—purchasing consistency at the cost of interposing the conception of a miraculous person without parallel in the world' (pp. 418–419).

Underlying Alexander's 'theology', which has been described as pantheistic, is the notion of the emergent universe which *includes* God rather than is transcended by him, for He is thought of as grounded in the primal 'stuff' of Space-Time. God's, indeed, is not a completed nature, but is for ever in a state of becoming. Alexander's thought leads to the conclusion that, as He who possesses, with the universe, the *nisus* towards deity, He is the eternal 'not-yet', the ideal God in embryo. It is not erroneous to deduce, further, that the emergent God is not the Creator in the theistic sense at all. The kind of emergence which Alexander has in mind does not greatly assist us in our enquiry for a category which covers the differentia of the *Kyrios* in contradistinction to the human quality which is merely a transcendent gift; for deity as something *realized* in personality would not, *ex hypothesi*, be deity at all, but perfection of manhood. Applied to Christology this would mean that, if the Lordship of Jesus is thought of as an emergent quality, that which emerges is not, in the religious sense, deity, but merely what orthodoxy, in its criticism of Adoptionism, has considered to be a form of human perfection, though according to Christian doctrine what Alexander describes as 'something which transcends in kind the most transcendent manhood' approximates fairly closely to the conception of the 'Lordship' of Jesus.

While, therefore, there is a genuine difficulty in interpreting religious ideas in philosophical terms, it is hardly possible to find in emergence as Alexander conceives it even an adequate analogy by which a relation between the two might be satisfactorily established. Alexander, to be sure, envisages emergence as a kind of pyramid (as does Lloyd Morgan[1]) with Space-Time as its base, out of the upper level of which 'deity' is the final emergent quality; but his 'deity' is conceptual rather than actual, the potential 'not-yet', and is not to be equated with God.

Further, the conception of a number of superimposed levels 'emerging' into each other and yet at the same time independent and self-consistent, as in Dr. Thornton's interpretation of the philosophy of graded organisms, is schematic rather than empirical. We do not see in 'mind' a quality in continual emergence from matter; there is matter and there is mind. We do not know if it is an 'emergent' from matter or whether the 'soul' or the spiritual consciousness is an epigenesis of matter-mind. Mind is not emergent from, say, a stone, or even from all organic matter. A plant doubtless possesses some sort of nervous system, and some plants are capable of a reflex strategy or even of aggressive action suggesting rudimentary consciousness. But a tree does not exhibit this characteristic and does not produce anything remotely resembling mind. There are different kinds of organic life, some of which show traces of mind and some of which do not; and despite some modern deductions from molecular theory that the basis of organic and inorganic matter is the same, it is nevertheless a fact that the arrangement of electrons in one type of matter (perhaps 'animate' is a more accurate term than 'inorganic' in this connection) does not produce mind, whereas in another arrangement and in conjunction with the biological factor, it does.

It would appear, then, that though 'mind' is higher in the structural scale than matter, it does not necessarily emerge from all forms of it. Matter is not that which, through some inherent *nisus*, naturally produces mind; it is doubtful if 'mind' emerges from it at all. Yet mind is supervenient on matter without being a logical deduction from it. Mind is not a necessary concomitant of matter, though, as far as is known, it is dependent upon it.

If, however, the time-factor is introduced, it is apparent that there was a 'time' when, excluding the Divine Mind, mind was not, though forms of animate matter may have exhibited mental

---

[1] Cf. Lloyd Morgan's Gifford Lectures *Life, Mind and Spirit* and *Emergent Evolution*. See especially lecture X in the former and lectures I and VII in the latter, where God is thought of as present in all levels of emergence. Morgan distinguishes between *emergents* and *resultants*.

qualities within their own sphere of reference of which we have no knowledge; they may even have evolved a conception of deity which, because of the lack of means of communication, is also outside human detection; we do not know, though it is improbable. But we can say that there have emerged 'new' qualities which were not there before, or qualities which have so far advanced that their primitive foreshadowings may be considered to belong to a lower order of being, not merely to a less-developed stage of the same order; and the characteristic of 'emergent' qualities is that they are 'new', for if nothing emerges, as Lloyd Morgan has said, there is nothing more than a regrouping of events. Emergence does not mean a regular line of continuous development, logically pursued from the beginning, but the occurrence of novelty at certain points. Life and mind, it is accepted, are such novelties; there was a time when they were not, and then they were 'there'.

The highest manifestations of mind are, in the time-scale, comparatively recent. Man's highly developed capacity for invention, the music of a Beethoven, the enormous developments in every sphere of life since the Renaissance, could not have been foreseen by primitive man as a natural growth of his latent talents, nor could an anthropologist deduce them from his studies of primitive culture. At certain times 'new' qualities have emerged without any evident preparations; others are a more heightened development of what was already latent and can be characterized by distinction of degree rather than of kind. The point at issue is whether supervenient qualities in the pyramid are an evolution of some inherent quality or *nisus*, or whether the gradation which it depicts is caused by the intervention of something from outside. Alexander supposed an upwardly emergent process from basic Space-Time, from the inorganic to the organic, to life, mind, and finally to deity: a scheme which describes, roughly, any form of emergent evolution, though it is not apparent that Alexander thinks of 'deity' in any theological or spiritual sense. Indeed, He whose body is Space-Time and who is not-yet because deity is always the *next* empirical quality to emerge as the result of cosmic *nisus* is not, as we have said, the transcendent Creator according to Christian theology, nor the ultimate causation of the emergent process as He is, for example, in Lloyd Morgan's stimulatingly suggestive philosophy.[1] Alexander's 'God' is the universe in evolution; and even if this is the philosophical, not the religious, idea of God, it is but another example of the non-correspondence of philosophical, or at any rate of some philosophical, and theological terms, of the inadequacy of the translation of the one into the other, and of the truth of William Temple's statement that 'philosophy never in fact goes beyond apprehension of the formal principle of Deity'.[2]

Despite, however, the special character of Alexander's idea of emergence, the principle of emergence, in a general sense, is by no means irrelevant to the consideration of Christological reinterpretation in non-mythological terms. Whether qualities 'emerge' as it were by some process immanent in the world, some vitalistic or hormic *nisus*, or whether they are induced to emerge by the intrusion of some act of will, that is by some teleological impulse from outside, is not a matter of which proof is forthcoming; what we are faced with is the fact of emergent qualities and their differentiation from other qualities. Are we, for example, justified in suggesting that the quality or attribute of 'Lordship' in Jesus was a 'quality' emergent as something new within the order of creation, as life and mind must have been, or is it something introduced from 'outside'? and if so, is it within the same sphere of causality as other outstanding, but at one time non-evident, human phenomena? Is it something which may, at some future time, be repeated?

This last question is clearly unanswerable, for we do not know what may or what may not recur except in a world organized on the principle of strict determinacy; certainty in any case belongs to past, not to future events, at any rate in the incalculable world of mind, where nothing is predictable. That tomorrow will come, that summer will recur next year, and that the mixing of the same two chemicals will yield the same result in five years' time, are so probable as to amount to a certainty, for these events belong to the cyclic order of nature or to scientific law. But we

---

[1] *Emergent Evolution*, pp. 208 ff., and in *Evolution in the Light of Modern Knowledge*, 1925 ed., p. 162.
[2] *Christus Veritas*, p. 175.

do not know if there will be another composer of the magnitude of Beethoven, though we can be reasonably sure that the future will produce musicians of competence. There are reasons, based on probability, for believing that there will always be men of a high degree of spiritual sensibility. There are, however, no reasons for believing that another figure of the spiritual dimension of Jesus will 'emerge' as the result of an evolutionary urge. Christianity has always ascribed that finality to him which belongs to the realm of the non-recurrent. There are no *philosophical* grounds for not believing in the recurrence of such a high level of spirituality as the title 'Lordship' implies, for a quality which has 'emerged' once may do so again at a different point in the evolutionary series. From the standpoint of religious belief, on the other hand, there is no expectation of such recurrence; what has happened as Revelation has happened once and for all, and there is no need for it to happen again nor is there any likelihood that it will. Where personality and purpose are concerned it does not follow that emergent qualities will recur, for non-recurrence is the special differentia of the realm of the personal and the historical. Recurrence and continuity are not necessary conditions of evolutionary emergence; the culmination of the process may occur in one person or in one event at one point in time. An inherent, immanent, though directive purposive *nisus* may reach fulfilment and culmination once and for all without reproduction or repetition.

In the non-personal realm, however, emergent qualities can be thought of as recurrent, for the character of the emergent or resultant is predictable. Neither copper nor sulphuric acid is blue; but when the two combine blueness is the result, and the copper sulphate possesses qualities which neither copper nor sulphuric acid possesses individually. Blueness, copper sulphateness, are 'new' qualities which are predictable of every application of sulphuric acid to copper, and the new chemical characteristics resulting are emergent. They were not there before, though they are neither 'higher' nor 'lower' than their components.

In the field of the historical and the psychological, that is in the field of the personal, an emergent result by combination, even in genetics, cannot be predicted except within certain limits. The operation of Mendel's law is predictable with regard to the culture of peas and the pigmentation of animals; but the result of the fertilization of the human ovum, except in the case of physical characteristics, is generally speaking unpredictable. Retrospectively it may be seen that this or that event was a probable result of a certain pattern of events or of a long line of development; but it can hardly be predicted from within the process itself; or if it is considered likely that this or that will result from a concatenation of historical circumstances, or from the intensive cultivation of spiritual hopes, there can be no accurate prediction of the time or the character of any eventual fulfilment or culmination; and even though a certain 'line' or movement may be a particular instance of other similar 'lines', it is possible that it alone, and not the others, may result in the culmination, and that the other patterns or expectations may find in it a kind of vicarious fulfilment, the attainment of the end of their own immanent *nisus*, although they develop their own particular patterns with their own form of apex. Karl Jaspers, for example, sees in the period *c.* 800–500 B.C. the 'axial' period both in the East and in the West out of whose womb sprang the movements which are now converging in world-history,[1] but only in one of its aspects, the religious history of Israel, was there a culmination which in Christian terms is called Incarnation, though non-Christians would deny that this was a culmination at all. Other culture-patterns produced different results.[2]

Now, in our enquiry into the possibly 'emergent' quality of that which caused the ascription to Jesus of the title *Kyrios* in a sense in which it is not applicable to other historical figures, there are two lines of approach. He can be considered as the apex, so to

---

[1] *The Origin and Goal of History*, Kegan Paul, 1953.
[2] Lloyd Morgan distinguishes between a single and a complex evolutionary line. With regard to the former he says: 'It seems, as I think on the evidence, that the higher we ascend in the hierarchy—and especially when we reach human persons—the emergent complexity is such that it appears justifiable to say that no two persons are quite alike. Each person is an uniquely individual product along one of the many lines of advance—say Shakespeare, Goethe, Newton and Darwin. If this be so, the *nisus* towards deity on its strictly central line should culminate in one unique person, at the very apex of the pyramid. If an impartial historical survey should lead to the conclusion that the *nisus* towards deity has culminated in one unique individual, there is, as far as I can see, nothing in the naturalistic interpretation of emergent evolution which precluded the acceptance of this conclusion.' If, however, *all* lines of advance represent a *nisus* towards deity, 'even so the unattained, as such, seems to imply that which is not yet' (*Emergent Evolution*, p. 31).

speak, or, as Dr. A. T. Cadoux has expressed it, 'the culminating achievement of a universally active process',[1] or as the culmination of a particular movement in history, namely, the developing religious consciousness of the Hebrew people. The latter may be considered first, for it permits of less speculation and arises from the appreciation of a historical-religious pattern of events which can be surveyed in its completeness.

3

One aspect of the theme of the Old Testament is the progressive revelation of God and a nation's progressive capacity for the acceptance of the revelation. It is also the account of the manner in which a people considered itself to be 'chosen' by God 'out of all the peoples of the earth'. It was in the light of this awareness that the history, in great part, came to be written. Throughout there was apparent, especially during the prophetic period, a considerable gulf between the actual and the ideal: between what the nation actually was and what it should be, for its kings and military men were often enough little more than bandits and its aristocracy exploiters of the poor.

It seems that this cleavage between the actual and the ideal ran right through the history of the people, from the dawn of national life, through the conflict between Moses and his people and the ethical judgments passed on kings, culminating in the emergence of the prophetic religion, whose representatives during the 'axial' period made a universal and permanent contribution to religion. These men were socially and sometimes politically minded and possessed a strong sense of the ethical quality of history. Their vision was of a God concerned with social justice, national righteousness, and national mission, and also with other nations who created the situation which gave meaning to the national mission. How far the religion of this period was coloured by Messianism it is hard to say, for it was through the eyes of later interpreters that the Messianic import of the Old Testament was seen. Yet there is substantial reason for believing that the expectation of the Messianic leader or deliverer was entertained fairly

[1] *A New Orthodoxy of Jesus and Personality*, p. 135.

early: an expectation which later, under the pressure of historical circumstances, developed into apocalyptic. What is clear from the reading of the Old Testament and the apocalyptic literature of two centuries before Christ is the extraordinary capacity of a people for spiritual vision. The devotion of the prophets, the piety of the psalms, the magnificent dialectic of the Book of Job, and the intense awareness of the national mission interpreted religiously, bear witness to this unusual spiritual awareness and sensitiveness, if not in the body of the nation, at any rate in its more conspicuous members; and though we cannot select any one point and argue inductively from it some future moment when spiritual expectations would be fulfilled, in looking back at the history as a whole it is natural to suppose that a fulfilment of the expectation was hoped for. The combination of achievement and expectation provides some justification for the assumption that the people who were capable of producing the great prophets and psalmists were neither pessimists in regard to history nor exaggerators of their own spiritual prowess in their idealization of the deliverer who was to come.

Now the Messianism which emerged from the later Jewish hope possessed a twofold characteristic: it was mythologically futurist in so far as it anticipated a divine action to come, and concerned with the historical past in so far as the Messianic deliverer was conceived to be of Davidic lineage. That is to say, he belonged to the historical series which ran like a thread through the various strata constituting the history and also embodied in history an intention which lay beyond it. The Messiah both belonged to history and was thought of as God's response to history. As a transcendent figure he was later conceived in mythological terms, but this did not detract from his participation in and his consummation of history by virtue of his historical lineage. He would emerge as the historical deliverer (sometimes as a superhuman, pre-existent figure), yet not on his own account or through the pressure of the historical moment, but rather as the result of divine intention. History and metahistory are inextricably intertwined, for it is through the action of God that history is made to yield its fruit and that historical potentiality emerges in a reality which is both transcendent over history and immanent in it. In this way it may be suggested that the whole accumulated tradition of Israel, historically pin-pointed, so to speak, in the travail of introspection and the anguish of hope, was precisely that out of which an unusual manifestation of the spiritual would emerge, both as a 'new' thing and as the result of the interaction of historical-religious forces.

That the New Testament people saw in Jesus this manifestation is beyond doubt. He was the 'Promised One'; genealogically he was represented as of the line of David (as he may well have been), and as the culmination of the movement of revelation which characterized prophecy (Heb. 1:1). Indeed, this historical-spiritual fulfilment is the theme of the early preaching in the Acts. But Jesus was also regarded as the transcendent Word from beyond. To the modern mind, with its different time-vista, this notion of fulfilment is strange, especially when it is realized that several centuries elapsed between the Messianic or expectational prophecies as subsequently interpreted and the actual date of fulfilment.[1] It is as if the year 1900 were thought of as providing the fulfilment of hopes expressed in 1200 or 1500. We should hardly regard them as fulfilled expectations, possibly because our time-perspective is neither 'religious' nor eschatologically conditioned.

It is at this point that the historical as distinguished from the mythological aspect of the Christological problem is seen to emerge; for if the mission and person of Jesus are to be conceived wholly in terms of revelation and 'mythological' thinking, as the Word from beyond, and as the Incarnation of the Eternal and pre-existent Son, little purpose is served by regarding him as the culmination of a long period of historical development, as a 'new' emergent from the historical series. But if, on the other hand, in fulfilment of a historically conditioned hope, he was (as the

[1] Not even the naïve ingenuity of Wilhelm Vischer and other theologians who indulge in the so-called typological approach to biblical interpretation can justifiably read into the Old Testament a continuous expectation or prefiguration of a Messianic or any other kind of fulfilment. Mention should be made in this connexion of Vischer's *The Old Testament Witness to the Christ* (Lutterworth Press, 1949), which has been pertinently criticized by Brunner (*Dogmatics*, II, 'The Christian Doctrine of Creation and Redemption', appendix vii, pp. 209 ff.); A. M. Farrer, *A Study in St. Mark* (1951); and vol. II of Lionel Thornton's *The Form of a Servant*. Neither Vischer's prefigurative nor Dr. Farrer's postfigurative or retrojective typology is convincing.

Apostolic preaching held him to be) the culmination of this historical series traceable through the national history, he was not a sudden, unheralded irruption into history from outside, a temporary intruder from eternity into time.

It is from such a standpoint as is here suggested, then, that it may be argued that the 'new' quality apparent in Jesus as the numinous, the holy, which characterized his historical life, and that of Lordship which was ascribed to his metahistorical personality after the Resurrection and Exaltation, raising his 'historical' significance (using Bultmann's distinction) to the level of the *geschichtlich*, may be thought of as a once-for-all 'emergence' of all that was implicit in the deepest potentialities of a national history.

As for the non-recurrence of what may be supposed to have 'emerged' and the legitimacy of describing as emergent what has appeared only once, it may be submitted that its non-recurrence was bound up with a non-recurrent series of historical and religious events. A national history does not repeat itself in cycles; once it has happened, it has happened, and if the non-recurrent is the result of that series of events or circumstances, and these are considered, as a complete pattern, to be non-repetitive, a repetition of them is not to be expected, for the very *Heilsgeschichte*, the 'story' of salvation, is to be regarded as having happened once and for all.

The Jesus who is different from any other historical person and whose differentia consists in his continuing 'existential' impact on man, however, belongs to the human-historical series.

It was not possible to predict from within the history, or from history combined with the idealized form of the expectation, what would be the character of the Christ. When he came, it was his differentiae which convinced men that he was the one to whom history and faith were considered to have pointed, *though they were not the differentiae which were expected*. The recurrence of the phrase 'according to the Scriptures' (however valid or invalid according to our standards the principles of exegesis may have been) shows that it was to the historical series that the early Apostolic age turned in its apologetic; it was unaware of any contradiction between the historical and the emergently meta-historical. Although they were not in a position to survey the course of the history of Israel in the manner of a modern biblical student, the Apostles interpreted the history religiously as its meaning was disclosed to them in the Old Testament in terms of the concept of fulfilment (Acts 3: 12–26; 7: 2–53). The Messiah was not thought of as a bolt from the blue but as one of whom Moses had said that 'a prophet shall the Lord raise up unto you of your brethren, like unto me' (Acts 3: 22). The method of interpretation does not matter: what is of importance is the manner in which the early Church considered the Lord to be in the line of historical expectation and promise as they were understood, and the fact that the one who was acknowledged as *Kyrios* was in the prophetic tradition.

The other line of argument presents fewer tangible possibilities. Whereas it has been submitted that the character of the history of Israel was such as might be expected to lead to the emergence of a unique personality within the historical series and yet who appeared also by the purposive intention of God, it is not so easy to contend that the qualities covered by the term 'Lordship' are a natural culmination of human evolution as such, or that they are, in Alexander's terminology, the highest achievement of the *nisus* towards deity.

The evolutionary approach to Christology has not been developed with any great thoroughness, though it has been touched upon by a number of British Liberal theologians. Dr. A. T. Cadoux, for example, has advocated this treatment of the problem of Christology.[1] The presence of God in Jesus, his argument runs, was not different from His presence in other men, and that if He is not in us as He was in Jesus it is because 'it is not God's desire that it should be so', though He could be so if He wished. We should see in Jesus the 'culminating achievement of a universally active divine process', 'the culmination and not the antithesis of God's ordinary way of working in the world'. 'Jesus is the full emergence of the divine immanent in the universe.' 'The divine outgoing that works in, and is the very being of the

---

[1] *A New Orthodoxy of Jesus and Personality*, pp. 135 ff.

universe, is, in the conscious and full co-operation of Jesus, carried to its highest and intensest phase of effectiveness.' Dr. Cadoux continues:

> If we start with the notion of a God who might be more in, and to, mankind than he generally is, then the utter self-giving of Jesus to his fellows is unintelligible. . . .
>
> If, in asking how we are to think of Jesus, we start from the relation of God to man as implied in our ethical activity and as given explicitness by Jesus, we shall find that our experience of him as a man without superhuman advantages over his fellow-men brings us to see that he is, not only entirely divine, but the consummate concentration of the divine, unique throughout the whole range of being. . . . In us the goodness is incomplete and the fellowship [between us and God] broken: we have misused the divine to most undivine ends; even the noble have fallen short, for if to the making of man there went a divine self-giving to the uttermost, then the human heart that is to respond truly and wholly to God must be one in which there are combined the most sensitive and inclusive spiritual understanding and the most passionate and heroic devotion. And it is in Jesus that we find this and see that which has its being and freedom in the outgoing and self-giving of God rendered back to God in complete devotion, so that in him there is an unequalled wholeness of the divine: God is more wholly God in him than elsewhere. Jesus is the full emergence of the divine immanent in the universe.[1]

The incarnation of God, Dr. Cadoux proceeds, works 'through what shows outwardly as a process of evolution'.[2] 'The subject of Christian thought is not God in Jesus alone, but God in humanity as interpreted, centralized, and consummated in Jesus.'[3] The process of human history should be thought of as 'culminating in Jesus', though at a mid-point in time rather than at the end of history.

Now, the difficulty here is that the differences between God and the world and between God and man are broken down into what might clumsily be called a kind of pantheanthropism: God is 'in' all men, he is immanent 'in' the universe, but He is 'more

---

[1] *A New Orthodoxy of Jesus and Personality*, pp. 137–138.
[2] Ibid., p. 139.
[3] Ibid., p. 140.

wholly God' in Jesus than anywhere else, and Jesus, it would seem, is what all men could become if God had not a good reason for not desiring it. While agreeing with Dr. Cadoux's reasons for reject-ing the idea of pre-existence and the metaphysics of much orthodox theology, we can find little evidence for the belief that Jesus is, so to speak, the completion of all the potentialities innately resident in human nature. In Dr. Cadoux's view the divinity of Jesus is both the flower of evolution and the form of God's imman-ence.[1] Yet there is little to show that human nature as such is what Jesus was if only God wished it to be so. The human scene is not such as to encourage the belief that 'man is akin to God, made by God of the very being of God', though in questioning this optimistic statement one should avoid the other extreme which considers man, since the 'Fall', to have lost the image of God to such an extent that there is no longer any 'point of contact' between him and God.[2] Left to himself, however, man does not rise to the Christ-level, and if to do so were a naturally evolutionary process, it is strange that this potentiality for emer-gent divineness should have been non-recurrent. Christian theology has been right in holding that what man was unable to do for himself God was obliged to do by His intervention in history.

It is not being suggested that Dr. Cadoux has ignored the difference between man and God; indeed, he admits that the difference between God's goodness and man's is that the latter is derivative, and that man's 'kinship' with God does not resemble his kinship with his fellow men or with a human father. There is 'an essential difference between personality in God and in man that is not adequately described by saying that human personality is imperfect and the divine personality perfect'.[3]

[1] The interpretation of Incarnation in terms of immanence (a modernized version of the logos-doctrine) is also prominent in other representatives of British Liberal theology, e.g., H. D. A. Major, *English Modernism*, p. 154: 'The Logos Christology lends itself admirably to modern ways of thinking as seen in the doctrine of Creative Evolution and Divine Immanence'; C. E. Raven, *What Think Ye of Christ*, pp. 26 ff.; W. Temple in *Foundations*, p. 259; Miall Edwards in *The Lord of Life, Grefydd a Bywyd*, pp. 109 ff.; W. R. Matthews, *The Future of Christianity*, pp. 110 ff.

[2] e.g. Karl Barth, *Kirchliche Dogmatik*, I, pp. 251–252.

[3] Op. cit., pp. 125–126. Dr. J. M. Wilson shares in this emphasis on continuity and culmination in emergent immanence. 'The facts of evolution,' he says, 'and continuity are indicating that the chain of mind reaches up to the Creative Spirit, to God Himself, and that the supreme manifestation on our earth of the Divine in that chain is Jesus Christ. This is not to abate one jot of the Christian claim that

Nevertheless, this kind of evolutionary thinking results in the statement that 'we must recognize that God is, and is to be found, in the whole creative process that culminates in Jesus, no less than in the creative initiative from which this process proceeds'. This does not seem to discriminate between various parts of the process, and it is questionable if the 'whole' creative process culminates in Jesus (though this is the theme of the great Christological passages in the Epistles); for sub-human forms of life not possessing mind can hardly be thought of as emergently fulfilling themselves in the spiritual culmination in Jesus. Many of the manifestations of the creative process fail to indicate the probability that they will culminate in moral goodness, and it would therefore be erroneous to think of evolution as a continuous process or *nisus* towards spiritual perfection. Further, evolution, in the strict meaning of the word, is a biological concept. The unique is the 'sport', and may not recur. It is not a unit in the evolutionary series. If Jesus could be thought of in evolutionary terms it should be legitimate to say: 'There is the apex of the creative process: there is the summit of the evolutionary pyramid. If only we go on for a long enough time, that is what we are all capable of becoming.' This is to substitute a humanistic optimism for biblical realism. The main differentia between Jesus and humanity consists not in achievable degrees of goodness, but in the absolute holiness which is not a product of evolution. The *Kyrios* is more than the supremely good man as the completion of an immanently human process of development.

4

When we turn to St. Paul it is apparent that, though he did not write in ignorance of the 'historical' Jesus, his emphasis was not on Jesus' continuity with humanity or on his pre-eminence over men as the culmination of the inherently human or of the divine alleged to be immanent in all men, but on the factors

---

Jesus was the Manifestation, the Revelation, of God in humanity, such as none other has been. Not one jot. It is not to lower Christ, but to raise our thought of man; it is "taking the manhood into God"' (*Evolution in the Light of Modern Knowledge*, p. 504).

which differentiated him from other men, some of which, it is being contended, indicate mythological thinking. Jesus is the means of salvation the scope of whose activity is commensurate with that of the Holy Spirit itself. He is the principle of human unity and solidarity (Col. 3: 11) and of the consubsistence of creation (I Cor. 8: 6, etc.) Although he 'went about doing good' it is not on his goodness, which may be taken for granted, that Paul dwells, but on his spiritual ascendancy over human life and on his being in a unique degree the receptacle of the divine indwelling, though the Christian is also a temple of the Holy Spirit. It is not in the principle of immanence which, in some form, is shared, at least potentially, by man as something which he has in common with Jesus that Paul finds primary significance, nor in Jesus' solidarity with humanity alone, though this, too, he takes for granted. The introduction to Romans (Rom. 1: 3–5) shows that for Paul Jesus was, at any rate in this phase of his thought, of the 'seed of David' and 'declared' (ὁρισθέντος) to be 'the Son of God with power' by virtue of his holiness and resurrection, which is consistent with the primitive kerygma;[1] nevertheless, this is not where the chief emphasis lies but on Jesus' divine Sonship and Lordship, which are his essential differentiae, and there is no suggestion that these are capable of being modernized into immanental 'evolutionary' attainments or that Lordship is in the same category as man's status as a potential or even actual son of God. True, we all cry 'Abba, Father': through the spirit we are children of God and heirs to His promises (Rom. 8: 15 ff.); and although we are 'sons of God' the full revelation of our sonship will be in the future and will be the work of the Spirit rather than a natural progression from one condition to another. Paul's thought may be complicated, at times elusive and ambiguous, and sometimes obscure; but it does

---

[1] Bousset cites this passage in support of the 'mythological' character of Paul's Christology. Jesus is the pre-existent Son; the πνεῦμα ἀγιωσυνης is more than personal holiness, namely 'the higher Wisdom of the Son'. Here, as with πίστις, Bousset is determined to establish Paul's debt to Hellenistic ideas. Even in this passage Jesus is less of the seed of David than the 'mythological' Son. 'The earthly career of the Son of God is for him [Paul] the presupposition of his present exaltation' (*Kyrios Christos*, pp. 146 ff., 152–153). Cf. also E. F. Scott's view that had Paul not been converted to Christianity 'his thought would have most certainly followed the line of Philo and Hellenistic gnosis' (*The New Testament Idea of Revelation*, p. 167). It certainly diverged at many points from Rabbinic Judaism.

imply discontinuity between Jesus and the human in man, between the indwelling of God in him on the one hand and His presence 'in' man as the temple of the Holy Spirit on the other. For Paul the otherness of Jesus is the decisive constituent in his Christology.

Elsewhere in the New Testament Jesus is described as the 'one Mediator, the man, Christ Jesus',[1] or the High Priest whose saving efficacy depends upon his solidarity with man; yet here, too, the emphasis is on that which Jesus does *not* possess in common with man.

The Synoptic Gospels, too, though less markedly and less theologically, indicate this bewildering quality of otherness. Despite the clarity of the historical emphasis of the earliest Gospel and its relative freedom from mythological and theological elaboration, something more than the implication of mere humanity underlies it. It is, after all, the 'Gospel of Jesus Christ, the Son of God', which, if not the terminology of the narrative itself (except on one or two occasions), states the reason for its composition. We have already seen, however, that, according to the Synoptic tradition, which may be presumed to be as close to an eye-witness tradition as can be hoped for, there is present in Jesus the 'numinous' quality which strikingly differentiates him from others. His supersession of the Mosaic law by his own legislation, his being the New Torah, carries with it not so much a defiance of tradition but the certain consciousness of its fulfilment in himself; and the Q saying Matthew 11: 27 shows that the divine-human intimacy in Jesus is different in character and not only in degree from ordinary human knowledge of God. Similarly the reported incidents of the walking on the water, the feeding of the five thousand, and above all the Transfiguration, witness to a perplexity and awe on the part of the disciples which call for explanation in other terms than those which would be applicable to superior human achievement.

It is, however, to the fact of the Resurrection that we must turn if the absolute uniqueness of Jesus is to be appreciated.

---

[1] The term Mediator is used on four occasions: Hebrews 8: 6; 9: 15; 12: 24; I Timothy 2: 5. Paul's use of the term in Galatians 3: 20 is in a different kind of context.

This is not the demonstration of a human *nisus* towards deity, or the seal of human evolution, though Paul does not hesitate to regard it as an indication of the kind of form in which man is destined to live in another dimension of existence (I Cor. 15: 19 ff., 46). Even if shorn of all the allegedly fanciful and mythical accretion found in the Gospel accounts of the occurrence, it does not appear as that of which man is intrinsically capable by virtue of what Dr. Cadoux describes as a 'universally active divine process' or the 'full emergence of the divine immanent in the universe'. For it is not of personal survival after death in general that Paul is speaking but of the unique resurrection of Jesus and his transference by it to the metahistorical dimension. It is the Resurrection which entitled Jesus to the name *Kyrios* which is above every name. Yet it is metahistorical not in the sense of being merely a post-historical mode of existence, the natural 'next higher' level, in the terminology of emergent grades, supervenient on the historical series. The Resurrection is not represented in the New Testament as belonging naturally to the order of creation or nature or historical existence, but to the realm from which the numinous quality in Jesus is derived. It cannot be regarded as evolutionarily implicit or predictably emergent in a human person.

The contention at the present stage of the argument, then, is this. Though Jesus belonged to history and was regarded by the New Testament tradition as essentially a historical person and human if only to the extent of obviously sharing the characteristics of human nature without its sinfulness, it was not primarily in possessing human qualities heightened and purified in an exceptional degree, but rather in possessing what might be called holiness to the nth degree, that he was considered worthy of the title of Lord. For the New Testament writers this differentia was such that the Lordship of Jesus could be described only in mythological or near-mythological terms: no others were adequate to account for his transcendence and for the experience of 'existential' encounter.

It is here that any attempt to solve the fundamental problem of Christology is doomed to failure, and where the heart of the paradox of the 'human' and the 'transcendent' is to be found.

Jesus as Lord was addressed or regarded as the historical figure who was known about by his contemporaries, though it is doubtful if those who knew him called him by the title *Kyrios* during his lifetime.[1] Yet as one who had lived as man he was given this title because of something which did not implicitly belong to the human order. The object of the Jewish expectation, to which Jesus came as a divine response, as he was the response to the totality of human need, was conceived both in historical and mythological terms: historically as the divinely appointed King in the Davidic line, mythologically as the Son of Man, the Man from Heaven of apocalyptic magnitude and magnificence, the supernatural judge whose future coming would coincide with a cosmic dénouement. The conception of the Man from Heaven, it is possible, influenced some forms of Christological speculation and belonged to the group of mythological ideas associated with the pre-existent Logos or Incarnate Son. All these conceptions, it is maintained, are summed up in the title *Kyrios*, which belongs to the human series in so far as it refers to a historical personality, and also to the more-than-historical and more-than-personal dimension through transcendence over history. The categories of historical evolution and biological evolution are inadequate as a means of reducing the mythological thinking, though they may be illuminating up to a point. They do not, however, do justice either to experience or to the claims made for Jesus Christ by the existential factor inseparable from the Christian's encounter with Christ, or to the witness of the New Testament, even allowing for the difference between its view of the world and that of modern man.

5

If we reject the notion of pre-existence as both improbable and not deducible from the known data, besides being not implied in any well-attested Synoptic *logion*, we are left with the picture of Jesus as one whose knowledge of God was unique and complete. The most significant saying in the Synoptic Gospels in this connection is the Q *logion*—Matt. 11: 25–27), which is

[1] With the exceptions already mentioned.

paralleled by the Johannine 'I and the Father are one' and the prayer of John 17. Even when allowance is made for the peculiarly Johannine interpretation and the complicated character of the world of ideas which forms its background, it is unwise to under-rate the importance of the Johannine utterances, the substance of which, even if clothed in the writer's idiom, should not be hastily dismissed as original composition. They are virtually an elaboration of the Q *logion*, and throughout the great discourses the impression is created that between Jesus and God there existed an intimacy far deeper than between any other son and his parent, and that this profound *gnosis* was natural. Jesus speaks as the filial ambassador of God: 'I have not spoken of myself: but the Father who sent me gave me a commandment, what I should say and what I should speak' (John 12: 49). 'I can of myself do nothing' (5: 30). 'The same works that I do bear witness of me that the Father hath sent me' (5: 36). 'As the Father hath sent me, and I live by the Father . . .' (6: 57). Jesus is 'in' the Father, who is 'in' him. There is a mutual in-dwelling or interpenetration. He who has 'seen' Jesus has 'seen' the Father; yet the Father is greater than the Son (14: 28). The love of the Father towards him is the pattern of Jesus' love for the disciples and for their love towards one another. Even in the moment of deepest anguish and abandonment the Father is with him (John 16: 32; Mark 14: 36 ff.). Although the Fourth Gospel opens with the great pronouncement about the co-existence and identity of the Word and God and the historical In-carnation of the Word, the theme is not overtly mentioned again: Jesus is not called the Logos but the Son; indeed, in the light of the later elaboration of the Logos-Christology of the post-Apostolic age it is noteworthy that the Johannine reference is so unassuming. Even though it states the theme of the Gospel in more or less philosophical terms it does not add substantially to the under-standing of the Gospel, in as much as it would remain a coherent unity if the Prologue were removed or had not been written. The remainder of the Gospel is not conspicuously the story of the Logos become flesh, of the Divine Wisdom walking as a man among men; formally, at least, it is the account of the ministry of one who was the Son of God in a special sense, living in unbroken intimacy with the Father, bodying forth His love, proclaiming His will, and performing his works. It was left to later theology so to dehumanize the historical Jesus through its elaboration of the Logos-doctrine that its Johannine form appears simple in comparison.

It is, however, in the Fourth Gospel that the highest reflective Christological affirmations of the New Testament occur: the pronouncement about the Word and the words of Thomas, 'My Lord and my God' where the term 'Lord' is given its fullest numinous content. The main theme, however, is the Sonship of Jesus the Word. This is much more than simple filial relationship to God or the culmination of evolving immanence. It is described in John as in the Synoptics as the result or condition of God's redemptive purpose, and it is possible, we maintain, to understand it in terms of this purpose without reference to mythological conceptions. It may be regarded as the result of divine 'adoption' (as in the kerygma of Acts) or as election without any loss to the full affirmation of faith, for it means a mutual knowledge so complete that the mind of the Son expresses the mind of God: a Sonship involving such unity with the Father that the Son is wholly drawn into the divine nature as the divine nature is drawn into the life of the Son. The Synoptics and the Fourth Gospel are equally emphatic, though the former are less elaborately explicit, in showing that Jesus' Sonship does not arise from human choice but from divine action: whether the demonstration of this is found in the Lukan incident of the visit of the boy Jesus to the Temple, the divine pronouncement at Baptism, or the Johannine declaration of the pre-temporal character of his Sonship. The precise manner in which this perfect filial-paternal relationship was achieved lies beyond human knowledge. Berdyaev has written of the 'interpenetration of the human and the divine', and that, no doubt, is as far as one can go, even though one cannot say *how* the human and the divine interpenetrate in Jesus. It is the perfection of such interpenetration which constitutes not only Jesus' Sonship but also his Lordship, the title which admits his holiness and implies recognition of his redemptive vocation as the chosen one of God who, because of his chosenness, claims the homage and faith of the Christian.

Now, both the terms—Sonship and Lordship—emphasize the distance of Jesus from ordinary humanity: the former because of the uniqueness of the human-divine relationship, and the latter because it implies the *Kyrios-doulos*, 'Lord-servant', relationship of Jesus to the believer: a relationship involving a distance which has been minimized, or at any rate not accorded a sufficiently conspicuous position, by the more liberal type of Christology which tends to overlook the transcendent element in the person of Jesus. For Paul Jesus was *Kyrios* because he was the Son; the terms are inseparable or complementary. They imply a significance which is more than historical: it is *geschichtlich* as well as *historisch*. For it was the Resurrection which is the attestation to the more-than-historical permanence of the pre-eminence of the Risen Saviour: to the nature of the historical mission of Jesus and to the transcendent element which must be acknowledged if, in Kierkegaard's term, Jesus is to be regarded as always 'contemporary' and if the historical revelation is to pass into permanent availability for faith.

Now, the issue is whether an anagogic Christology preserves the essential meaning of the katagogic (or, in Harnack's term, pneumatic), which, it is contented, is mythological in form, and whether the conceptions of Sonship and Lordship lose anything of their decisive significance for Christian thought and faith through being interpreted in terms which exclude the need to think of Jesus as an eternally pre-existent and divine being appearing as a man or of God as 'descending' to live a human life. If the authority of the New Testament is sought it is seen to provide evidence of both approaches to the problem: one may choose whichever one prefers. But the former has not been regarded as the orthodox understanding of the Incarnation. In its adoptionist form it was considered heretical, though it was advocated as late as the eighth century, when the Bishop of Toledo was attacked for sponsoring the view that Jesus was the 'adopted' Son of God: a view which was condemned at three Frankish synods. A later version of this Christology was Socinianism. In one form or another it is an attempt to understand the person and mission of Jesus in minimally mythological language. One criticism of it, as Dr. Thornton held while wrestling with the problems of how

Absolute Actuality could be incorporated into the time-series, on the one hand, and on the other how the human organism could be taken up into the level of deity,[1] is that for this form of Christology God (Dr. Thornton borrows a term from Temple) is 'adjectival'; and Dr. L. W. Grensted, in criticizing the kind of liberal Christology represented in his view by Harnack is that it 'cannot in any way make intelligible the "exaltation" of Jesus to be God'.[2] But here there is a curious contradiction. If Jesus *is* God he cannot be 'exalted' to be God. He is already exalted by virtue of his Godhead. Yet the New Testament does not teach this at all. It teaches that Jesus was exalted to be Lord, not *Theos* but *Kyrios*. Dr. Temple, too, lays himself open to the charge of inconsistency when he says at one point that Jesus 'is not a man exalted to perfect participation in the Divine Nature or Life; He is God manifest under the conditions of humanity',[3] while elsewhere he writes that Jesus 'was aware of an intimacy with God which He found that other men had not experienced. He interpreted this as a call to fulfil the promise of the Messiah who should come. The Voice that hailed Him at His baptism called Him to begin the Messianic work'.[4] With the second view we have no quarrel: it is what is being advocated in this book; but it is in flat contradiction to the first, for he who is 'aware of an intimacy with God' can hardly be the same as that God 'living a human life'. The second view is close to the Adoptionism which Temple was criticizing, for it is nearer to the view that Jesus was 'exalted to perfect participation in the Divine Nature'. Throughout Temple's great book there is evident this struggle between seeing the need to do justice to one kind of Christology and at the same time endeavouring to preserve the precious emphasis of the Catholic tradition. This tension, and the inconsistency which accompanies it, should be attributed to the influence of the mythological type of Christology which is under discussion, though a philosophical approach is being employed to support it.

What, however, matters is not the truth or otherwise of

[1] *The Incarnate Lord*, pp. 229 ff.
[2] *The Person of Christ*, p. 174.
[3] *Christus Veritas*, p. 139.
[4] Ibid., p. 121.

Adoptionism but whether the principle behind it is capable of application to the Christology of *Kyrios* as we are expounding it, for its essential meaning is that God 'chose' Jesus into Sonship and 'sent' him to be the medium of revelation and the instrument of redemption, which does not exclude the interpenetration of the divine and the human, the perfect filial *gnosis* of the Father, the absolute holiness which is the distinctive differentia of the Christ from humanity in general. Whether this constitutes, in Dr. Thornton's words, 'a new level of the old series' or not is of secondary importance; the primary factor is the establishment of perfect mutuality, the meeting of a movement from the side of God and from the side of man, which is found in Jesus the Lord. It is expressed, amid the arithmetical and philosophical complexities of the Athanasian Creed, in words which appear somewhat strange in such a document: 'not by conversion of the Godhead into flesh, but by taking of the Manhood into God': a succinct statement of the anagogic Christology, whatever else the Creed may affirm.

For the present it must suffice to state that the affirmation of the Lordship of Jesus is fundamental to the Christian faith and that, in Paul's words, no man can say that Jesus is Lord except by the Holy Spirit. 'If thou shalt confess with thy mouth the Lord Jesus, and shalt believe in thine heart that God hath raised him from the dead, thou shalt be saved.'

Such is the declaration of evangelical faith. It sums up the Gospel and is capable of a liberal range of interpretation. It is the affirmation of the sufficiency of the Jesus of history and also of his exaltation into the object of faith. Further than this one cannot go without, in the one direction, dissolving Jesus into an amiable moralist of humanistic unitarianism, or in the other, erring through obscuring the genuinely historical by the imposition of a mythological manner of thinking which is associated with an obsolete world-view.

CHAPTER TWO

THE LORDSHIP OF JESUS AND CREATION

I—CHRIST AND CREATION

I

The attempt to understand the place of Jesus in the human order and to evaluate the significance of the New Testament Christology within the framework of the concept of the mythological necessitates an investigation into the New Testament conception of the relation of Jesus to creation. For Paul, John, and the author of Hebrews, as we have seen, considered Jesus not only to belong to the human order by virtue of his manhood (even if this was at times conceived only in formal terms), but also to be Lord of creation and co-creator by virtue of his eternal Sonship. It will be necessary, too, to deal further with the place of Jesus in the evolutionary process. For if his Lordship is to be understood historically he must belong to the order of nature as well as to supernature. Before, however, proceeding to an examination of this relationship of Jesus to creation the New Testament statements about it may be briefly summarized.

Jesus is the 'name' above every name; every knee should bow before him 'in heaven and on earth and under the earth' (Phil. 2: 10). He is the principle uniting all things 'in heaven and earth' (Eph. 1: 10). He is the 'first-born of all creation, for in him were all things created', the means by which God reconciled to Himself 'all things whether on earth or in heaven' (Col. 1: 15). He is the 'Second Adam' (I Cor. 15: 45); through him God 'created the world'; he 'upholds the universe by his word of power' (Heb. 1: 2). Much of the Pauline soteriology assumes the reversal of the relationship of Adam (and through him of humanity) to the created order, which, like man, is in need of redemption. In short, the New Testament theologians ascribe to Jesus the supreme place in the universe and also represent him as the agent

of creation. It is necessary to enquire into how far this is mythological thinking.

For the Gospels contain or reflect no knowledge of this high
Christology, and any thoughts regarding Jesus' place in creation
which are to be found in them are suggestive rather than explicit.

Thus while the nature-miracles do not point to any doctrine
they suggest that in his mastery over natural forces Jesus was
exhibiting his Lordship over them. 'What manner of man is this,
that the sea and the winds obey him?' He is one who is believed
to walk on the water (whatever natural explanation there may
be of this, if there is one at all). He multiplies the loaves and feeds
the crowd. He raises the dead to life and is not himself subdued
by death. That is to say, the natural laws governing the place
of man in creation do not apply to Jesus. After the Resurrection
he is no longer subject to space and time as they are generally
understood. The Christian belief in his presence in the Church
shows that in any adequate conception of the person of Jesus
something more than the merely 'natural' is involved. He is the
Prince of Life (Acts 3: 15), whereas the created order is subject
to death.

The biblical picture of creation is concerned with origin, not with the process
of becoming. The scientific world-picture, on the other hand, knows nothing of
creation as an act but is concerned with the observation of the process. Ultimate
causality lies outside the scope of science, for this would bring it into the field of
the theological in so far as a creative, purposive cause is postulated. When a
scientist such as C. Lloyd Morgan sees in the 'hormic schema of development'
evidence of purposive mind and attributes 'the whole sweep of evolutionary
advance' to 'spiritual agency' in terms of Divine Purpose, he is introducing
into the contemplation of creation a factor belonging to the theological or
philosophical sphere (*Evolution in the Light of Modern Knowledge*, p. 182), for a
conscious purpose or end implies a Purposer or one who designs and decides the
end in view and is therefore to be conceived as being present at the 'beginning'
—that is, anterior to creation. For creation is a process, not a point in time or a
succession of definite moments, as in the Genesis story, which may, mythopoetically, be thought of as a telescoping in terms of divine causation. In the
Old Testament creation is a finished picture, a completed scene which God the
cosmic artist contemplates with enjoyment and pronounces good, as an artist
looks with approval at the picture which he has just painted or the sculptor
at the figure which he has completed. As a finished product the universe of
Genesis resembles the work of an artist rather than the object of scientific

investigation. In Job and the Psalms God is again represented as rejoicing in what he has made (Job 38 ff.; Ps. 104, etc.), and among the prophetic writings Amos 5:8 and Isaiah 40:20 ff., show God to be the creator of a vast system in comparison with which man is very small. The psalmists and prophets were impressed by the majesty of God as revealed in the finished splendour of His creation, which is usually described as the object of His aesthetic contemplation. Philo was in advance of his age in his comments on Genesis 2:1, for he thought of creation as a continuous process. 'It is quite foolish to think that the world was created in six days, or in a space of time at all. Why? Because every period of time is a series of days and nights, and these can be only made by the movement of the sun as it goes over and under the earth. . . . It would therefore be more correct to say that the world was not made in time, but that time was formed by means of the world . . . God never leaves off making, but even as it is the property of fire to burn and of snow to chill, so it is the property of God to make. . . . Whereas things produced by human arts are finished and stand still and remain as they are, the products of divine skill, when completed, begin again to move.'[1]

For St. Paul creation is neither static nor worthy of admiration. As found in Romans 8 it is not the artistic magnificence of the finished product which engages his attention but its woeful incompleteness. The creation is subject to vanity or futility (ματαιότης), not through any waywardness of its own, but through the will of 'him who subjected it', though whether Paul means by this that Satan and not God was responsible is not indicated. However the state of bondage to corruption originated, creation awaits universal redemption. The passage is brief, and doubtless capable of more than one interpretation, and it is perhaps too easy to read into it a modern notion such as evolution or development which was foreign to the writer. Thus Dr. C. E. Raven describes Paul as 'the first to propound a coherent scheme of creative evolution and thinks of God as creatively co-operating with the creature in its age-long travail (*Natural Religion and Christian Theology*, I, p. 34). In the Pauline view creation derives its significance from the scheme of redemption, and is itself, like man, the object of redemption: perhaps 'redemptive evolution' (if evolution of one sort or another there must be) would be an apt term. What he meant by the imperfection of creation can only be guessed; but that he believed it to be subject to futility and decay is plain.

The Gospels contain no thought-out basis for a doctrine of creation or a particular view of nature. Jesus speaks of nature illustratively. Nature is impartial in that the sun bestows its benefits on just and unjust, and no sparrow falls to the ground without the knowledge of God. As there is no reference in Jesus' teaching to the doctrine of the Fall and to the mythopoetic picture of creation which is its presupposition, it is not legitimate to attribute to him ideas about the origin of evil as the disruptive factor in creation. That God tolerates good and evil together is suggested by the parable of the tares, but this has clearly eschatological import which has to do with judgment rather than

---

[1] *The Allegorical Interpretation of Genesis* (*Legum Alleg.*), 1:31, 32.

with creation. The demons are exorcised; miracle appears, in Heim's words, as 'the mighty act in which God confronts the demonic powers which seek to maintain themselves in opposition to Him despite His self-revelation' (*The Transformation of the Scientific World View*, p. 190).

The Fourth Gospel adds little that has not already been said by Paul. The words of the Prologue in verse 3 are in the Pauline tradition, and the same difficulties as to origin apply to them as will be seen to apply to the similar words in the Pauline Epistles. Reitzenstein (*Poimandres*, p. 244) considers that they are connected with the Hermetic formula. Norden (*Agnostos Theos*, p. 354 *et ante*) sets the phrases in Colossians 1: 16ff. and ἐξ αὐτοῦ καὶ δι᾽ αὐτοῦ καὶ εἰς αὐτοῦ τὰ πάντα side by side with John 1: 3, comparing them with the Latin text of the *Asclepius* (*Hermetica*) *sine hoc nec fuit aliquid* (*nec est nec erit*), *omnia enim ab eo et in ipso et per ipsum*. Other phrases of the Prologue he finds to correspond closely to Hellenistic formulas (p. 348: see the whole discussion in Appendix IV, pp. 347 ff.). The significance of these Hellenistic parallels consists in making us ask the question: Does the Prologue express John's views about creation, or was he merely making use of stock phrases and adapting them to his Christology? If the latter, his cosmology is, like Paul's, linked with a non-Christian Hellenistic thought-world. The formal relationship of the Johannine phrases to the Hermetic formula is certainly striking, as is the similarity of the same kind of phrase occurring in Paul to other examples of extra-biblical terminology. (*Vide* further C. H. Dodd, *The Interpretation of the Fourth Gospel*, pp. 10 ff.) In post-Apostolic writings the idea of Jesus as creator is given even more lyrical and elaborate expression than in the Epistles (e.g. the Epistle to Diognetus, vii, and Irenaeus also, following Paul and John, identified Jesus with the Creative Word who became flesh.

2

In order to understand more fully the implications of New Testament thought for the notion of the Lordship of Jesus over creation it will be profitable to examine in greater detail what has only been briefly touched upon and particularly the ideas implicit in the great Christological passages in the Epistles to which fuller reference has already been made. We shall then proceed to the consideration of the Lordship of Jesus over creation as modern thinking understands it, whether the notion is mytho-logical, and, if so, what should be done with it to divest it of its mythological content. For, if the bold conception of the Cosmic Christ, and of the redemption of creation through him, are not a form of theological extravagance or a piece of rhetoric, it is desirable to enquire into how far the New Testament view of creation is consistent with a modern view of the cosmos. This will lead further to the consideration of Jesus' place in creation as well as his pre-eminence over it.

The two most frequently used terms for 'creation' are κτίσις and κόσμος, to which should be added τὰ πάντα as denoting the totality of all created things. κτίσις can mean (1) the act of creating (Rom. 1: 20; II Pet. 3: 4); (2) creation as the result of this act, that is, the total created order (Rom. 1: 25; 8: 39; Heb. 4: 13; Col. 1: 15, 23); and (3) the individual creature, which is often not easily distinguishable from (2), as in the foregoing references, and in Romans 8: 19–22, where the term is ambiguous.

Examples of the use of these terms are as follows:

I. Creation (κτίσις, also 'creature').
(1) Romans 1: 20—'from the creation of the world'.
   2 Peter 3: 4—'from the beginning of creation'.
(2) Romans 1: 25—'they worshipped the creature/creation'.
   Romans 8: 39—'nor any other creation/creature'.
   Hebrews 4: 13—'nor is there any creature'.
   Colossians 1: 15—'the firstborn of all creatures' (or all creation).
   Colossians 1: 23—'every creature under heaven'.
In Romans 8: 19, 20, 21 κτίσις can mean either 'the creation' or the created person, though in verse 22 the whole of creation seems to be implied.

II. 'All things' (τὰ πάντα).
   Colossians 1: 16—'all things were created' (twice).
   Colossians 1: 17—'before all things', 'by him all things'.
   Colossians 1: 20—'by him to reconcile all things to himself'.
   Here 'all things' presumably refers not only to the visible earth but also to the cosmocrats: the unseen spiritual intelligences such as angels and demons.
   I Corinthians 8: 6—'the Father, of whom are all things'.
   I Corinthians—3: 21—Here 'all things are yours' means everything in this present world and in the world to come.
   Ephesians 1: 10, 22—'all things in Christ'.
Whereas τὰ πάντα includes κτίσις, i.e. the creation, it is a more explicitly comprehensive term in that it suggests more than the created physical order, namely spiritual beings as well.

III. The world (*κόσμος*).

This means

(i) The ordered universe (Acts 7: 24; Rom. 4: 13; I Cor. 3: 22; Phil. 2: 15; 'lights in the world').

(ii) The inhabited earth (Col. 2: 20; John 1: 10; 4: 22; Rom. 3: 6; I Cor. 4: 13; II Cor. 5: 19, etc.).

(iii) In the Johannine sense an evil order: I John 4: 4; John 7: 7; 14: 17, 27.

In the Johannine Prologue the Logos is the agent of creation: *τὰ πάντα* is here synonymous with *ὁ κόσμος* (1: 10); *κτίσις* does not belong to the Johannine terminology. Although John does not refer to Jesus by name as the Creator but speaks of the Word and the Light, the conclusion cannot be avoided that the Prologue regards Jesus (Logos) as the creator of the world and as present in the world which he has made. The principle here enunciated is the same as that which is found in Paul and Hebrews ('by whom also He made the worlds'—*αἰῶνας*—a term which Paul does not use as a synonym for *kosmos* or *ktisis*. In Paul, John, and Hebrews it is Jesus the Son through (*διά*) whom the creation came into being. The idea of creation is bound up indissolubly with the pre-existence of the Son, for he (Col. 1: 17) was 'before all things', and his centrality to creation is emphasized by Paul by the use of the prepositions *ἐν*, *διά*, *εἰς*, and *πρό*: all things 'subsist' 'in' him. He is the author and ground of all being; he cannot, therefore, be part of the series and of the order of creation. He is above it and was prior to it. He will survive it as his own (the 'heir' of all things). He is not only pre-eminent in status and supreme in the hierarchy of being: he was eternally prior to it in time.

The 'cosmic' Christ, then, is at the heart of the Christology of the Epistles and of the Prologue to John and cannot be regarded as less than fundamental. The references to creation through Christ, however, are by no means extended, those in Colossians consisting of only a few sentences which sound like formulae and are similar to those occurring elsewhere. The passage Ephesians 1: 10, 21–22 refers to Jesus' cosmic pre-existence rather than to his being the agent of creation, and the reference I Corinthians 8: 6 is brief. Paul does not extensively elaborate the conception, though the argument, sometimes adduced, that he states it as one which should be assumed to be accepted by the recipients of the letters because there is no evidence that it was disputed is hardly convincing, for it may be taken for granted that there was not enough generally diffused theological acumen in the early church to offer a reasoned disputation. It may be accepted as a main structural constituent of Pauline thought, though how far it is poetically metaphorical, or how far it should be understood literally as expressing the conviction that Jesus actually created the universe, cannot be determined.

A consideration relevant to the discussion of Paul's creation-Christology is the question of the originality or derivation of the phraseology of the crucial passages which have been cited, together with the similar phrases in John and Hebrews, and of how far New Testament writers were merely adopting a religious formula generally current in the contemporary world. Lightfoot[1] acknowledges that the Alexandrian philosophy underlies the whole of Colossians 1: 15–17 and that the Alexandrian phraseology is an important aid to its understanding; indeed, the whole passage, in his view, could be equally applicable to the Logos. The term *pleroma*, too, though not necessarily Gnostic in its associations, was prominent in some Gnostic circles to whose ideas Lightfoot devotes some space.

More significant, however, is the recurrence of a phrase such as Romans 11: 36—'for of him and through him and to him are all things', which Norden[2] compares with the words of Marcus Aurelius (*Meditations*, IV, 23): ἐκ σοῦ πάντα, ἐν σοι πάντα, ἐις σὲ πάντα, which the Emperor applies to Nature, the Pauline phrase being, in Norden's view, a borrowed addition to the previous passage. Further instances of this kind of formula are I Corinthians 8: 6; Colossians 1: 16; Ephesians 4: 5, Hebrews 2: 10, the phraseology being almost exactly the same as the Stoic formula. If John 1: 3 is added the area of borrowing is increased, and the evidence for the extra-biblical origin of this formula, which Norden submits in detail, is convincing. The same idiom is found in the anonymous pseudo-Aristotelian writing

---

[1] Commentary on Colossians, *ad. loc.*
[2] *Agnostos Theos.*, pp. 240 ff.

Concerning the World (περὶ κόσμου): 'all things are of God (ἐκ θεοῦ) and through God (διὰ θεοῦ) they cohere (συνέστηκεν) for us' (cf. Col. 1: 16; I Cor. 8: 6). A similar version of this formula occurs in Sallustius' *Concerning Gods and the World* (περὶ θεῶν καὶ κοσμοῦ) dating from the second half of the second century: 'he who makes all things to subsist by his own power makes all things to subsist together with himself'. The evidence adduced by Norden together with other instances lends support to the conclusion that the New Testament writers made use of Stoic-Hellenistic phrases which were widely diffused and clearly standardized, even though some of the documents in which they are found are post-Apostolic. It should be assumed that they had long been in general use. There is little doubt, for example, that Colossians 1: 17, 'and in him all things consist' (καὶ τὰ πάντα ἐν αὐτῷ συνέστηκεν), is derived from a world of thought both Jewish and Hellenistic, though the terms used are not quite identical. In the *Poimandres* the notion of 'all things' cohering in or being sustained by the Logos occurs as 'Holy art Thou, who holdest all things together by the Word' (ἅγιος εἶ ὁ λόγῳ συστησάμενος τὰ ὄντα),[1] while in Ecclesiasticus 43: 26 the variant is 'and by his word all things consist[1] (καὶ ἐν λόγῳ αὐτοῦ σύγκειται τὰ πάντα). Dr. Rawlinson, however, prefers an exclusively Old Testament sanction for the formula, and cites C. F. Burney's elaborate interpretation of the Hebrew text of Genesis 1, illuminated by Proverbs 8: 22, which turns the Colossians passage into a complicated riddle.[2]

It would appear from this, then, that Paul, in particular, was transferring to his Christology not only Wisdom-concepts from the late Jewish tradition (possibly influenced by Hellenism) but also Hellenistic-Stoic terms current at the time and thereby practising a kind of intellectual syncretism analogous to the cultic-Christological syncretism which Bultmann regards as one of the characteristics of the early church.[3] Paul's habit of thought is

[1] *Poimandres*, 31. R. Reitzenstein (*Poimandres*, p. 338) adds the variant reading συνιστάμενος πὰ πάντα, which is almost identical with the vocabulary of Colossians 1: 17. Text also in Scott, *Hermetica*, I, p. 130. It is highly probable that Jewish influence is present in the Hermetic writings. See C. H. Dodd, *The Bible and the Greeks*, Part II.
[2] *The New Testament Doctrine of the Christ*, p. 164.
[3] *Das Urchristentum*, p. 195 (1949).

certainly eclectic, and the importance of this transference is considerable, for it is highly relevant to any estimate of the validity of Paul's terminology as binding on later ages. A complex of ideas taken over from one field and transferred to another may have illustrative value but it is not necessarily binding in reference to the new field. Marcus Aurelius applied a theological formula of the Stoic philosophy to Nature as Paul applied it to Jesus. What is involved is whether we are committed to accepting as predicates of Jesus terms which Marcus Aurelius and other pagan writers applied to quite different objects.

We have remarked briefly upon the picture of agonized imperfection which the passage Romans 6: 18–22 suggests: a passage which Bultmann describes as a 'mythological speculation about the future'[1] and the expression of a Gnostic mythology of the fall of creation, for the whole picture is, in his view, in complete and pessimistic contrast to the conception of creation as implied in the teaching of Jesus and of the Old Testament as a whole.[2] In this context *ktisis* is now usually translated 'creation' (Moffatt, RSV), though the Authorized Version, in using the word 'creature', may be more accurate, for the conception of the human creature is easier to envisage than is the whole creation. The difference between the two, however, need not be pressed. Nature in the sense of creation in its totality is personalized and represented as animate, for it awaits with 'eager longing' for the revealing of the Sons of God.' The passage may be interpreted as indicating Paul's conception of the universe as in some sense psychic, for in the cosmology of the time, as we have shown, the cosmos was thought of as inhabited by spiritual intelligences. Creation is, moreover, in some way subjected to 'futility' ($\mu\alpha\tau\alpha\iota\acute{o}\tau\eta\varsigma$).

It is to be assumed, then, that Paul regarded creation as something 'living' which had gone wrong or which was vitiated not only by imperfection but by evil, decay ($\varphi\theta\acute{o}\rho\alpha$), and meaninglessness. It is clear, therefore, that, like its human component, it was in need of redemption, though nowhere in the passage is Jesus actually set forth as its redeemer. On the contrary, in verse

---

[1] *Die Christliche Hoffnung und das Problem der Entmythologisierung*, pp. 57–58).
[2] *Theology of the New Testament*, p. 173; *Das Urchristentum*, p. 198.

38 Paul seems to regard the creation, consisting, as a totality, of life and death, as something which is capable, by virtue of its own nature, of acting as a separating force between Christ and the Christian, but which, despite its power and malignant hostility, is doomed to ultimate frustration. Paul may well have observed creation in its malignant, if not malevolent, aspect, and because of the hideousness of the corruption disclosed, and of the universal prevalence of predatory cruelty and destructive potency, concluded that, like himself, like man as such, it was involved in some primordial fall which required rectification. Indeed, it may be held that creation appears to display a malevolent purpose more sinister by far than malignance; for nature is not only predatory but is ingenious in being so. As Sir Charles Sherrington has said, the redia battening on the snail, the liver-fluke and the anopheles (malaria parasite) are the product of evolution. 'Nature has evolved in this plasmodium a means of inflicting pain and distress to an extent calculable but practically unimaginable.' 'Life's prize is given to the aggressive and inferior life, destructive of other lives at the expense of suffering to them, and, sad as it may seem, suffering in proportion as they are lives high up in life's scale.'[1] The observation of this predatory character so evident in nature supports Paul's gloomy view that the creation is 'subjected to futility' (if *ktisis* is translated 'creation'), for in many fields of experience it is meaningless rather than, judged from the human standpoint, meaningful. Whichever way *ktisis* is translated, the meaning of the passage is that imperfect man is involved in imperfect creation and that as man must be redeemed from sin, so must nature be redeemed from decay and apparent meaninglessness.

What the 'setting free from bondage to decay' means Paul does not say. He does not indicate whether, in a redeemed state, there will be any more death, or whether the cruelties of sub-human life will vanish. The hope of cosmic redemption is hardly the anticipation of the Messianic-Utopian vision of Isaiah 11: 6-9. Indeed, there are so many obscurities in this passage, eloquent though it is, that it is not easy to find in it a consistent pattern of thought. But, the 'creation and we ourselves', it is true, have groaned 'in travail

[1] *Man on his Nature*, pp. 374, 367.

together until now', if this is taken to mean that human error, imperfection, and sin have their counterpart in the internecine conflict evident in nature both in the animal and the insect world; but *how* this is to be redeemed Paul does not indicate. He does not, at this point, explicitly maintain that it will be achieved through the cosmic effect of divine action in Jesus. The whole material universe, it seems, resembles the human body, the flesh, in that the flesh is the domain of death and decay; and just as Paul hopes for 'the redemption of our bodies' (8: 23), that is the material part of us, so does he await the redemption of creation, of the physical part of the totality which is animated by invisible demonic and angelic beings.

Now, whereas in Romans 8 the idea of the supreme Lordship of the cosmically redemptive Christ receives no clear expression, in the great Colossians passage and its parallels nothing is said about the meaninglessness and decay of creation or about its redemption, though Paul refers to the reconciling principle operative in Jesus as of universal application. The emphasis is on his spatial and temporal pre-eminence and filial priority, 'born first of all creation' ('before all the creation'—Moffatt). Neither in Colossians 1 nor in Ephesians is Jesus represented as the redeemer of a cosmos which has gone wrong, vitiated as it were through a primordial twist or fall. The theme is the subordination of creation to him. There is to be a kind of cosmic reconciliation, if 'all things' (Col. 1: 20) is synonymous with creation; but there is no suggestion of futility and of decay from which, in Romans, creation is doomed to suffer.

If this affirmation of the creational centrality of Jesus appears extravagant to the modern mind, to which the notion of Jesus as Creator-Logos made manifest for the purpose of universal redemption is foreign and mythological, it should be considered within the context of contemporary reference. The only sure method of presenting the essence of the faith was by asserting Jesus' absolute supremacy over the whole of creation. It was primarily a doctrinal not a cosmological affirmation; for in a world where idolatry (the worship of the 'creature', Rom. 1: 23–25) and the fear of spiritual beings still threatened belief in the sovereignty of the one God as revealed in Jesus Christ, the latter could be given no secondary place in creation. It was necessary to think of him within this context as prior to creation in order that any notion of subordination through derivativeness should be rejected. Only in this way could the centrality of Jesus be adequately safeguarded. Creation was ·to be understood in terms of the Lordship of Jesus, who was not one of the many mediating beings but the possessor of sovereignty in his own right: a *Kyrios* in the full sense of the word.

The emphasis on the implications for Christology of the biblical doctrine of creation is the subject of much contemporary theology, which stresses the interconnection of creation and redemption. Though Brunner is less committed to the exposition of the biblical story of creation than is Barth, whom he criticizes for his excessively allegorical interpretation (*Dogmatics*, II, p. 39), he follows the lead of the New Testament epistles. 'All that is taught in accordance with Scripture about the revelation of God in the work of creation,' he writes, 'is to be understood "christologically". There is no other revelation in creation save that which derives its being from the Eternal Son or Logos' (*Dogmatics*, II, p. 29). 'The love of God is the *causa finalis* of the creation. In Jesus Christ this ideal for Creation is revealed.' The Old Testament story, however, is not the starting-point for a Christian doctrine of creation. This is found in the New Testament. 'From Him [Jesus] alone—and not from the Old Testament story of the Creation—can we understand what God's creation of the world really means' (ibid., pp. 13–14). The notion of 'Adam in Paradise' is no longer tenable and is quixotic and reactionary (pp. 46, 49).

Barth (*Kirchliche Dogmatik*, III/ 1–3) devotes much space to the doctrine of creation. His treatment of it is to expound, in III, 1, the Genesis story clause by clause; he does not relate the Christian theology of creation to the scientific-philosophical conception, and his method suggests an ambiguous position in so far as he expounds at great length (much as Philo did) a non-factual account as though it were factual. He admits that the Genesis story is a saga (rather than a myth), but without examining the validity of the terms and conceptions employed. The whole order of creation is to be interpreted as leading up to Christology. 'The view that man owes the fact and manner of his existence, together with all reality differentiated from God, to Divine Creation, is fulfilled only in the acceptance of and the response to the self-witness of God, that is, in belief in Jesus Christ, in the knowledge of the realization in him of Creator and Creature.' 'We believe in Jesus Christ when we believe in God the Almighty Creator of Heaven and Earth' (*KD*, III/ 1, p. 19). 'The whole bible speaks prophetically and typologically of Jesus Christ when it speaks of Creator, Creation, and the creature' (p. 24). 'We have the assurance that Jesus Christ, considered from all points of view, is precisely the key to creation' (p. 30). 'For him who believes in Jesus Christ the *Creator* has appeared on the scene in His Person' (p. 34).

This is, of course, the interpretation of the cosmic Christology of the New

Testament and of the early theologians, and Barth, in an extended discussion of Jesus and the Logos as agent of creation, comments that not only God the Father but the Son Jesus Christ is the Creator of all things, which is implied by the ascription to him of the title *Kyrios*, though Barth admits that the New Testament writers ascribe to Jesus exactly what Philo ascribed to the Logos and the 'synkretistische Cosmosophie' to Hermes, Tot, and Athene, and the Zoroastrians to Mithra (see the excursus, pp. 54–59).

In the second part of the Doctrine of Creation (*KD*, III/2) Barth expounds the Christian theology of man the creature, and it is significant that Christology is central to the discussion of this human aspect of creation. As he does not consider cosmological pronouncements to be the legitimate concern of theology he does not discuss the place of man in the cosmos, that is, in relation to any particular view of the universe, relevant to a *theological* understanding of man in creation or to a Christian anthropology. To this theological understanding, however, the understanding of Christ is a precondition; hence Barth deals here at greater length with Christology than elsewhere. Man—Christ—Creation are inseparable concepts. Man exists *in* the cosmos, which is meaningless without him, just as he cannot be imagined without the cosmos; but he cannot be understood except in reference to Jesus Christ. For Barth, therefore, Christology is essential to the understanding of creation.

Barth makes only parenthetical references to the *Weltbild* of the physical and biological sciences and does not relate man or Christ to creation as it is represented by them. Nor, unfortunately, does Arthur Titius in his monumental *Natur und Gott* (Göttingen, 1926), which offers a masterly and thorough exposition of the scientific world view in all its aspects from the quantum theory to psychology. As a lucid account of the whole field of modern scientific thinking Titius' book is an astonishing achievement. It is, however, less a contribution to theology than an indication of points of contact and compatibility between science and religion, and in this respect serves a useful purpose. It devotes far more space to *Natur* than to *Gott*. Barth rightly points out (*KD*, III/2, p. 4) that it cannot be regarded as a comprehensive theological enquiry into a doctrine of creation, and in an extensive comment on Titius (pp. 96–98) he expresses the view that the book suffers from the kind of nebulous liberalism which is naturally abhorrent to him. Instead of a theology, he says, it confronts us with a 'religious idea' to which the author does his best to do justice. While Titius' work, from Barth's point of view, is woefully incomplete, a similar criticism in reverse might be applied to Barth's, which, while massively theological, takes little account of the *Weltbild* and its significance for religion so painstakingly expounded by Titius (pp. 299–654), whereas it is the examination of the implications of this for the Christian doctrine of man and creation which would appear to be of great importance. Consequently, by limiting the scope of his anthropology Barth also limits that of his Christology and is therefore prevented from giving adequate consideration to the question of the relation of Christ to creation, though he deals at length with the manhood of Jesus but without attempting to relate it to the physiological antecedents which cannot be separated from the notion of man or Christ *in* creation. But if the Pauline presentation of the Cosmic Christ is accepted there is no need for this; for Christ was prior to, not part of, creation.

Two further approaches to the subject of science and theology and hence to the Christian conception of creation, Karl Heim's *Christian Faith and Natural Science* and *The Transformation of the Scientific World View* (E. tr., S.C.M. Press, 1952–3), and Dr. C. E. Raven's Gifford Lectures entitled *Natural Religion and Christian Theology* (Cambridge, 1953), are, like Titius' work, concerned more with the scientific than the theological attitude to creation. The latter's chapter on 'Christ and the Universe' deals with some of the issues raised for Christian theism by man's experience of evil and by the existence of sub-human cruelty and imperfection which Raven relates to Roman 8, though here again (doubtless because of the limitations imposed by the character of his enquiry) there is little discussion of the Christological implications in so far as the question of the relation of Christ to creation is involved. In any case, as one of the few surviving Modernist or Liberal theologians he would be disinclined to deal with it as biblically as do the post-Liberal theologians.

A. D. Galloway (*The Cosmic Christ*, Nisbet, 1951) comes to grips with the problem of how an impersonal creation can be redeemed, though the philosophical difficulties implied in cosmic redemption are considerable. He recognizes (p. 203) that the New Testament view of nature and creation belongs to another age and to a culture which the modern man cannot take seriously, and that the question of its interpretation becomes very difficult in terms of twentieth-century thought. But whereas the idea of the redemption of the physical world order is hard to grasp, so also is it difficult to reject because of man's place in the physical cosmos; otherwise there is involved a dualism of which one form is Gnosticism and another the Kantian attempt to separate man's life as part of the cosmos from his life as personal being (subject). Dr. Galloway sees a philosophical solution to the problem when we encounter in Jesus 'the complete ascendancy of meaning over existence' (p. 257). 'Personal redemption and cosmic redemption are not two separate things, the one subjective and the other objective. They are correlative aspects of one and the same thing' (p. 240). He admits that neither the problem nor the answer yields to systematic analysis; we are driven back, like the New Testament writers, to symbolic language. Dr. Galloway does not examine the New Testament affirmations about Jesus as the agent of creation, which he probably regards as a wholly mythological conception; nor does he, in spite of a valiant attempt, succeed in offering a reinterpretation which actually assumes the redeemability of the physical universe; nor does he suggest in what way it could be thought of as redeemable, except in terms of a transformed subject-object relationship.

E. C. Rust's *Nature and Man in Biblical Thought* (Lutterworth Press, 1953) is a careful exposition of the biblical concepts rather than a theological interpretation of them elucidating the biblical meaning of both the agency of Jesus and the notion of cosmic redemption (pp. 236 ff.). He briefly suggests (pp. 294 ff.) directions which a modern understanding of it might follow, relying on the doctrine of the Trinity as conceived by the Apologists as a basis. The author of the 'new' creation must also be the author of the 'old', for 'His Lordship in redemption carried with it a Lordship in creation'. What, however, Paul and Hebrews affirm is the personal creative agency of one who was the historical figure Jesus of Nazareth, and that he, Jesus, was actually he who created the universe. In the last resort there has been, in my view, no satisfactory answer to the difficulty encountered by the modern mind in the apostolic and mythological affirmation, which is neither a necessary explanation of creation nor a constituent *sine qua non* in the concomitant notion of the pre-eminence of Jesus over creation. The separation of the pre-existent Son (Logos) as creator from the Jesus of Nazareth who is his incarnation is not a legitimate answer to the question set by the problem, for it raises insuperable difficulties in the way of regarding Jesus as human.

3

From the foregoing account of New Testament thought about Jesus and creation two things emerge as indisputable. Firstly, it is Jesus the Incarnate Son who is the author not only of redemption but of creation: not as an entity hypostatized as the Logos or Holy Spirit (in the Philonic sense) as a functional activity of God, but Jesus Christ the pre-existent Son. This is at any rate the formal affirmation of the Colossians passage, I Corinthians 8: 6, Hebrews 1: 1, and John 1: 1 ff. implying that Jesus is not continuous with creation but anterior to it. Secondly, because of this aetiological priority he is pre-eminent over all created things. Implied, though not always explicitly stated, is the further notion that this cosmos, of whose creation he is the agent, is to be the subject of redemption. How far are these ideas inalienable from the comprehensive conception of the Lordship of Jesus over creation? Are they reducible to precise terms acceptable within the framework of a less mythological type of thinking, or are they still to be considered as a mythological affirmation which cannot be dispensed with? If so, what is to be done with them? For it is clear that St. Paul's terminology affirms that through Jesus Christ, the *Kyrios*, the creation came into being.

In the first place it should be stated that this claim was not propounded by those who, in the Synoptic Gospels and Acts, were personally in contact with Jesus, but by later minds after a process of reflection on the presence of Jesus in the Christian community and on their personal experience when confronted with the total picture of his life, death, resurrection, and reconciling work, and with the experience of the Holy Spirit. That both the New Testament and contemporary theology affirm the centrality of Jesus in creation has been already indicated in the foregoing excursus. Whether the precise form given to this conception of centrality in the New Testament is valid or binding on later ages is another question. It is inevitable that notions which came naturally to a much earlier age should be questioned by others possessing a completely different background of thought and taking for granted quite other presuppositions.

Now, we have stated that there is ample evidence in the Gospels for believing that Jesus, to put it no higher than this, was a numinous personality, convicting others of sinfulness by the power of his holiness, and aware of his unique relationship to God the Father. There are, however, no sayings, nor are there any actions, in the Synoptic Gospels indicating either that Jesus regarded himself as co-creator (even in pre-mundane form), or that his impact upon his contemporaries was such as to give currency to the idea. That he asserted his power over 'nature' was evident to the originators or the earlier transmitters of the Synoptic tradition who may well have been eye-witnesses of the incidents described.[1] The miracles of healing were regarded as victories over demonic beings, discarnate embodiments of evil in a sense similar to that in which the cosmic intelligences of the Pauline thought-world were conceived. He could exorcise demons, give sight to the blind, heal the lepers, make the lame walk, and raise the dead, was rightly considered to be superior to the 'powers' which distort life and militate against the positive aspect of creation: a superiority which attained full and overwhelming expression in the Resurrection through which Jesus asserted his power over corruption and death itself.

The miracles of nature were, to Jesus' contemporaries, in the same category as those of healing. There may be a natural explanation of these incidents; we do not know; but unless we assume the complete dualism of life and matter, and that inanimate matter is fundamentally different in structure from animate

---

[1] 2 Peter 1: 16 may be expressing a genuine Petrine statement embodied in a much later document than Peter could have written.

matter, it is unwise to indulge in negative dogmatism as to what is or what is not possible. If, as is implied by biblical writers, the universe, as they understood it, was not inert but 'psychic', and the findings of atomic physics lead to a non-mechanistic conception of nature in which the division between the organic and the inorganic has been eliminated,[1] no limit may be logically applied to the ability of one 'in whom dwelt the fulness of the Godhead bodily' to manipulate it. Even though it is dangerous to read into quantum mechanics and the principle of 'indeterminacy' too great a theological relevance, and though on the whole matter still 'behaves' according to the principles of Newtonian physics, whereas the atomic microcosm does not, it is, to say the least, not improbable that the Power who created matter still remains its master, and is able, when He chooses, to behave accordingly. There is some justification for Titius' description of 'eternal natural laws' as a 'pseudo-scientific mythology'[2] and for refusing to regard the supernatural as contranatural. The supersession of the mechanistic physics provides a theoretical reason for concluding that nature may be plastic material in the hands of one who was in unbroken communion with the Creator and who was specially entrusted with his redeeming mission. There are, however, only a few miracles which can be definitely described as nature-miracles, and these are of such a character as to be susceptible of some alternative explanation, though there is no *a priori* reason for assuming that they may not have occurred. It may at least be contended that Jesus' association with creation may take the form of being the instrument through whom works the Power who created the universe, though it is doubtful if this is what the Apostolic writers meant.

The miracles of healing, however, cannot be cited as evidence of *unique* powers, though the manner of their exercise was unusual. The world of the time was not unfamiliar with such performances, and the present growing concern with the ministry of healing as part of the ministry of the church has shown that 'miracles' quite as remarkable as those performed by Jesus are not unknown today; some of them, indeed, according to published reports, are

[1] K. Heim, *Christian Faith and Natural Science*, p. 101.
[2] *Natur und Gott*, p. 584.

almost instantaneous. The ability to perform acts of healing is not in itself an assurance that the performer is to be identified with the Creator, even though the power which makes them possible may be supernatural; and whether spiritual healing is *fundamentally* different from medical healing is at least, in theory, arguable, for both may be different methods of calling into action the natural biological tendency to achieve wholeness, and expressing what Titius calls *Ganzheitskausalität*[1] and Monakow *das biologische Gewissen* or Syneidesis[2]. I am not questioning the immense significance of the healing ministry of Jesus: I am merely stating that, by itself, it is not of such a unique character that the creation of the universe can on its account be ascribed to him.

Further: Jesus did not perform miracles in order to show that as the Incarnate Logos-son he was the Co-creator or the agent of creation but that he was the Messiah. Such, at any rate, is the meaning of his reply to the disciples of John the Baptist. As for the character of the Messiah, the later Jewish conception of this figure was, it has been maintained, wholly mythological, and it was precisely this kind of Messiah that Jesus rejected.

If, moreover, we consider the supreme miracle, the Resurrection, it does not of itself point to the conclusion that he who, by the decision of God, overcame or passed through the final moment of death which is the end of all living creatures was himself the creator of the natural order of which death is as much a part as life. Such a conclusion is not a self-evident deduction for the modern Christian, though it may have been for St. Paul, for he does not transfer to his Christological interpretation of cosmology the thought-categories of the Hellenistic age which were natural vehicles for St. Paul's thinking. For what Paul did, as by a stroke of genius, was, so to speak, to change the labels. Whereas (as Barth has said) the Hellenistic religions attributed the creation to Tot, Hermes, and Athene, Zoroastrianism to Mithra, and Hellenistic Judaism to the Logos, Paul attributed it to Jesus, which shows how far he was prepared to go in applying mythological thinking to historical personality.

---

[1] Which might be translated as 'causality directed towards the achievement of wholeness'.
[2] See below, p. 173 f.

There is, further, no soteriological necessity for belief in creation 'through' Jesus the *Kyrios*. The experience of salvation does not carry with it as an inevitable concomitant the belief that the Saviour Jesus is the Creator-Logos, but if it is contended that it was He who 'dwelt' in Jesus, God reconciling the world to Himself, who was the Creator, this both states the doctrine of the Incarnation and does justice to one aspect, at least, of St. Paul's thought. For if this is the content of his Christology no exception need be taken to it.

Now modern faith—and this is where demythologizing according to Bultmann is relevant to our problem—is more inclined to consider the experience of redemption, which was the source of the Apostle's Christological speculation, and of the language in which he describes it, existentially rather than cosmologically. In his insistence on this Bultmann is to a great extent right. The cosmological Christology does not add to our understanding either of Jesus or of creation, though it expresses not only Paul's 'existential' experience but also his view of the universe. There is a sense in which the 'saved' person enters into a new existential awareness through his relation to Jesus, and transcends the cosmos, whether it is regarded as meaningful, meaningless, or merely neutral towards human endeavour. It does not mean that there has been any objective change in the cosmos, but that the subject-object relationship has changed and that man no longer feels himself to be estranged from creation. Evil is no less evil; only it ceases to exercise jurisdiction over the Christian. The cosmocrats, in Paul's mythological language, no longer have power over him. There has come a change over his understanding of his situation in the world. Suffering remains suffering, though it may lose its malignant character. The blow of the disaster is no less severe, but it is not finally devastating. It is not the ultimate factor in existence. Sin still remains, though it has lost its corrupting power over him who has been delivered from it. Death remains as the final biological fact, but without its sting or its victory. The grave yawns, but it does not finally close over the soul. Affliction still remains as a universal content of experience, but it is not the last word. Man shares in Jesus' transcendence of the 'world' (in the Johannine sense). Such is the meaning of words of the Fourth

Gospel: 'In the world you shall have tribulation, but be of good cheer: I have overcome the world.'

4

Salvation, σωτηρία, is the achievement of spiritual wholeness; it has to do, etymologically, in most languages, with health: 'salus', 'iechydwriaeth' (in Welsh 'iechyd'=health); the Saviour is the Iachawdwr, the Heiland, the 'Healer', the bringer of spiritual soundness and integration, the initiator of the reversal of the process of fragmentation or estrangement which makes a man feel that he is not part of the cosmos but a lost creature who has intruded into an unfriendly or neutral creation: one who, in St. Paul's telling phrase, is 'alienated from the life of God.' It is not only of creation that the *Kyrios* is author, but, in biblical phrase, of salvation; he is the bringer of 'healthy' or 'healthful' transformation of the whole personality and the impetus to our revaluation of our existence in the presence not so much of creation but of the Creator.

In the light of this, the more closely the idea of 'cosmic' salvation is examined, the more perplexing does it become. Soteriological action upon myself is something that I can conceive and experience in terms of my own 'existential' situation. It is something of which I am aware becaue it happens to me, and I can be aware of its happening to others because they can communicate their experience to me, or at least inform me about it, in ways which I can understand. In other words, because I know, or can know, what deliverance, 'healthness', means to me I also know, or can know, within limits, what it means to other beings like myself. It may not make them or me less imperfect: it does break down 'the middle wall of partition' and bring them, and me, into the household of God and the fellowship of the saints.

It is less easy, however, to imagine what the redemption of creation means, nor is there any solution to the problem of the relation of the concept of redemption to an impersonal order, the world of τὰ πάντα which includes the impersonal and inanimate as well as the animate and the human. The great Pauline conception of a suffering creation, a creation which suffers as does the human creature, waiting for deliverance from 'bondage to corruption', 'groaning and travailing until now' in cosmic anguish, is magnificent; but it is difficult to decide exactly what it means, for this ascription of personality to the cosmic whole is in itself a form of mythological thinking. Unless its redemption means the cessation of human suffering and the perfection of at present imperfect natural processes, the overcoming of what appear to man to be contradictions and the elimination of demonic distortion until the perfection of Paradise is attained, the meaning is elusive.

Moreover, to interpret the redemption of creation in terms of evolution is hardly permissible. Evolution, though not necessarily incompatible with providential guidance and control, is by no means to be identified with it, though as usually understood divine creation and evolution are considered irreconcilable, for the latter is not a theistic conception. In the strictly Darwinian sense it is no more than a description of *how* things happen, a 'phenomenological description of the emergence of life-forms'.[1] Evolution, moreover, appears to be indifferent to values, at least in the sub-human world, though in the human world it might mean the achievement of transcendence rather than mere adaptation. Indeed, the most highly developed type of life is frequently maladapted to its environment. A 'redemptive' evolution would rectify this state of things; as yet, however, the evidence of such rectification is not conspicuous. Creation, judged from the only standpoint from which judgment is possible, namely from our own situation in creation, is still, and is likely to remain, the scene of ineluctable warfare. But it is at least possible that we may be mistaken in making such a judgment.

There is another point of view: notwithstanding his exalted opinion of himself, man must face the possibility that by some standard of values yet to be made known, the bacillus and the cancer cell possess importance, mystery, and beauty comparable to these attributes in the human organism. He must also reflect on the inescapable fact that the world of bacteria is highly complex, that it was presumably intended to be so, and that there is a *prima facie* case for suggesting that micro-organisms shall

[1] A. Titius, op. cit., p. 768.

inherit the earth; and that man—viewed from this standpoint—is a mere intruder who occasionally gets in the way, with interesting consequences to the individual and the species. When we consider the life-cycles of many of the parasites that infest man and the lavish provision made for their survival, it is abundantly clear that somewhere in the scheme of things considerable importance is attached to the existence of these creatures. A similar line of thought is possible when considering malignant growths. Most of us visualise the development of living organisms through the same process of gradual evolution. It is conceivable, however, that within this framework of change, nature deliberately indulges in an occasional experiment designed on a different plan—a mitotic caper amounting to frenzied exuberance—achieved maybe by some curious twist of the ordinary cell metabolism. What seems to us a tragic waste of life may in fact be recorded as a stroke of genius in the laboratory notebook of the Divinity Himself —an aberration from the norm full of promise for the future, vitualised in terms of millions of years.[1]

Such is an interesting possibility propounded by a distinguished physician and one which perhaps brings closer than it had hitherto seemed the idea of a conscious creation whose dimension of existence and of consciousness may be apparent to the Creator but not to man.

Further: the cosmological scene is so vast that there is no fixed point from which we can judge it to reflect a process or pattern conforming to design. 'Appeal to design,' writes Sir Charles Sherrington, 'has lapsed as an argument, and that leaves Nature acquitted not only of good but of evil', or, to put it more positively, Nature displays what from the human point of view is both good and evil. Man can, it is true, 'tame' the physical world up to a point and adapt it to his own purposes. This, however, does not indicate evolution *within* the world of nature but the transcendence of man over it and the result of his ingenuity in modifying such parts of it as are within his immediate reach.

[1] I am indebted to Dr. Stanley Alstead, Regius Professor of Materia Medica and Therapeutics in the University of Glasgow for permission to quote from a paper entitled 'Reflections on the Philosophic Background to the Practice of Therapeutics' prior to its publication in *The Lancet*, Dec. 1954, though this passage does not appear in the published article.

Improvements in the fertility of soil, the growing of wheat in the Arctic, the domestication of the horse, the cat, and the dog, are examples of this mastery over the non-human aspect of creation. But even here there can be reversion to type given the required conditions, and it does not appear that the hyena or the snake or the shark shows any marked tendency to domestication as part of an immanent or providential evolutionary process. That man has become by 'emergence' rather than by adaptation a spiritual being in a sense which cannot be predicated of his earliest ancestors[1] is not an illustration of evolution in the strict sense of the word (for it is a biological concept); for man, as Barth has maintained at great length, can in the last resort be understood only theologically. He has become a 'living soul' and is therefore redeemable.

It may, of course, be possible that an anthropocentric survey of creation is doomed to failure in attempting to predict what form it will eventually take; God may have a higher destiny for the animal world than we can imagine from our point in time, though certain insects have changed little, some of them not at all, during the last two hundred million years, and the capacity for destruction has even grown through the emergence of higher types of life on which micro-organisms can prey. So far, however, evidence of the capacity for transcendence of environment in the subhuman world is not conspicuous, though in the biological order, even on this subhuman level, there is at least the possibility, whatever the degree of improbability, of spiritual emergence, not in terms of natural evolution (which would mean that spirit is an epigenesis of matter) but under divine creative action as part of the divine purpose. For if the cosmos is thought of as something 'outside' of God over which He no longer has any control, and not as something of which evolutionary change is merely a formal mechanism appointed by Him for the fulfilment of a

---

[1] The mental and spiritual attitudes of 'primitive' man in his observable condition are extremely complex and represent traceable potentialities of later developments (cf. John Murphy, *Primitive Man*, Oxford, 1927); 'primitive' in this sense means, as Dr. Murphy says, 'the mind of the savage of the present day who is at a low state of culture, and in religion as in other respects is at the levels probably occupied by early man'. If his spiritual apprehension is not a form of 'adaptation', is there not implied (apart from the fact of physical structure) something resembling a 'special' creation such as is mythologically indicated in Genesis?

purpose into which we have at present no great insight, we are committed to a kind of cosmic or metaphysical dualism which from the first excludes any likelihood of redemption: that is, of deliverance from evil and imperfection, in forms appropriate to various levels, by which the cosmos, in the Pauline sense, is subdued. And if evolution is creative as well as adaptive and creation is a continuous process, if the cosmos *can* be regarded as 'psychic'[1] or panpsychic, there may be a dimension, appropriate to its own kind, but inaccessible to human perception, on which redemption is at least conceivable as a possibility. Each field of life may have a different kind of self-awareness, just as there are great differences between the nervous systems of mammals and non-mammals. There is an immense difference between the world of deep-sea life and that of the termites, as there is between the self-awareness of man and that of the higher mammals, though it may not be as great. All have a certain group or social consciousness and all reveal similar reactions in terms of fear and aggressiveness on the most primitively instinctual level. The one common factor is animation and instinctual urge, life as $\beta\acute{\iota}o\varsigma$; as $\zeta\omega\acute{\eta}$ it would appear to exist within the human field alone.[2] Where there is animation and instinctual behaviour it is not impossible that mutations and 'psychic' developments in the sub-human world might lead, over a long period of time, to the growth of an embryonic spiritual consciousness, or at any rate to the development of a level of mental perception out of which it might grow. The organic scheme of reality discloses an order in which the molecule emerges into the cell, the inanimate is superseded by the animate, the organic is differentiated (for practical purposes) from the inorganic, though there is no movement from the one to the other. The stratification remains constant. The stone does not develop animation and become self-propelling, though complex forms of life have, somehow, developed from simpler forms.

---

[1] Cf. Raven, op. cit., II, pp. 145, 156 ff.

[2] The late J. M. Hickson, the Australian healer, however, describes how, during one of his healing tours, he healed a dog by the laying on of hands (*The Bridegroom Cometh*, Methuen, 1937). Saint Brendan is said to have preached to the fishes, and Saint Francis to the birds. They may have well done so, though with what effect is not known. There is, however, nothing inherently absurd in the supposition that there are depths at which human holiness finds itself *en rapport* with the animal consciousness.

The unicellar organism, however, does not become a star-fish or a horse by its own volition.

Nevertheless, it is improbable that the sub-human world will develop a spiritual consciousness similar to man's, or that the higher mammals will progress beyond their present level, though the theoretical possibility should not be excluded.[1] Brunner, in some important comments on the differences between man and the animals, has stated that the main difference is not that man has a 'psyche' and the animal has not: the boundary between the two lies

> where the Bible sees it: in the fact that man has been created in the image of God, in the spiritually responsible personal being of man. It is not the intellect, but the spirit related to God, which distinguishes man from the animal. Even the highest animal does not show a trace of spirit, of the possibility of ideation.[2]

The animal can communicate by means of signs, but it cannot talk.

It is apparent, too, that the release of 'creation' is attendant upon the 'revealing of the sons of God': an anticipation which is somewhat lacking in clarity. Dr. Galloway is of the opinion that objective thought can recognize only two interpretations of the phrase 'cosmic redemption': the first a 'full-blooded interpretation which looks for some objective change in the material condition of the universe', and the second 'a subjective alteration in man's outlook' which will so enable him to re-estimate the world around him as to be equivalent to a renewal of the world'.[2] This is really an 'existential' interpretation, for he suggests that the distinction made between the two conceptions of 'cosmic

---

[1] Dr. Julian Huxley (*Evolution in Action*, 1953, pp. 107 ff.) observes that sub-human species have all reached a blind-alley stage. Birds have not improved as 'flying machines' during the last 20,000,000 years, though there have been new species. From the evolutionary standpoint it would seem that only human individual development is open; the animal future is, in Huxley's opinion, closed. See also his *Evolution: the Modern Synthesis*, 1942, pp. 566 ff., where he observes that if man were wiped out it is highly unlikely that his animal next of kin would take the step to conceptual thought. If evolution is to be thought of as progressive, it is because of the emergence of man as the dominant type.

[2] *Man in Revolt*, pp. 418–420.

[2] *The Cosmic Christ*, p. 239.

redemption' is false, and that it is through encountering in Christ the ascendancy of meaning over existence and the 'overcoming of the "it" ' in Christ that the idea of cosmic redemption is given meaning. This, however, suggests a way of escape from the dilemma rather than its resolution, though it is an attempt to translate the mythological thinking of St. Paul into philosophical and theological intelligibility. It evades the dilemma because what Paul evidently meant was an objective material change in the universe, an ultimate release from personalized cosmic anguish and from subjection to futility and decay to a personal being who had so subjected it. A new outlook on the world, though it would make a great difference to man, would not necessarily make any appreciable difference to the cosmos, and, for example, change the character of the shark or the tubercle bacillus or prevent the grey squirrel from destroying trees on a large scale.

For St. Paul's eloquent and moving words imply a personalization of creation which can only be accepted as mythological, which was, perhaps, what he himself intended them to be. If the notion of cosmic redemption is poetry and not a cosmological implicate of Christology and soteriology, it would be wiser to accept it as such and not to build a theology upon it; for ultimately the sphere of redemptive Lordship is that sphere where it is personally acknowledged and experienced, namely in the life of the Christian. We would do well to attend to Brunner's warning against a slack use of the term, as for example in relation to the state or any institutional organization, for Christ's Lordship is a reality only where men 'bow the knee', namely in the Church, without which there is no true Lordship, which is a reality only where people *actually* obey his will.[1] On the other hand, *we do not know* what would be the total effect of a total human redemption, for if man were released from his subjugation to sin and imperfection there might be no more hostility between himself and the animal world, though this can hardly happen until men are delivered from hostility towards one another.

If a further avenue of approach is sought to the question of the redeemability of creation, an indication of it may be found, speculatively, in the philosophy of

[1] *Dogmatics*, II, p. 302.

hormic vitalism as a form of biological monism in which the dualism of man and nature is overcome, at any rate where animate nature is concerned. An example of this may be found in the writings of Constantin von Monakow (1853–1931), whose biopsychological philosophy has some affinities with certain types of modern scientific and philosophic thought such as the 'holistic' evolution of J. C. Smuts and the principle of entelechy as propounded by Hans Driesch. Monakow denied that his hormic vitalism had much in common with the latter and with other neo-vitalistic theories, which, in his opinion, were too vague and unscientific, whereas his own theory of what might be called syneidetic hormism provided, in his own view, a scientific justification for introducing value-concepts, such as conscience, into the scientific field. The great neurologist's philosophical ideas are concentrated in his *Introduction Biologique à l'Étude de la Neurologie et de la Psychopathologie* (written in collaboration with Raoul Mourgue of the Sorbonne in 1928) and a series of long essays appearing originally in the Schweizer Archiv für Neurologie und Psychiatrie and collected by his pupil and successor at the Zurich Institute for Psychiatry and Brain Anatomy, Dr. M. Minkowski, in a volume entitled *Gehirn und Gewissen* (Morgarten Verlag, Zurich, 1950). For a more detailed account of Monakow's life and philosophy see my article in *The Expository Times*, May, 1952.

The fundamental concept governing Monakow's philosophical and scientific outlook is what he calls *syneidesis* or the 'biological conscience'. This he regards as the automatic principle of regulation in the biological field protecting the organism from danger and constituting the urge towards wholeness and balance and restoration when damaged. Life is a 'prospective process in which the individual and successive generations are guided towards the infinite'. The so-called human conscience has its basis in the protoplasm itself and in the biological and psychological presuppositions behind organic life. Where there is a tendency to disintegration the 'biological conscience' comes to the aid of the organism and restores the balance, in both the physical and the psychical realms, where it takes the form of a moral corrective to dysgenic and disruptive forces. Religion—that is, the highest human spiritual activity—is the most refined expression of this basic biological conscience and belongs in the first place to the world of instinct. Monakow therefore ascribes to it a place of fundamental importance: it is not of late appearance, nor is it an epiphenomenon. 'The roots of religion do not lie,' he wrote in *Religion und Nervensystem*, 'as civilized man likes to imagine (in the language of popular psychology) in his feelings and in his preoccupation with the uncertainty of his fate, in the fear of death and the quest for security . . . but far more in those remote levels of development prior to the emergence of the conscience and the ideas which belong to it, where biological urges (which are directed towards the maintenance of the life-plan) predetermine the psychic growth of developing man.' What Monakow means is that religion is the 'spiritual' or higher expression of the same fundamental urge as is found in the biological (i.e. non-human world of life) and that it is not alien to or superimposed upon life but inseparable from it, its roots lying deep in the *syneidesis* or biological conscience.

There is no need to elaborate Monakow's basic ideas, which he applies to biology, psychology, psychiatry, and sociology. It is enough to say that, in his view, the *hormé* is supplied by nature and therefore religious activity is not separated from the basis of organic life; it is not less spiritual because of (according to Monakow) its biopsychic origin. Monakow maintained that his conclusions were based upon scientific observation, and if this is so it provides some justification for supposing that there is a field of consciousness common to man and the rest of animate nature, and that if this *hormé* has in man developed into a spiritual apprehension of reality and the 'Einstellung auf die Unend-lichkeit'—the striving or self-direction towards the infinite—the basic poten-tiality for its development may also reside in the sub-human world. Monakow's hypothesis also indicates the common psychical endowment of 'nature' and man. The sharpness of the dualism man-nature is thus lessened, though the fundamental difference between man and inanimate nature remains. If, through some primeval 'fall', the 'life force' (as N. P. Williams suggested in his *The Ideas of the Fall and of Original Sin*) as it were 'went wrong' and became vitiated from the start, the possibility remains that both creation and man are in need of redemption. There is, however, no limit to speculation along these lines.

5

Finally: it is with reluctance that the mind which is not at home in mythological thinking attends to the notion of either 'fallen' humanity or 'fallen' creation. If the idea has any validity it can apply only to a being who is able to make decisions. What-ever may be the scope of its application in the human field, the idea of 'fallenness' can hardly be considered to apply to the process of change from a primordial gas or galactic nebula to a condensation or a development into countless solar systems. In this connection it is manifestly true that the mythological thought of the New Testament cannot be understood cosmologi-cally, and if an attempt is made to understand it in this sense, the result will inevitably be confusion.

It is here that the existential interpretation of mythological thinking advocated by Bultmann is relevant, and perhaps no-where more so than in the interpretation of what Paul says about cosmic redemption. While Paul is eloquently describing a cosmo-logical situation whose ultimate redemption is visualized and is placing Christ at the apex of the order in whose creation he has participated, he is at the same time describing the human predica-ment as that which involves man in a total reaction to his world.

Not only creation but man is subject to the dominion of meaning-lessness and decay; the *Sein-zum-Tode* (Heidegger) is the ineluctable condition of existence. Man waits for the redemption of his body and soul. As Paul says in another context, he awaits deliverance from the body of this death. Here at any rate Paul represents man in his state of *Geworfenheit*, 'thrownness': *Sorge* (anxiety) is that which inspires the hope of eventual redemption. Man (Rom. 7) is torn by the dilemma in which he must choose or decide but cannot; and whether he will or not, he has no choice but to continue in the creation which forces upon him the will to the understanding of self and of existence. He is caught up in the system described in Romans 8: 38–39 which is somehow antithetical to the realm over which God is sovereign. From this human predicament of which the constituents are tribulation and distress, persecution, and so on, the 'love of God which is in Christ Jesus' is the only means of deliverance. In this sense, for St. Paul, Christ stands beyond the existential situation, the realm of decision in which the decision cannot be made as long as man inhabits an unredeemed creation. In this context at least Paul conceives of man as compelled to ask fundamental questions about himself and his ultimate destiny as he is confronted by the fact of the imperfect cosmos in which he himself is inextricably involved. Quite apart from the notion of Christ the co-creator of this 'fallen' or 'travailing' cosmos, it is clear that, if we bring together the various strands in his thinking, Paul considers Jesus the *Kyrios*, the exalted Lord, to be him who, because of his transcendence over creation, can alone deliver man from his thraldom to futility and decay. If this notion of a personalized, suffering creation is mythological thinking, it is legitimate to understand it, as Bultmann says, not cosmologically but anthropologically. Paul is writing formally about the creation: actually his theme is man in and confronted by the cosmos, and his bold, imaginative thought gains in depth and penetration when so interpreted. Although man is the thing formed, that is, a κτίσις, and as such has no right to dispute the justice of God, the question 'Why hast Thou made me thus?' (Rom. 7: 20) nevertheless arises from the profundity of his awareness of the character of his own being; and the Colossians passage, which is the most eloquent of all Paul's affirmations of total reconciliation through Christ, is equivalent to a promise of the removal of all the contradictions in which both man and nature are enmeshed.

The conception of the cosmic Christ, however, is more than mythological, just as its significance is wider than its 'existential' implication. Although it is not primarily cosmological in import, it should not be dismissed as cosmologically valueless, for it speaks not only of the person as the subject of redemption but also of the nature of the universe which is the setting of that redemption. The theme of Paul's bold speculation has to do not only with the immediate but with the ultimate. As Brunner has said, the point at issue is not a purely cosmological question 'but rather a question of whether I recognize God as my whence—my Creator—my whither, my destiny'.[1] It is Jesus, the *Kyrios*, according to the New Testament, in whom this question receives its answer, and what St. Paul magniloquently affirms (in mythological terms) is that our destiny within the order of creation is illuminated by the centrality of Christ. Indeed, as Brunner points out in commenting on the existentialist interpretation of Paul's cosmology, unless I know my whence and my whither I have no understanding of my own being at all. That is to say, the ultimate significance of the place of Christ in creation is necessary to my self-understanding and appreciation of it is prior to it. What matters is not the truth or otherwise of the affirmation of the creative function of Jesus Christ, the *Kyrios*, but the fact that in him the Creator God is revealed and made intelligible and makes our destiny intelligible. Paul's statements about Jesus and the cosmos are 'objective' in so far as they affirm the character of the divine purpose for man and state that this purpose, which is concerned with our ultimate destiny in the universe, is clarified in our knowledge of the Lord who reveals God as the source, ground, and goal of being.

[1] *Eternal Hope*, p. 189.

CHAPTER THREE

THE LORDSHIP OF JESUS AND CREATION

II—CHRIST IN CREATION

I

Christian theology has always insisted upon the manhood of Jesus, though with varying emphasis; but it has often done so in a way which has tended to represent it as 'adjectival', to use a term which William Temple applied to the deity of Jesus, as conceived by adoptionist Christology. The theological presuppositions of orthodox Christology, however, were such as to make it difficult to regard Jesus as wholly man in a sense in which manhood would be understood today and would be predicated of one who belonged to the order of creation through his full participation in the human series. Yet the Nicene, Athanasian, and Chalcedonian definitions of the faith were so framed as to safeguard the genuine manhood of Jesus, and the Synoptic Gospels, if the Matthean and Lukan prologues are excepted, do not suggest that he was other than one born in the normal manner. The prologues, however, are the expression of mythological thinking: angels engaging persons in conversation, the proclamation of a birth to which only one human parent contributes, a heavenly choir enunciating its message to the shepherds, and the rest of the descriptive details of the Christmas narrative, are not data which could be treated objectively by a historian. Whether we believe in the virginal birth of Jesus or not, the character and method of these narratives are those of the mythopoetical imagination at work on a sacred theme, though there is no convincing *a priori* reason for refusing to believe that God should have chosen this as the appropriate manner for the entry of Christ into the world. The belief in the Virgin Birth goes back to a very early period, and even if there are grounds for believing that the narratives were not part of the

Gospels in which they occur, and that originally the Lukan material was of Palestinian origin and incorporated into the third Gospel, the fact that two differing traditions testify to the belief indicates that it must have been current within a decade or two of the Resurrection.

Dr. Paul Winter, in a recent examination of the language of the Lukan prologue, concludes that it could not have come from the same pen as the rest of the Gospel but must have existed in literary form as a Hebrew writing (*New Testament Studies*, Nov. 1954, p. 121). The Hebraic origin of the narratives has long been known. Thus Plummer (*Luke*, I.C.C.) makes the pleasing, though unsupported and improbable, suggestion that Mary herself may have written the Lukan prologues, and James Orr (*The Virgin Birth of Christ*, 1907) reckoned with their Semitic origin. Dr. W. Manson (*Luke*, Moffatt Commentary) thinks that the narratives may have had an independent circulation before their corporation in the Gospel. Yet although its basis is in the Synoptic Gospels and presumably was included in them because of its early currency, the belief in the Virgin Birth was not part of the Apostolic preaching. Douglas Edwards' argument that because the doctrine was believed at the end of the first century it *must* have been taught by the Apostles, is unsupported (*The Virgin Birth in History and Faith*, 1941, p. 32), for nowhere outside the first and third Gospels is there any reference to it in the New Testament. Edwards (whose book is strongly polemical) interprets (as others have done) John 1: 13 as indicating familiarity with the belief, and G. H. Box (*Dictionary of Christ and the Gospels*, II, p. 805) considers that it may lend it 'presumptive support'. Actually the verse should be read in connection with John 3: 15–16, as it has to do with the sarx-pneuma antithesis, not with the birth of Jesus (cf. C. H. Dodd, *The Interpretation of the Fourth Gospel*, p. 224). Barth (*Kirchliche Dogmatik*, 1/2, pp. 187–221: 'das Weihnachtswunder') provides a masterly exposition and survey of the field and has the weight of the Christian tradition behind him. He describes Brunner's questioning of the Virgin Birth as casting 'twilight over his whole Christology'. He says that he can only sigh over it and that the less said about it the better (p. 201). While Barth defends the doctrine he is, however, at pains to distinguish between the divine 'conception' of Jesus and his divine 'generation'. The Holy Ghost, he says, was not the father of Jesus. 'The phrase *conceptus de Spiritu Sancto* . . . does not mean that Jesus Christ according to his human existence was the son of the Holy Spirit. It affirms, rather, and as emphatically as possible . . . that Jesus Christ had no human father. The fact that the Holy Spirit took the place of a man in this miracle does not in the least mean that He did what a man does. That Jesus was conceived by the Holy Spirit does not mean that he was *engendered* by the Holy Spirit' ('dass Jesus vom Heiligen Geist *empfangen* ist . . . heisst also nicht, dass er vom Heiligen Geist erzeugt ist'). Then what can it mean, if not this? (*K.D.* 1/2, p. 218). Dr. Vincent Taylor, who carefully examines the Gospel narratives, suspends judgment on the historicity of the tradition, concluding that 'what is doctrinally irrelevant is not likely to be historically true' (*The Virgin Birth*, p. 129, 1920); though it should be added that it is not necessarily true even if it is doctrinally relevant. I have little to add to what Brunner has written on the matter (*The Mediator*, pp. 322 ff.), and my agreement is with him rather than with Barth, though his treatment of the question is not comparable with Barth's in scope. In Brunner's view what matters is the fact of the miracle of the Incarnation, not the allegedly miraculous manner of its occurrence, which is an impediment to belief in Jesus' full manhood. Liberal-Modernist opinion, as may be imagined, has tended to reject the Virgin Birth. See, e.g., C. J. Cadoux, *Catholicism and Christianity*, pp. 348 ff.; J. F. Bethune-Baker, *The Miracle of Christianity*, p. 11; W. Sanday, *Bishop Gore's Challenge to Criticism*, p. 19, *Form and Content in the Christian Tradition*, p. 9, where 'supernatural' birth is explained as 'an influx of Deity into manhood'; H. D. A. Major, *English Modernism*, pp. 127 passim, 98 ff.; Percy Gardner, *Exploratio Evangelica*, pp. 239 ff.; J. M. Thomson, *Miracles in the New Testament*, pp. 137 ff. Bishop Gore (*A New Commentary*, II, p. 320), finds myth inadequate as an explanation.

From several points of view the arguments used by Dr. J. G. Machen in vindication of the doctrine and of the historicity of the gospel narratives are impressive, for in his massive and erudite investigation of the question he defends them on textual, linguistic, historical, and theological grounds;[1] and it must be conceded that there are difficulties in understanding why an evangelist such as Luke, who appears to have been careful in consulting his sources, should have incorporated a tradition so manifestly at variance with human experience, unless he was naturally inclined as a man of his age to accept without hesitation any tradition testifying to the supernatural conception of the *Kyrios*. It is the Lukan narrative, further, which preserves the most manifestly mythological elements in the story, though they are entangled in narratives which have a less fanciful colouring. Yet when the cogency of the arguments in support of the Gospel tradition is admitted, the narratives nevertheless remain stubbornly mythological in character and detract from the complete manhood of Jesus instead of confirming belief in it.

For what is involved in the Birth-narratives is the question of Jesus' relation to creation by virtue of his manhood. On the one hand the divine parentage safeguards his transcendence over creation, while on the other his human parentage establishes at

---

[1] *The Virgin Birth of Christ* (1930).

least formally his position within it. The Virgin Birth, so to speak, gives him a foot in both worlds.

The narratives, however, are in a different category from St. Paul's ascription of cosmic pre-eminence and co-creatorship to Jesus as the pre-existent Son. Both are formally statements of facts about Jesus, the one in brief terms borrowed from current Hellenistic thought, the others extended narratives claiming to be a bona fide account of how Jesus came to be born and of the circumstances antecedent to and attendant upon his birth. St. Paul ascribes to Jesus a pre-natal status; the Birth-narratives, with all the appearance of myth, tell not *how* a *pre-existent* divine being became man, but how the Son of God was born. Paul, who assumes the pre-existence of the *Kyrios*, says nothing of his birth; the evangelists say nothing about his pre-existence. The differences between the two have their source not in two different approaches to fact, but in two different kinds of mythological thinking. In any case, the Birth-narratives clearly represent two quite different traditions with very little in common. In Luke's version, which is the more elaborate and literary of the two, the angelic announcement is made to Mary; in Matthew's to Joseph. Matthew 1: 18–25 appears to be a self-contained *pericope* with no mention of the place of birth. Chapter II begins as if it were a separate document, also complete in itself. 'Now when Jesus was born in Bethlehem of Judea' reads like the beginning of the Gospel, not like a continuation. Indeed, nothing is common to the two narratives except the announcement of the miraculous birth, and in each case the circumstances are different. They are not even complementary, though they are not contradictory; and the question is made more confusing by the alleged historical indication in the Lukan material that Jesus and John the Baptist were second cousins or at any rate kinsmen, for which there is no foundation in any of the accounts of the public ministry of Jesus nor in Josephus's account of John's mission or his reference (if its genuineness is accepted) to Jesus. In other words, as F. C. Burkitt has said, the precise manner of the birth of Jesus is not a matter which historical criticism can establish.[1] Either of the traditions *in itself* might be entitled to

[1] *The Gospel History and its Transmission*, p. 350.

serious historical consideration; but the existence of *both* traditions so different from one another creates a confusion out of which historical order cannot be established. That both go back to an early date is undeniable, but, as Dr. Vincent Taylor wrote over thirty years ago in his monograph on the subject, a myth could have sprung up 'new born' as soon as the parents of Jesus were dead.[1] The matter is further complicated by the fact that none of the alternative theories offered is satisfactory, least of all the suggested derivation of the tradition from pagan analogies. On the other hand, had two of the Gospels and all the epistles and the Acts been silent about the Resurrection, and if the only two existing accounts of it had been found in narratives as different from one another as are the accounts of the birth of Jesus, there would be considerable hesitation in assessing their historical worth. As it is, all the Gospels attest its occurrence, and it is mentioned or implied in the major Epistles of St. Paul. The doctrine of the Virgin Birth, moreover, is virtually inconsistent with the notion of pre-existence, as Bultmann has observed,[2] for he who was born by generation from the Holy Spirit, as it were, can hardly be considered to have existed before his birth. The myth-world contains its own inner contradictions. The tradition, nevertheless, must be ancient, and was accepted by the Church at an early date, though the theoretical objections to it, as is shown in Justin's Dialogue with Trypho, were understood. Yet if there is an outstanding instance of myth in the New Testament it is this.

The Birth-narratives, then, whether regarded as historical or mythical, remain. They are part of the Gospel story and their Christological implications cannot be ignored. If they are treated as a statement of historical fact, as has been done by a great part of the Christian church, they should be accepted as the only authentic accounts of how Jesus was born, that is, by conception by the Holy Spirit. If they are regarded as beautiful traditions mythologically expressed, they still remain embedded in the New Testament. The sceptic may treat them as pious fiction; the

---

[1] *The Virgin Birth*, p. 126.
[2] *Kerygma and Myth*, p. 34. Cf. also C. H. Dodd, *The Interpretation of the Fourth Gospel*, p. 260 and footnote.

theologian cannot dismiss them with a gesture. Whatever else lies behind them, two things are clear: the exceptional place which they ascribe to Jesus in the order of creation, and the fact that his sinlessness and transcendence over the human order to which he belonged by virtue of his manhood are to be attributed to a special cause, namely divine intervention and preservation. The Christological consequences of the narratives, however, must be faced: that it represents Jesus not only as involved 'organically' in humanity, but also as separated from the human series by a radical discontinuity with it.[1] From the standpoint of demythologizing the problem which confronts us is this: how can the discontinuity, which the Birth-narratives indicate, be upheld without appealing to its sanction in the miraculous, that is to say, without involving a radical disruption of the human series to which Jesus, by virtue of his manhood, belongs? With the question of whether the miraculous birth is necessary to the doctrine of the divine Sonship we are not at present concerned, nor are we questioning the historicity of the tradition because it describes a miracle, but because this kind of miracle is by its very nature neither accessible to historical investigation nor the subject of rational explanation. Ultimately the birth of Jesus may be as much a mystery as the Incarnation itself.

In pursuing the Christological implications of the Birth-narratives, then, we shall begin by considering what warrant there is in the Synoptic Gospels for the assumption that Jesus transcends not creation (with which we have already dealt) but the human order to which he is related by his manhood, that is, by the human factor in his parentage. We shall enquire into whether the miraculous conception is the only supposition on which the emergence of the unique filial relationship implied in the Synoptic tradition and throughout the New Testament rests, or whether, by analogy, other fields of enquiry will lend support to the Christology which the Virgin Birth affirms in mythological terms.

---

[1] Yet the author of Hebrews (2: 17) states that 'it behoved him *in all things* to be made like unto his brethren'.

Brunner, in a striking passage,[1] has referred to Jesus' complete detachment: a characteristic which emphasizes the numinous character of his personality and points to his transcendence over 'historical' situations to such an extent that we might appropriately describe it as 'disinvolvement'. This is not only a conspicuous feature of the Fourth Gospel's interpretation of Jesus: it is also indicated in the Synoptic tradition itself. For there is a kind of ambiguity, or paradoxicality, in Jesus' attitude towards any event or situation: he is 'in' it and yet at the same time he gives the impression of being wholly uninvolved in it. This disinvolvement is revealed in his objective attitude towards it as of one who deals with it with complete authoritativeness and as an onlooker whose judgment upon it is unerring. Even at the age of twelve his reply to his parents in the Temple shows that he has only a partial loyalty to his family; he is by no means fully involved in it and therefore claims the right to detachment from it. He declines to be involved in an adjudication in a dispute about property; he reserves the right to condemn one party and not the other, as in the *pericope adulterae*. He is apparently indifferent to the storm on the lake. As one uninvolved in the pursuit of earning his living during his public ministry he summons others from their vocations, though he does not command them to leave them permanently. He is not committed to obedience to the Judaic law but claims the right to disregard it together with ritual observance. In the Fourth Gospel he speaks significantly of 'your Father' and 'my Father' rather than of 'our' Father. When he is asked a question the incident usually ends with the interrogator himself answering questions. This happens regularly and suggests that it is not *his* business to answer questions but to ask them.[2] He obliges the rich young man and the Scribe to answer his counter-questions and to pass judgments on themselves: an indirect technique suggesting and reinforcing this impression of disinvolvement and authoritativeness. A striking example is his behaviour at his trial, for the impression created by

[1] *The Mediator*, pp. 364 ff.
[2] Cf. H. Thielicke, *Fragen des Christentums an die Moderne Welt* (1948).

the Gospel narratives is that he is a spectator of the proceedings rather than one judically involved in them, and ultimately we are made to see that it is not he but his accusers who are on trial. And while he commends to others the disinterested *agape* of God, he shows few signs of human *philia* or *eros* in so far as this implies being profoundly involved in personal relationships of a binding character.

This disinvolvement is especially noticeable in his relationship with his family, not one of whom was among the Twelve. Indeed, his family seems to have been hostile: a prophet is not without honour except among his own people and in his own country. According to the Synoptic Gospels none of his family was present at the Crucifixion, though John refers to the presence of his mother, and it was one of his remoter followers, Joseph of Arimathea, not his family, who asked Pilate for his body. In the Fourth Gospel he is said to have addressed to his mother the brusque words, 'Woman, what have you to do with me?' (Moffatt), a question which commentators have tried unsatisfactorily to explain away. Again, he who does the will of God is his brother and sister and mother. And the Fourth Gospel contains the words in which Jesus commends his mother to the care of the disciple whom he 'loved' (the only instance of personal affection in the Gospel) while the rest of her not inconsiderable family were still living. Paradoxically he who was to be more responsible than anyone for the esteem in which family life is held seems to have refused involvement in it himself.

Now there may be an example here of the 'withdrawal' which Toynbee considers to be an attitude typical of men with a particular sense of mission. The difference between the aloofness or disinvolvement of Jesus and the withdrawal of the politically dedicated revolutionary, or St. Paul retiring to the wilderness, is that that whereas these were involved in bringing about a visible or this-worldly institution such as the state or the church, Jesus was 'involved' in something wholly other, namely, the transcendent Kingdom of God. Incident after incident in the Gospels could be cited in which this disinvolvement is unmistakable.

One incident, the Transfiguration, illustrates this numinous detachment in a striking manner, for more than any other pre-Resurrection narrative it emphasizes the sense of awe which the disciples experience in the presence of something which indicated the gulf separating them from Jesus. In this problematical moment in which the interpenetration of flesh and spirit, of the phenomenal and the noumenal, reaches a unique climax in the career of Jesus, there is set forth a kind of anticipation of the complete transfiguration wrought by the Resurrection. There is no satisfactory reason for doubting its authenticity, though the narrative as it stands doubtless contains some mythological embroidery. Bultmann's assumption that it is a Resurrection story is quite unconvincing.[1] The numinous details of the occasion are clear enough: all three versions refer to the shining garments, the overshadowing cloud, and the supernatural 'voice': details which should not be dismissed as mere myth or the product of the imagination working in retrospect. Clearly it cannot be investigated 'historically' or by direct cognition, but it is an event of which notice must be taken in any Christological discussion. However the form of the narrative may have been influenced by Old Testament archetypes, something of such tremendous significance happened that the transmitters of the tradition could only describe the sheer awe experienced in poetical terms with an Old Testament reference. As Schweitzer has suggested, the Confession of Peter in Mark 8 comes more naturally *after* the Transfiguration,[2] for it is reasonable to suppose that an occasion such as the latter would naturally lead to Peter's recognition of Jesus as the Messiah.

The culmination of this 'disinvolvement' and numinous apartness is the Resurrection: the final and incontrovertible demonstration that his transcendence is not over events alone, but over death. Here the detachment is complete. Jesus appears and moves within the dimension of this world, otherwise he would not be perceptible, but the Gospel narratives make it clear that he

---

[1] *Theology of the New Testament*, p. 27, *Die Geschichte der Synoptischen Tradition*, pp. 278 ff. Bousset (*Kyrios Christos*, p. 61) considers the incident to be an intrusion (Fremdkörper) in the Gospel narrative and the most supernaturalised incident in the Gospel. A. T. Cadoux (*The Sources of the Second Gospel*, p. 33) is of the opinion that the Transfiguration and the Caesarea Philippi incident are variants of the same occasion from two different sources. See, however, A. M. Ramsey's discussion of it in *The Glory of God and the Transfiguration of Christ* (1949).

[2] *The Quest of the Historical Jesus*, p. 381. The rearrangement would contribute to solving the perplexing problems which Schweitzer enumerates.

is at the same time independent of any space-time dimension humanly measurable, and, according to the narratives, he is no longer subject to the limitations imposed by 'solid' matter. Here again the Johannine Gospel cites significant words: 'Touch me not (RSV do not hold me), for I am not yet ascended to my Father'.[1] His detachment is such that there shall be no tactual relationship between himself and Mary.

It is this distance between himself and man that one aspect of the Birth-narrative is concerned to emphasize. Jesus is no ordinary member of the human race and thereby likely to sin or to be involved in human situations, for he is 'bodily' the Son of God by a human mother. Here is safeguarded the element of transcendence while the concession is made to his place, even if the connection is not complete, in the human series. He who in the literal sense is born of the Spirit as well as of the flesh belongs to both worlds, the worlds of 'above' and of 'below', to use the Johannine terminology. If the underlying motivation in organic life is the propagation of the species and the will to life (what Titius calls *Arterhaltung* and *Selbsterhaltung*), these are not prominent in Jesus; indeed, he seems to be indifferent to them. He is the exception in the series, though others have also disregarded life and self in the prosecution of some purpose or in witness to the truth. Perhaps, moreover, Jesus may be even thought of as the perfect example of the tendency to individuation which is evident in the highest organisms. At any rate, disinvolvement through detachment or renunciation is a characteristic feature of the 'otherness' of Jesus.

Now the title *Kyrios* implies this transcendence over common humanity;[2] even as a secular title 'Lord' carries with it a distinction and a difference from the ordinary commoner: it is a title of respect, an indication of special worth and of an elevation

---

[1] The present form of this saying, however, is curious, as its implication is that Jesus must not be touched *as long as* he has not ascended, with the corollary that he may be touched after his ascension. It also appears to contradict Jesus' invitation to Thomas in John 20: 27.

[2] As Barth has stated, the title *Kyrios* was one which was conferred after the Resurrection on the historical Jesus: it is the *man* Jesus who has risen from the dead; and in the tenth chapter of the *Dogmatik* dealing with creation Barth has finally affirmed the full manhood of Jesus, rejecting the 'two-substance' Christology in the interest of his complete manhood (*K.D.*, 111/ 2, p. 394). Barth writes of the retrospective 'transference of this name to the man Jesus'. Indeed, he strives to emphasize the manhood and in doing so refers to personal qualities to which little or no attention

of status. Applied to Jesus it denotes his elevation to a position which deserves more than reverence or recognition, namely obedience, self-surrender, commitment, and, for some, worship due to a divine being together with the Father and the Holy Spirit, though he himself did not demand it.

A figure completely transcendent, however, completely exalted above humanity, as it were projected from another world into this or abdicating from a position of cosmic sovereignty and co-creator-ship with God, cannot be considered as belonging fully to the human order and hence to the realm of creation. Yet the man-hood of Jesus, the real and not apparent manhood, if it is to be more than a description or a disguise, must belong in all essentials to this realm. A christophany or logophany is not a man. Much of the barren Christological controversy of the first five centuries centred in the discussion of whether the constitutive principle in our Lord's person was divine or human, whether it was the Logos or his human nature, what was the character of his human and divine consciousness. To the modern mind this sounds remote and academic, for manhood is to be defined in terms of human qualities which establish an unbroken relationship both on the psychological and physiological levels between a species and a member of it. The Church, however, was concerned about a matter of vital importance: the preservation of the belief in the genuine manhood of Jesus. Yet to speak of 'impersonal humanity', as theologians have done, is to raise confusing issues.[1]

---

is paid in the Gospels. For example, it is not stated that Jesus thought reflectively, laughed, or rejoiced (3/ 2, p. 396). His inner life and his physical life are as good as ignored. On the other hand, it is not stated, says Barth, that he did *not* do these things. Although Jesus is 'der ganze Mensch', 'der Mensch für andere Menschen', there is a fundamental difference between Jesus and men which consists not only in his sinlessness but in 'the mystery of his identity with God' (3/ 2, p. 82). He is wholly man, but there is in him that which is outside the human order.

[1] A comparatively modern treatise, for example (Dr. H. M. Relton's *Study in Christology* (1916)), represents the limit to which one can go in reinterpreting the Christology of the ancients, and the author's perception of the inapplicability of a notion such as 'impersonal humanity' is not replaced by a more helpful alternative. If Jesus was man, he must have been a particular man, namely Jesus of Nazareth, and the employment of concepts such as 'anhypostasia' and 'enhypostasia' does not clarify the matter, though Dr. Relton, I gather, would not deny that Jesus was *a* man. The difficulty about this kind of interpretation, however, as Dr. D. M. Baillie points out (*God Was in Christ*, p. 91) is that it is an impediment to the understanding of Jesus' 'having a human experience of God'. Cf. also L. W. Grensted, *The Person of Christ*, p. 177.

Now the Virgin Birth is to this extent self-contradictory or ambiguous in that it takes away with one hand what it gives with the other. The theological doctrine is designed to safeguard the sinlessness of Jesus by implying that the human act of normal conception is to be regarded as sinful, that is, that what is essentially of the divinely-ordained order of creation is something to be discarded if God is to incarnate Himself in man. But unless Mary was sinless (as she may have been), which is what Roman Catholic doctrine states, the entail of sin could have been transmitted through her as well as through Joseph. Both the doctrine of the Incarnation by means of virginal birth and the dogma of the Immaculate Conception stress negatively, if unwittingly, the factor of heredity in so far as the sinlessness of Jesus presupposes a departure from a normal biological process because of the transmissibility of the sinful disposition. In order that the Son of God, that is to say, a completely new factor, may appear, there must be a radical break with creation through the substitution of the Holy Spirit for human paternity. While admitting, with Brunner, the miracle of Incarnation, we cannot avoid asking whether this miracle requires, as its concomitant, discontinuity within the human order. Brunner considers that the doctrine of the Virgin Birth would have been abandoned long ago were it not that dogmatic interests appeared to be concerned in its retention. He questions it partly because it indicates a disparagement of normal procreation and because it means that God did not take upon Himself *all* that was human.[1] Or can there be such discontinuity which is not incompatible with belonging wholly to creation through complete and normal membership of the human race? For the very notion of Incarnation implies an irruption from without into the order of creation, or, as Berdyaev has expressed it, of the noumenal into the phenomenal world; indeed, the emergence of any genius (though we are not including Jesus in this category) represents both continuity and discontinuity at the same time, a givenness and something that is given, an innate possession and a transcendent endowment. Christologically this is expressed in the transcendent Lordship of Jesus over creation and his transcendence within the human

[1] Op. cit., p. 324.

189

order through the quality of his self-consciousness on the one hand, and through his complete manhood entitling him to membership of this human order on the other. Both sets of relationships involve forms of discontinuity, though the implication of the doctrine of the Virgin Birth is that such discontinuity is, on the biological side, radical. If the introductory chapters of Matthew and Luke are rejected as historically untrustworthy because of the improbability of their contents or because the narratives are mythological in character, or for any other reason, assent to the 'fact' to which they attest is not required. If, on the other hand, it is agreed that they should be retained because they are part of the Gospel narrative and because they enshrine a truth with which the Christian faith cannot dispense, or because they make a permanent impact on faith through their imaginative appeal, it is necessary to enquire into the character of what they affirm and into how far it can be stated in non-mythological terms, and also into whether what is thus stated is an essential part of the structure of Christian belief.

3

The problem with which we are concerned is that of relating the unique to the general, the exceptional within creation to creation, the Incarnate Lord to sinful man; in other words, it is a fundamental problem of Christian metaphysics and Christology. As Dr. Lionel Thornton approached the Christological problem in terms of an adaptation of A. N. Whitehead's philosophy of organism, it will be equally legitimate for us to approach the same problem in the form in which we have stated it from an analogous point of view. Assistance may be received from considering the nature of variation in terms of artistic creativeness, that is, in terms of analogy taken from the world of values.

In the first place, it is the emergence of the wholly new which, in the form of the non-generic which results from creativeness, distinguishes man from creation, from the order of nature, and it is by means of it that he succeeds in transcending it. As Berdyaev has pointed out in what he has written about creativeness, man is able to bring being out of non-being through himself being a creator. The primary creative impulse, he says, 'takes place outside the objectified world, outside the time of this world; it happens in existential time, in a flash of the present; it knows neither past nor future. A creative act is a noumenal act',[1] though it is revealed in the phenomenal world. Creativeness is the making of something new that had not existed in the world before[2] and cannot be deduced from anything. It presupposes non-being, the μὴ ὄν, and the creative act issues from the depths of this 'meonic' being which is the source of 'primeval, pre-cosmic, pre-existent freedom in man'.[3] Creativeness, Berdyaev continues, has a dual aspect: there is the primary creative act in which man stands face to face with God, and the secondary creative act in which he faces other men and the world.[4] It is a characteristic of personality as a whole and not a specific gift; the aim of creative inspiration is to bring forth new forms of life,[5] though objectification in Berdyaev's opinion has to do with the world of necessity, whereas creativeness is the realm of noumenal freedom.[6] In any case, creativeness means the bringing into being of the new, which means a break with what has gone before. Personality is a 'break with the world-order'.[7]

The main sphere of creativeness is art. Through his exercise of the creative impulse, which is the domain of freedom, man transcends the physical nexus which binds him to creation, for nature, and the sub-human world, know nothing of free creativeness in this sense. Through being himself 'new' as an individual and through being the one who creates and brings the 'new' into existence, he transcends the phenomenal, objective world. We speak, metaphorically, or by the method of personification, of nature doing this or that, as though 'nature' acts by intention, as for example in 'compensating' or 'rectifying'. But 'nature' does no such thing by deliberate intent: the impersonal, the phenomenal, cannot 'behave' as does the personal and the noumenal. In nature events 'happen'; they are not premeditated.

[1] *The Beginning and the End*, p. 181.
[2] *The Destiny of Man*, p. 126.
[3] Ibid., p. 127.
[4] Ibid., p. 128.
[5] Ibid., p. 129.
[6] *The Beginning and the End*, p. 59.
[7] Ibid., p. 136.

Nature does not create the sunset because 'she' wishes man to see something beautiful; but man creates a work of art depicting a sunset which is more than the reproduction on canvas of any particular sunset. It is in this transcendent act of creation, through obedience to the impulse of creativeness, that he so to speak imposes form upon nature and by so doing transforms the material provided by nature into that which is not nature: the expression of his aesthetic experience which is art.

It is at this point that the concept of evolution, which has to do with creation and not with creativeness, is seen to be not wholly applicable to the factor of newness. Although the meaning of the term has been modified or reinterpreted by the addition of terms such as 'emergent' or 'creative', the 'evolving' quality is not new but merely the same thing in process of gradual change. It should be possible at any point in the process to observe the thing in the act of evolving. Evolution does not involve a break within the series (except in the form of a 'sport' or freak, and it is doubtful whether this is actually a step in the evolving process) but only an imperceptibly slow transition from one point to the next.

Human creativeness, whether applied to invention or art, is in a different category. But here again there is a distinction. The process of creation differs from that of invention, even though the invention is a 'new' thing; for artistic creation is less dependent on rearrangement and conformity to practical purpose. There is less givenness in it because of the antecedent factor of non-being. The aeroplane, radar, atomic bomb, or electronic brain are at first 'new', but they are made of substances which were already 'there'. Once they have been made they can be exactly reproduced by mechanical means. The prototype is 'new', but it is repeatable; otherwise it is not a prototype.

A work of art, however, is both 'new' and unrepeatable, though it can be reproduced in print or copied. The copy, however, is not identical with the original creation, which retains its quality of once-for-allness and unrepetitive uniqueness in a manner which cannot be predicated of a functional instrument. The latter belongs to the phenomenal world, the world of createdness, of *ktisis*. A work of art, the fruit of creativeness, is neither fully

reproducible nor reproductive, for the creative impulse summon-
ing it out of 'nothing', out of Berdyaev's 'meonic depths', does
not recur in the same form. The artist, if he possesses what Goethe
called the *unendlich schöpferische Geist*, the infinitely creative spirit,
will continue to create out of it; but every creative impulse, each
imaginative vision, differs from all others, as does the resultant
work of art. The next in the series of nine symphonies would not
be another Ninth Symphony but a Tenth. To reprint or reper-
form the Ninth does not make it a tenth. The great Van Eyck
altar-piece at Ghent may be photographed many times; but this
does not as it were add to it numerically. The impulse in which
it was conceived and the resultant delight in its execution, through
its effect upon the spectator, are continuous and inexhaustible.
But whatever the form, each result of creativeness means a new
thing, a break in the numerical order of things. Left to itself
creation, that is the objective world, would not have produced
it; and the work of art, in its non-recurrence, possesses finality
and uniqueness. Berdyaev, by straining the word beyond its
original connotation, calls it eschatological. The new thing, for
him, is eschatological. As art it may also be apocalyptic in a
sense in which other things are not, for it offers a vision of the
noumenal world.

This newness, however, this unrepeatableness, is not miraculous,
nor is it within the evolutionary process, though it does not run
counter to nature. Rather is it outside nature through transcending it. It is within the totality of creation if this is thought
of as τὰ πάντα, the sum-total of all existing things. Such totality
is a kind of cosmic monism: nothing can be outside it. Yet even
if this is so, the new thing, the work of genius, was not implicit
in creation, for it was unpredictable, and it is non-recurrent.

Now an argument deriving from the consideration of the
character of a work of art as the result of the creative impulse
may seem to be too remote from the doctrine of the Incarnation
as set forth by the first and third evangelists to merit serious
consideration; but if there is validity in analogical argument,
what we are seeking to establish by its means is that the Incarnation can be thought of as an act of divine creativeness emerging
from the noumenal being of God Himself. This, indeed, is its

basic meaning, and one which is not affected by belief or disbelief in the particular manner in which it is represented, especially when there is involved in it a mythological mode of thought. For what the Birth-narratives describe is the self-realization of God the subject in the objective world in terms of personality, which can only be apprehended phenomenally. The method is secondary. Whether it was achieved in the precise manner described by Matthew or Luke, or whether by a katagogic movement on the part of God and an anagogic movement on the part of the Son meeting at a point and at a moment designated as Incarnation, is not of primary importance. What is of importance is the once-for-allness of the act, the final, eschatological unrepeatability of the event, to which nothing less than mythological thinking is able adequately to testify. Through Jesus man becomes a 'new creature'. Jesus in this sense can be thought of as the creative impulse of God continuous in human experience. To this extent he belongs, like the creative impulse described by Berdyaev, neither to the past nor the future. 'Jesus Christ the same yesterday, and today, and for ever' (Heb. 13: 8): that is to say, Jesus belongs to the past-present-future which is the existential time limited to no moment in chronological time. In this sense Jesus, the *Kyrios*, is noumenal being revealed in the phenomenal world. Like all persons, he appears on one level out of non-being; on the other he participates in the biological continuity of the race. To employ Berdyaev's phraseology again: as the result of the primary creative act Jesus stands face to face with God, and secondarily face to face with other men and the world.

We see from this in what way continuity and discontinuity can exist together without being contradictory. As man Jesus is continuous with humanity; unless this were so the evangelists would not have taken the trouble to include even contradictory genealogies of Jesus in the prologues to their Gospels. It is true that ultimately his lineage according to Luke's list is traced back to God,[1] whereas Matthew's stops at Abraham. What matters is that the genealogy is given, for it establishes Jesus in a historical

---

[1] Either Luke failed to see that this was not necessary if the story about Jesus' birth was true, or he was making doubly sure.

line. That the two lists differ does not greatly matter; nor does the curious inconsistency that they purport to give an account of Jesus' ancestry through Joseph, who (according to the doctrine of the Virgin Birth) was not his father. These are important only to those who seek history in the narratives. What matters is that they testify (among other things) to Jesus' solidarity with man. And this, too, is the meaning of the story of his birth. The principle of continuity is established.

It is, however, the discontinuity which should be regarded as the main characteristic of the Christological implication of the mythological thinking represented in the narratives. To its assertion belong the supernatural details of the stories; for the appearance of supernatural beings and the picturesque presentation of this criticial moment in world-history are the tribute of the religious imagination to the coming of the Son of God into the world. Jesus the *Kyrios* is discontinuous with creation as man is, for the world of nature, the cosmos, is the objective world which man transcends and with which, through transcending it, he is discontinuous. Man is in the created series and is yet not of it: his relation to creation is therefore ambiguous. He is continuous with creation in being a creature and thus has an immanental relation to it, and as a physical being he is generically related to the rest of his species. But he transcends nature through his ability to create. He is *in* nature through being able to procreate. He is superior to the cosmos which has it in its power to overwhelm him. That is the truth which was expressed in the eighth Psalm long before Pascal.[1] And like man, Jesus in virtue of his humanity is 'above' creation and in this way discontinuous with it. As man, the noumenal being, transcends the phenomenal world both by comprehending it and by occupying a higher plane of existence, so can it be said of Jesus that he is 'above' all things, pre-eminent over them, as the spiritually creative and as himself the 'new'. He is an interruption of the order of nature,

---

[1] 'Man is but a reed, the weakest thing in nature, but he is a thinking reed. It does not take the whole universe to crush him. But were the universe to crush him, man would be nobler than his slayer, because he knows that he dies and that the universe has the better of him' (*Pensées*, Art. VI, § 347). For Pascal the greatness of man consists in his transcendence over nature through thought. Even his awareness of *la misère* is an example of such transcendence.

as is all individuality, and at the same time an interruption, by virtue of his uniqueness, of the human order.

To say this, however, is not to include Jesus with other individuality or with other examples of creativeness and createdness; it means only that these categories are applicable to him and that a Christological problem can be illuminated by thinking of Jesus in terms of continuity and discontinuity, of continuous organic relationship and of discontinuous newness which implies interruption and transcendence, as well as of immanent relationships, rather than in terms of evolution or predictable emergence.

In saying this, however, we have done little more than affirm that within the context of the created series there can arise a new thing, the unique, that which possesses a creative, eschatological potency, without introducing any miraculous factor to explain it and yet at the same time without implying a contradictory relationship to this series. The Birth narratives, like the Christology based upon them, postulate not only discontinuity within the series but a radical interruption of it from without through the intervention of the Logos or of the Holy Spirit itself performing the act of procreation. What they affirmed, and what the New Testament often formally affirmed, is that the pre-eminence of Jesus over man and creation is not to be expressed in terms generally applicable to man or creation, though the Epistle to the Hebrews (2: 9 ff), significantly enough, speaks of the Lordship of Jesus in terms of the eighth Psalm, of which the subject is not a supernatural being but man. The author leaves us in no doubt about the solidarity of Jesus with man and hence his direct relationship to the created order which includes man, though in this passage the Stoic formula 'for whom are all things and by whom are all things' (verse 10) is employed.

We have used, in our approach to the problem of interpreting non-mythologically the New Testament forms of the doctrine of the Lordship of Christ over creation and the conception of his deviation from the human order within that order, analogies drawn from other fields. We have suggested that within the series of the created order there is an organic continuity and at the same time discontinuity, while the discontinuous nevertheless remains paradoxically continuous. Man, as a biological being, is continuous with creation; as a spiritual being he is discontinuous with it and transcendent over it in a way in which the animal world is not. He is, however, not wholly subject to creation, he is not merely a being who, in Pringle-Pattison's phrase, is 'organic to nature': he himself is a creator and is able to produce the new, the discontinuous, and the non-recurrent. He lives in the world not only of cosmic or historical time but (as Berdyaev has expressed it) in the existential or 'noumenal' time, which is the source of all creativeness.

The relevance of this can be realized when it is seen that what is significant about Jesus is not only his solidarity with man and creation but also the things which distinguish him from them. Berdyaev[1] has rightly said that though the very greatest of minds are dependent upon the world-environment, it is not what they receive but what they bring, that is, the new principle, that which had not previously existed in the world, that is of primary importance. History and environment, though they have a contributory importance, are wholly inadequate to explain the appearance of Jesus, and the biological factor of heredity can hardly be invoked with success in the absence of sufficient knowledge about the relation between biological inheritance and the transmission of spiritual qualities. The superlative phraseology of St. Paul's Christological testimonies (in which there is no indication of knowledge of the Virgin Birth) and the matchless narratives at the beginning of the first and third Gospels mean that the Lordship of Jesus is not derived from his unique setting *in* creation but from the creative newness which he, as *Kyrios*, brings to cosmos and creature.

For the 'new' creative force has appeared. It is eschatological and continuous through its *geschichtlich* impact upon mankind. The spiritual creativeness of Jesus does not cease, though it may appear to be intermittent and more in evidence at some times than at others. It is a creativeness which does not have its source in creation, that is, in the phenomenal world, but in the noumenal, the world of spirit. If the Lordship of Jesus is understood in this sense, the doctrine of the Incarnation may be seen to mean the confluence or interpenetration of the divine

[1] *The Beginning and the End*, p. 164.

and the human, of the phenomenal and the noumenal, in a historical personality. Man is inseparable, as a creature, from the cosmos, and because Jesus belonged to creation as well as embodying what is beyond creation, because of his spatio-temporal setting in the world, he, too, was involved in creation. But because he transcends the natural order (for this is the meaning of the Resurrection) and stands over and against man as well as with him and for him, because, that is, he is on God's side as well as on man's, he may be properly described as the *Kyrios* pre-eminent over the cosmos. In Scriptural terms, he is the Lord of all.

It is this that the Birth narratives emphasize in vividly pictorial manner. Their latent as distinguished from their manifest meaning is that Jesus, in the words of the Fourth Gospel, was 'from God'. Without these narratives there would have been the Birth, but no Christmas in the sense of a memorable picturization or dramatization of the occasion which alone is able to preserve the ultimate truth of what they set out to state. In the last analysis we do not know how much is myth and how much factual kernel, embroidered by tradition, they contain. They have become, in a broad sense, Christian archetypes without which thought, ritual, liturgy and doctrine would be impoverished.

4

There remains one further approach to the Birth-narratives: the interpretation which, in Bultmann's view, is appropriate to the translation of mythological thinking into other terms, namely their 'existential' significance. What is the 'existential' impact of mythological thinking about the birth of Jesus? We are, be it observed, not speaking of *fictional* thinking, for the myth may be no less than the divinely appointed means of conveying a truth which is more *geschichtlich* than 'historical'. In other words, if the *Weihnachtswunder*, the Christmas miracle, as Barth calls it, is not *really* and *essentially* about speaking angels, a moving star, royal astrologers, and a celestial choir ('cosmological' details!), what remains? What *is* it about? What it offers is not, judged by modern standards, a coherent intellectual system appealing to the reason, but rather a complex of vivid and memorable pictures which are not only liturgically and emotionally irreplaceable but powerful stimuli to man's self-examination and to the urge to consider whether there is anything in his experience of the structure of being on which they throw light. The propositional statement that 'the Word became flesh' in itself may mean very little. What the Word was, and how it became flesh, and why, are not indicated by the mere affirmation. It is, of course, a statement about the noumenal world entering the phenomenal, the Creator participating personally in His creation, the ineffably holy being embodied in visible holiness, the divine appearing as the human, with all the consequences which this has to our understanding of the nature of existence and our place within it. The Christmas story, in its pictorial form, confronts us with questions about the meaning of historical being; whether it has any relation to anything outside itself; whether the kind of existence which we know, the actual predicament in which we stand, is capable of transformation into a different kind of historical existence, whether the predicament can lose its distortedness, its being charged with all the contradictions of 'in-der-Welt-sein', 'Geworfenheit',[1] and anxiety, which occupy so prominent a place in the analysis of historicality and *Dasein* which Bultmann, following Heidegger, considers to be a truthful account of the structure of being: whether, in a word, we can be lifted out of our 'plight' into an awareness of harmony with the underlying structure of reality. If we cannot, then the New Testament message is meaningless, and its *kerygma* (as Unamuno described faith) a 'preaching in the desert at night',[2] and the hunger of immortality, *el hambre de inmortalidad*, insatiable. That evil remains an obstinate and intractable problem we are compelled to admit, but that the dissociations and dislocations evident in our human plight can be reharmonized is a basic proclamation of the Gospel. Empirically considered, history, as Unamuno believed, is a protesting, agonized, struggling history (*historia agónica*),[3] in need of redemption, and it can be redeemed not through itself but through something wholly other, something

[1] 'Being in the world', 'thrownness' (i.e., being 'thrown' into the world).
[2] *Ensayos*, vol. ii (1900).
[3] A theme which he wrote about in his *Agonía del Cristianismo* (1928).

which is as different from it as the Christmas stories are from naturalistic literature.

Viewed from this standpoint the *Weihnachtswunder* proclaims, in the language of myth (though not of the 'cunningly devised fables' of II Pet. 2: 15), that it is by divine intention and initiative that man is to be rescued from his predicament in his world, from the 'existential' anguish of which Kierkegaard, Unamuno, and Berdyaev have written: that is, through the sanctification of human life and the realization that only when his life *is* sanctified can both personal experience and institutions be delivered from the contradictions which disrupt them. To say this is not to minimize the importance of other approaches to the problems of living: the sociological, political, and technical, for example; it is to assert that, in isolation from faith in the divine transcendence over creation becoming immanent in it in personal terms, these techniques may encounter ultimate frustration.

The Birth narratives, whatever their origin, remain as a point of reference to which man can relate his situation, for their meaning is unmistakable: namely, that, in Brunner's words, 'with Jesus Christ... has come a new consciousness of existence'. Whether man submits to it or not is another matter, just as paying lipservice to the Incarnation through singing Christmas hymns once a year does not necessarily bring the singer into a new relationship to God or to the humanity which, according to the doctrine of the Incarnation, He has hallowed. The mere statement that 'the birth of Jesus Christ was on this wise' (Matt. 1: 18) may, or may not, be a 'factual' indication of how Jesus Christ was born; but the statement alone is a mere statement unless man participates in its meaning through permitting it to confront him with an existential challenge. What Berdyaev says about existentialism may be said to apply to the relation between faith and doctrine if we think of faith as 'subject' and doctrine as 'object'. 'What we for the time being may call existential philosophy,' he says, 'marks a transition from the interpretation of knowledge as objectification to understanding it as a *participation*, union with the subject matter and entering into co-operation with it';[1] and

---

[1] *The Beginning and the End*, p. 61. Cf. G. Marcel, *The Mystery of Being*, II, pp. 112–13. Marcel is writing here of 'objective' and 'non-objective' participation.

New Testament gives is that of one who came down to earth, was victorious over the hosts of evil and through his sacrifice on the cross, conquered the last evil, death, and demonstrated the final impotence of evil before returning to God.

In endeavouring to answer the question raised we shall have to enquire into how far the New Testament world-picture conforms to the mythological character described by Bultmann, into whether there is a truth behind it which both Bultmann and the 'modern' man have insufficiently appreciated, and into the character of the 'victory' of the *Kyrios* over this menaced realm. First of all we shall make some general observations on the problem of evil.

2

The rock which threatens to wreck all our idealisms and which challenges all theologies is the problem of evil. Without it, however, there would be neither idealism nor theology, for idealism is an attempt to overcome frustration and evil through the exercise of faith and hope, and theology is systematic thinking about the God who has intervened in Christ in this world-order which is partly subject to the dominion of evil. In the Gospels Jesus exhibits his power over the 'demons', and in a vivid, strange, apocalyptic saying which has nothing to do with space or time he describes his vision of Satan falling from heaven. The lives of people are ruled by demons until the moment of exorcism; the existence of man continues under the rule of Satan. These alien sovereignties are challenged by the Kingdom of God breaking in through the appearance of His Son. To that extent the New Testament presupposes a cosmic dualism of good and evil. As Berdyaev has said, evil and the fight against it form a dualism with its own 'sinister moral dialectic', for in this fight man himself becomes infected by it; in him the good and the evil encounter one another and interpenetrate. To the question 'What is it?' no clear answer can be given, though it is everywhere perceived phenomenologically as belonging to the structure of existence, 'a horrible fifth or sixth dimension of being' as Barth tellingly describes it.[1] Its elusiveness has frequently been

[1] *Kirchliche Dogmatik*, III/3, p. 619.

commented on.[1] It attacks personality and undermines even the physical creation; yet it is not, in the sense in which the term is usually understood, 'created'; a street or a garden 'goes' bad so that through decay what was once attractive and lovely assumes the form of physical hideousness which in itself exercises a kind of morbid fascination. In every aspect of life: in politics, in personal relationships, as sin, as falsehood, lust for power, the exploitation of sex, as ugliness, natural calamity, accident, cruelty, malignant disease, some forms of death, evil is 'there', and there is evidence of something which might be called primal evil which is prior to and outside 'original' sin. Indeed, evil, whether as a metaphysical problem or a personal, 'existential' experience, is one of the ultimate problems confronting human life; it is *the* problem of existence, and it is antecedent to sin because sin is only the manifestation of it in the human field. On sub-human and pre-human levels, too, there is in evidence this element of destructiveness, of anti-creation, present even in the decay of organic matter and in the corrosion of the inorganic as well as in the more elusive 'sinister' as a quality immanent in things. Whether as Barth's *Nichtig* or as Tillich's *Dämonische*,[2] or whether it is simply designated as the 'bad', there is what Tillich describes as a 'form-destroying irruption from the creative depths of things'. This 'evil', too, is as incapable of precise analysis as was the demonic according to Goethe's description of it to Eckermann as something which 'cannot be analysed by the understanding and intelligence',[3] though we are aware of it when it faces us. And if suffering, the sense of tension, estrangement, anxiety, and incompleteness are forms of evil, certain aspects of existentialist philosophy suggest that its exponents are somewhat sombrely preoccupied with these expressions of it. Heidegger in particular abounds in expressions such as 'die Unheimlichkeit des Daseins

---

[1] This is what Barth means when he says that the *Nichtige* lacks *Bestand* (substance). So also Brunner: 'It is of the essence of the power of darkness that it does not reveal itself, although it manifests itself. . . . It defies definition because it refuses to come out into the open and be made manifest.' 'It loves and understands the art of dissimulation, of camouflage' (*Dogmatics*, II, p. 143). H. Thielicke writes of its 'anonymity'. The demonic power hides itself behind an angelic mask. The Tempter never says, 'Come, let me instruct you in sin,' but offers the temptation in an attractive form (*Fragen des Christentums an die Moderne Welt*, pp. 198 ff.).

[2] *Das Dämonische: ein Beitrag zur Sinndeutung der Geschichte.*

[3] *Gespräche*, 2. 3. 1831.

als die Drohung', 'das Sein des Daseins als Sorge'; references to 'das Un-zuhause', 'Sein zum Tode', are instances of a Wagnerian preoccupation with doom and death as existential factors of primary importance.[1] Kierkegaard's *Angst*, Unamuno's *congoja*, and the existential eros-anguish of Berdyaev, are other examples, though the latter is free from the pessimistic Teutonic gloom of Heidegger, whom he describes as 'perhaps the most extreme pessimist in the history of philosophic thought in the west'.[2] Nevertheless, the feeling of estrangement, of the evil of not being able to fit in, the awareness of one's 'Un-zuhause', is one of the primary causes of unhappiness.

Indeed, it is this fact of estrangement, of the separation of subject and object, which existentialist philosophy finds itself obliged to take into account, for in it, and in the objectification of the subject, is found the exteriorization or alienation of the spirit from the world and from itself.[3] It reaches its peak precisely in the objectification of the subject, that is to say, when the subject is no longer treated as a subject but as a thing and is so treated in its encounter with the most ruthless of all forces, evil, which is at the same time the most radical challenge to any theodicy.

For it is in his encounter with evil that man knows himself to be at the mercy of something over which he has no control: whether he is the victim of the disease which preys upon him just as a metal is eaten away by corrosion or as an animal is consumed alive by maggots, or whether he is tortured by his fellow-man and thus comes to be regarded as no more than a means to an end such as the provision of information required by the torturer. He is aware of being a subject (otherwise he would not be aware at all) and at the same time he knows that he is being treated as an object, and it is this knowledge which exposes him to the full existential significance of the fact of evil. He is aware of the evil of evil, of evil *as* evil, precisely because it causes him to question fundamentally the character of the existence of which he is aware as subject. The animal may be aware of pain

---

[1] *Sein und Zeit*, § 39–53. These phrases may be translated as 'the sinisterness of existence (being) as menace', 'anxiety as the essence of Being', 'not-being-at-home', 'living' or 'Being towards death'.
[2] *The Beginning and the End*, p. 116.
[3] *The Beginning and the End*, p. 116.

as a sensation, but because he lacks the capacity for reflection and ideation he is most probably unaware of it as an evil. If tortured he reacts, physically, as does a person, because of the similarity of his nervous system, but, though he knows terror, he is not aware of the pain as torture, as is a person, for torture is the infliction of pain by a subject on another subject either for pleasure or as a means of extracting information or as punishment and is the expression of a definite purpose and the instrument of its fulfilment.

Similarly, as far as is known, disease is not an evil from the standpoint of the bacillus which causes it; it may even be a good in so far as it enables it to fulfil the law of its own being. It is not an evil for the animal unable to reflect upon it: it is a form of suffering. For a person a disease is an evil because, like any other form of evil, it compels him to ask questions about the universe, compelling him, above all, to ask why he is dealt with as a thing of no account by a form of life which he considers only as an unnecessary object. To be wholly in another person's power is perhaps the worst form of evil, for in this case the subject becomes in every sense an object, unable, in the depth of utter derelection, to affect his situation by an act of will through the exercise of his freedom or, as a personality, to transcend that situation. In Heidegger's terms, as a being with *Dasein* he is treated as if he were only *vorhanden* or *zuhanden*, numbered but not named, an instrument of policy.

According to the biblical conception of existence sin is man's rebellion against God, though evil was prior to sin. The serpent was already in the Garden (presumably as one of God's creatures) before the fruit was eaten. Sin was in this way the result of anterior evil, not the cause of it, for evil, in the biblical myth, is that which causes man to sin and to rebel against his Creator. As myth this biblical narrative about man in rebellion against God remains valid in a way in which an apodictic statement about it could not be, for it describes evil dramatically and exhibits it both as glamour and suffering, in its disguise and in its reality. This is true of the biblical attitude towards evil as a whole, for in the lurid glamour of paganism and of the *femme fatale* such as Delilah or Jezebel as well as in the merciless, impersonal,

Satanic evil which afflicts the Adamic paradise and afflicts Job, there is exposed in a memorable manner the universality and the desperateness of the human predicament. The Gospel narrative, too, throws into terrifying relief the ultimate consequences of political, ecclesiastical, and personal evil in the crucifixion of the Son of God, whose most solemn prayer was that man should be delivered from evil. Not only human experience but biblical testimony shows that evil is something 'there', antecedent to us, waiting for us, like a trap into which we walk or like the sinister darkness facing the Knight in Dürer's *Ritter, Tod, und Teufel*: hideous, menacing, and palpable. Whether it is a distortion of the will, or something with an objective, independent, 'personal' existence as it is depicted in the allegedly mythological language of the New Testament, are questions which demand answers, though whether anything approaching definitive answers can be offered is doubtful. Like the thing itself, the problems involved elude solution. Yet if, according to Christian belief, the Lordship of Jesus over creation implies his Lordship over a realm dominated in great part by evil, by the power of darkness, 'the prince of the power of the air', and therefore over the dominion of evil, the resources of systematic Christian thinking should be at our disposal in our endeavour to disentangle the complicated issues which emerge from our consideration of this most intractable of all religious and philosophical problems.

It is this intractable and elusive character of evil which makes it such a baffling and, apparently, insoluble problem and something more ultimate even than Kant's 'radical evil' and the will which is evil in spite of itself referred to in the seventh chapter of the Epistle to the Romans. For it is not merely an affair of the will or of the whole personality: it is anterior to these because we recognize in the evil decision or the evil act a manifestation of something ulterior of which they are the manifestation; for evil, we maintain, and to this Barth's conception of the *Nichtig*[1] lends support, is an aspect of existence much wider than the personal, much more comprehensive, even, than the notion of moral evil. The gaping abyss of nothingness, the sinister emptiness of the

---

[1] *Kirchliche Dogmatik*, III/1, pp. 426 ff., III/3, pp. 327–425, pp. 608 ff., where Barth discusses at length the *Nichtig* as the anti-creational principle. The terms

surrealist pictures of Giorgio di Chirico or Dali, the experience of the sinister as such, testify to a quality or activity fundamentally irrational and universally pervasive. As Brunner pointedly says, 'the more anyone knows what evil is, the more inexplicable does it become';[1] and though it is true that a man who has not yet perceived that evil 'is intertwined with the very roots of his personality' is a superficial person,[2] it is also true that he is equally superficial if he does not perceive that it is intertwined with the roots of existence. As a problem it can be solved neither philosophically nor theologically: one can do little more than analyse it phenomenologically and speculate and accept it as a structural element in creation. It is certain that it cannot be dismissed or treated, as some idealistic philosophy is regarded as treating it, as a prolegomenon to good or even, with Barth, as a *Schattenseite*, a 'shadow-side', of experience or as belonging to God's 'left hand'. It can, however, be overcome in its personal form and, if the spirit is strong enough, transcended in its impersonal form. But as far as we know it is unlikely to be abolished short of the final 'redemption' of creation, a conception which, we have contended, is difficult, if not impossible, to accommodate to satisfactory rational definition. That is why more realistic and frank thinking about the Christian doctrine of redemption and the conception of the Lordship of Christ over the dominion of evil is required. Both Barth and Berdyaev, and we might add Thielicke, tend to personalize, that is to say to 'mythologize', evil through attributing to it a kind of Satanism which deliberately mocks the divine (the 'myth of all mythologies', Barth calls the demons); they regard it as having only apparent power, though they at the same time admit its actuality, and agree that the victory over evil is achieved through the Cross. If Jesus is

---

which he uses are 'mythological', especially in the section on angels and demons. His discussion is very valuable in drawing attention to the ambiguous and dialectical character of evil and has points of contact with Berdyaev's treatment of the same theme. Cf. N. Berdyaev, *Freedom and the Spirit*, chap. 5, *The Destiny of Man*, chap. 2, *The Divine and the Human*, pp. 80 ff., *Spirit and Reality*, pp. 100 ff., *The Beginning and the End*, pp. 141 ff., and *passim*. He denies that there can be an ontology of evil, though it has existential significance. (Cf. my article, 'God and Negation', in the *Scottish Journal of Theology*, Sept. 1954, for an exposition of Barth's *Dogmatik*, III/3, § 50.)

[1] *The Mediator*, p. 144.
[2] Ibid., p. 141.

the victor, then the *Nichtig*, the evil opposed to God and creation or issuing from the depths of 'meonic' darkness, has no final power, and its reign is, finally, illusory. What we have to discuss is whether this is really so, or whether it is in turn the expression of a mythological approach to the problem of evil and the victory over it, and how far, first of all, the New Testament picture of evil is mythological in the sense in which Bultmann conceives the term.

3

In the New Testament world evil is neither elusive, ambivalent, nor abstract, but something with which man is able to come to grips. While, as we have indicated, the problem presents itself to some modern thinkers as having to do with something resembling a Japanese wrestler smeared from head to foot with grease in order to enable him to elude his opponent's grip, for the New Testament people it resembled the boxer who, though formidable enough, can be tackled by frontal attack and be knocked out. Indeed, in one way or another Jesus as the victor over evil has been represented as the one who deals evil, in the form of Satan, if not exactly a knockout blow, at any rate the decisive blow which from the moment of its delivery places the opponent at a permanent disadvantage. This is what is implied, for example, by Cullmann's interpretation of the Cross as a kind of D-day which is the prelude to the ultimate Victory-day.[1] For the Apostolic writers, as for Jesus himself, evil was not a philosophical conception or a metaphysical problem: it was essentially something very definite to be dealt with there and then. The hosts of wickedness were not concepts to be speculated about but an immediate 'existential' challenge to be accepted and enemies to be fought and defeated.

The striking thing, however, about the New Testament is not that it confronts us with a wide range of mythological representation of evil and its source but rather its restraint. A world-view as impregnated with mythological thinking as Bultmann alleges might be expected to intrude itself into almost every page of the New Testament, whereas what is noticeable is its

---

[1] *Christ and Time*, p. 141.

infrequency, though the 'mythical' character of the realm of evil is presupposed by it, but hardly more so than appears in Barth's chapter on angelology.[1] The mythological background is there, and though it emerges at unexpected points, it is not excessively conspicuous. Paul refers to 'bondage to beings that by nature are not gods' (Gal. 4: 8), the 'weak and beggarly elemental spirits', the 'elemental spirits of the universe' (Col. 2: 8, 20). There is a curious passage in I Corinthians 10 (vv. 20–21) referring to pagan sacrifice to 'demons' and admonishing the Corinthians not to drink the 'cup of the demons' and pointing out that partaking of the table of the Lord is incompatible with partaking of the 'table of the demons' ($\delta\alpha\iota\mu\text{ov}\iota\omega\nu$). His visit to Thessalonika was hindered by 'Satan' (I Thess. 2: 18). There are references to 'principalities and powers in the heavenly places' (Eph. 3: 10, 6: 11 ff) against whom, in contrast to 'flesh and blood', we contend. In II Thessalonians 2: 3 there is a strange passage about the 'man of lawlessness, the son of perdition', who may well be anti-Christ and whom the Lord will slay with 'the breath of his mouth' and whose activity is caused by Satan 'with all power and with pretended signs and wonders'. II Peter 2: 4, and Jude 6 refer to the rebellious angels cast into the nether gloom, and I Timothy 4: 1 speaks of those who depart from the faith 'by giving heed to deceitful spirits and doctrines of demons'. According to I John 3: 8 'the devil has sinned from the beginning', and the reasons for the appearance of the Son of God was the destruction of 'the works of the devil'. The author writes about the overcoming of 'the evil one' by the recipients of his letter (2: 13). The existence of the devil and of evil spirits who are thought of as his entourage is taken for granted; indeed, it is difficult to imagine how the reality of evil as a universal force could be otherwise represented than by personal objectification, even though its embodiments are apparent only in disguise, for Satan is a 'deceiver' (Matt. 4: 1 ff.; Rev. 12: 9; II Thess. 2: 9), and evil spirits (I Tim. 4: 1) are deceitful; the wicked one is mischievous (Matt. 13: 19, etc.). The Satanic legions, the demons, are responsible for mental illness, which is attributed to extra-personal causes.

[1] *Kirchliche Dogmatik*, III/3, pp. 426–623.

On the other hand, it should be stated that the New Testament is not wholly concerned with the objectification of the source of evil, which is thought of as endogenic as well as exogenic in origin. 'Sin is lawlessness' (I John 3: 4). Paul writes with great force about evil as the perversion of natural impulses (Rom. 1: 24–31), of the will as the seat of evil actions and decisions (Rom. 7: 13 ff.), and of the 'flesh' as the symbol of whatever wars against man's higher nature. The robust, realistic Epistle of James sees in desire the cause of evil actions: 'each person is tempted when he is lured and enticed by his own desires' (1: 14); evil, both social and individual, has its source in the mind (4: 1), and Jesus attributes wickedness to the evil imagination (Mark 7: 18 ff.). II Peter 2: 12 comments on the evil, disruptive activities of 'irrational animals, born of instinct', that is, those who pervert natural instincts: a passage which is also a condemnation of antinomianism, though the relevance of the whole passage is not very clear. The absence of references to the Adamic myth, too, is surprising in the light of the formidable place which this mythological picture has occupied in Christian theology.

If explicitly mythological references to evil are, on the whole (we are not considering the Apocalypse), not conspicuously frequent in the New Testament, though the demon-world is assumed, neither are allusions to the Lordship of Jesus over the Kingdom of evil, though it is clearly implied. John (I. 3: 8) gives as the reason for the Incarnation the destruction of the works of the devil, and according to Colossians 1: 13 God has 'delivered us from the dominion of darkness and transferred us to the kingdom of His dear Son'. In Hebrews 2: 14 Jesus is described as having partaken of human nature 'that through death he might destroy the power of death, that is, the devil'. I Peter 3: 22 refers to Jesus 'who is gone into heaven, and is on the right hand of God; angels and authorities and powers being made subject to him', which Cullmann considers to be an early Christian confession.[1] Underlying the whole of the New Testament, however, is the fundamental assumption of the delivering work of Jesus the

---

[1] *The Earliest Christian Confessions*, p. 60. The same kind of confessional formula is also found in Polycarp, Ignatius, and Justin, who explicitly refers to the 'subjection of every demon' and to Jesus as 'Lord of the demons'.

Saviour, for it is he who has empowered man to overcome evil, as he himself overcomes the Tempter and his demons, just as the demons are exorcized by his followers (Acts 16: 16 and elsewhere). The Cross is hardly as 'mythological' as Bultmann would have us believe, and there is little suggestion of that curious conception of the Atonement as a kind of 'transaction' or as a deceptive trick to cheat the devil: notions which are foreign to Apostolic thinking and which have in the past doubtless been responsible for so much false interpretation of the Gospel.

It is in the concrete encounters of Jesus with 'possessed' persons that the most impressive evidence is found of his power over 'mythologically' objectified evil, for it is here that he is shown to be casting out devils 'by the finger of God', and even if from the aetiological standpoint the Gospel presentation of evil in action, in actual possession of a person, is questionable as a description it is above criticism, and so far the investigation of possession as a psychopathological symptom has not led to a fully satisfactory explanation.[1] As the belief in 'demons' is regarded by Bultmann as one of the chief constituents of the mythological thinking of the New Testament, it is necessary to devote some space to its examination.

The phenomenon of demoniacal possession, so accurately described in the Gospels, in particular in the case of the Gadarene demoniac, should not be dismissed without further discussion by attributing belief in it to the primitive outlook of people naturally disposed by environment and tradition to regard it as a supernatural explanation of abnormal behaviour. In the words of M. J. Richet, possession is 'the invasion by the demon of the body of a living man, whose organs he exercises in his own name and at will, as if the body had become his'. 'In possession the spirit acts from within and seems to be substituted in the body for the soul

[1] Cf. H. J. S. Guntrip, 'Psychoanalysis and Exorcism', *The Congregational Quarterly*, April, 1952; T. Hawthorn, 'The Gerasene Demoniac: a Diagnosis', *The Expository Times*, December 1954. The latter article examines the case as that of a schizophrenic. In their book *The Devil* (E. trans. Gollancz, 1929), which approaches the problem of the Devil historically and medically, the authors, Maurice Garçon and Jean Vinchon, describe possession as 'demonic neurosis' and as a state of mind characterized by demonic fantasies and confusional insanity (pp. 169–275). Their question, Why are these patients demoniacs rather than mystics? suggests that there is something more behind the tendency to demoniac possession than mere psychic disturbance; otherwise why should not the disturbance assume a 'good' form?

which animates and moves it.'[1] This succinct definition accurately describes the examples of possession followed by exorcism in the Gospels, the truthfulness of which need not be questioned. K. T. Oesterreich has shown, in his detailed study of the subject, how general is this phenomenon, though he points out that it occurs chiefly in primitive societies and among uneducated individuals.

Oesterreich cites a large number of instances of demoniacal possession of various kinds which have this in common, that in all of them there seems to be an 'evil' personality (never a good one) either side by side with a normal one or actually taking its place, inducing automatic action and using the speech-organs of the patient (as in the cases of possession in the Gospels). A girl, for example, speaks with a man's voice, for which there would seem to be no physiological explanation. A decent person is transformed against his will into a hideous, raving, evil demoniac. 'This develops in the psyche a sort of secondary personality which directs the person's life against his will.'[2] For the time being, however, the personality is not secondary but dominant, and only exorcism is able to expel it. Janet[3] succeeded in 'exorcizing' a case of possession by the clever psychological method of somnambulistic suggestion, and held that the seat of possession was the unconscious. Oesterreich does not accept the assumption that a person is 'possessed' by 'demons', but seeks a psychological explanation which may be found in either auto- or heterosuggestion, hallucination, or guilt-consciousness. Its incidence is usually among people who already believe in possession. Although it is true that some cases might be accounted for in this way, this does not by any means explain the phenomenon of possession as a whole, and Oesterreich admits that the deep-seated effects of exorcism, as far as any descriptive accuracy is possible, are elusive, and that the mere affirmation of the connection between faith and the changes which it is thought to produce cannot be scientifically substantiated.

Between the two ways of accounting for demoniacal possession —either as endogenic or as exogenic—there is a profound

---

[1] *La Mystique Divine*, 1883, III, pp. 191 ff., 179, quoted by K. T. Oesterreich, *Possession, Demoniacal and Other* (E. trans. Kegan Paul, 1930, p. 83).

[2] *Possession*, p. 65.

[3] Ibid., p. 110, where this long treatment is described in detail.

difference. According to the former it is a manifestation of psychic abnormality, attributable, possibly, to the dissolution of the ego, whereas according to the latter it is the consequence of the actual indwelling by an objective spirit in the personality, which it for the time being completely transforms. In both cases the results are the same. The one, however, does not take account, as does the other, of evil as an independent force fundamentally distorting the normal personality, and, indeed, the characteristics of demoniacal possession are such that the psychological explanation (for example, of possession as a form of hystero-epilepsy or schizophrenia) are, within the limitations of present knowledge, inadequate. Some contemporary practitioners of divine healing, though they may not be professional psychologists, are convinced of the reality of the evil spirits which they have driven out by exorcism 'in the name of the Lord Jesus'. One who has spent many years in the East, and who has described to me cases in which he has practised exorcism with success, believes that he has actually 'seen' demons, and, though an Anglican clergyman, was on one occasion possessed during exorcism by a demon which left the patient only to invade him. J. M. Hickson, too,[1] describes how a woman who had tried to help an 'obsessed' maid was herself plunged into the same condition, and relates the distant exorcism by rebuke at a service in Tokio, in which case a woman had suddenly become 'out of mind, violent, and unmanageable'.[2] Hickson's book abounds in instances, described in detail, in which patients, chiefly women, and even including a baby who suddenly became hideously possessed, were cured by prayer and by the rebuke of the evil spirit 'in the name of Christ'. My informant has seen the same thing happen in mental hospitals where he has practised exorcism.

It should be emphasized that when confronted by such cases Christian 'healers' do not regard them as cases of psychical abnormality such as paranoia or schizophrenia. 'Where one is dealing with cases of obsession and possession,' J. M. Hickson writes, 'one is opposed by forces more subtle and more powerful than when dealing with physical diseases.' 'One felt the opposition

---

[1] *Behold, the Bridegroom Cometh*, 1937, p. 183.
[2] Ibid., p. 54.

of the powers of darkness.'[1] It is, indeed, difficult to understand how a baby in arms could display the symptoms of possession merely if it were an endogenic disturbance, and why it should have become normal again after exorcism, for it is questionable if a baby could respond in the same way as an adult, in which case the condition might conceivably have been the result of repressed guilt or heterosuggestion. A baby is unlikely to have been responsive to heterosuggestion, and is too young to produce symptoms of possession through guilt-repression and in any case would not entertain any belief predisposing it to accept the possibility of demoniac possession.[2]

Now, whether demoniacal possession is attributable to endogenic or exogenic causes, it presents the problem of evil in an acute form, for no phenomenon of 'angelic' possession is known. If the former, we must assume some kind of evil potency in the ego itself, even if the theory is advanced that, because the ego is not subject to the dimension of space and time, it can exist in a 'fluid' state and make contact at a deep unconscious level with another ego which can transfer its characteristics to the first. Possession, on any showing, is evil. The perversion and dislocation of the personality which it causes would appear to occur without any question of volition. The phenomenon poses the perplexing problem of the structure of the ego and of its stability,[3] even though it may be considered to be a form of psychic aberration. Though the symptoms are those of advanced lunacy, it is amenable to treatment, usually instantaneous, whereas the latter is not, except, possibly, by such a drastic method as leucotomy. It is this factor, more than any other, perhaps, which places possession in a category different from that of ordinary mental disease.

---

[1] Hickson, p. 137.

[2] Psychologists would probably attribute this kind of condition to the result of pre-natal shock or some such cause. This, however, does not explain it away: it only offers a different explanation. See further, a little brochure, *Signs Following* (Elim Publication Co., 1952), by W. F. P. Burton, a missionary in West Africa, who describes in detail the case of a woman who became 'possessed' after confessing her faith publicly; also L. D. Weatherhead, *Religion, Psychology, and Healing*, 1951, pp. 97 ff.

[3] The extraordinary case of a man whose sex completely changed and who had to re-register as a woman (*The Glasgow Herald*, 6 March 1954) suggests the possibility that, although such cases are unusual, the ego as such is an unstable entity, a supposition which confronts the Christian doctrines of creation and of providence with a difficult problem.

If, however, the exogenic explanation is accepted, as it was by Jesus and as it is by some Christian healers, profound metaphysical problems are raised. If demons exist in space, and can at any moment 'take over' a personality, by whose permission do they exist? Are they discarnate spirits? Does their existence not imply a dualism which Christian theology, enlightened by scientific thinking, is unwilling to admit, though it is clearly indicated in the New Testament? And if it is contended that it is chiefly among the ignorant that cases of possession are found, may not this be so because the barriers to resistance are likely to be weaker than in more developed societies and individuals? And there still remains the appalling experience of a very large number of people under National Socialism in Germany made capable of performing atrocities of such magnitude that 'ordinary' human evil seems to be an inadequate explanation of their ingenuity, extent, and calculated viciousness. It should be added, further, that whereas a complicated case of psychic abnormality is treated by a highly skilled practitioner over a usually lengthy period of time, and then not necessarily successfully, the Christian exorcist, assuming that the cause of the condition is exogenic, namely objective, discarnate evil, treats the patient on this assumption, and where results are obtained, they are usually immediate. If, however, this assumption is accepted, it means that we are left with the possibility of a polydaemonistic universe: a conclusion with far-reaching results for theology and somewhat startling consequences for the exponent of the view that the New Testament representation of evil is purely mythological.

For the dispassionate psychologist the term 'demoniacal possession', though it describes a fact of experience, belongs to the terminology of myth. If there are no 'demons', then to attribute a condition to their activity implies a belief in a mythological view of the world, and if there is no such thing as 'possession', discussion of it is unprofitable. If belief in such possession is a form of mythical attitude no longer possible for sophisticated man, and it is in fact to be equated with a superstition which psychology will in due course expose and fully explain, it is not easy to see how Jesus can be regarded as 'Lord' over a world peopled by imaginary spiritual beings.

If, on the other hand, the exogenic explanation of demoniacal possession as a condition caused by the actual taking over of a personality is accepted, Jesus' ascendancy over a demon-ridden world is established. He ordered demons to come out of people, and they obeyed. He perceived that the distress of those whom he was about to exorcize was not due to physical or psychical causes (though hystero-epilepsy may have been its accompaniment) but to the actual presence (as was thought) of something from a different dimension of being, namely from the world of darkness. His encounters with the possessed left him in possession of the field. In this sense he may be thought of as the Lord of a world in which the powers of evil, in this particular form, were quelled and defeated.

That the demons have been routed, however, is manifestly not the case, for neither Cross nor Resurrection has succeeded in putting them permanently to flight, and theological language which suggests this is misleading. For it is here that the mythological character of the idea becomes apparent. The Son of God comes down from heaven, encounters the demonic forces of evil, is crucified by them, but through his Resurrection, and through rebuking the demons in his earthly encounters with them, he defeats the armies of the demon-world and rescues man from their domination. This is the implication of much of the New Testament, and if this is what is meant by the Lordship of Jesus over evil it must be admitted that it is mythological thinking which takes little account of things as they are. For if 'defeat' means anything it means the complete surrender, disintegration, or decimation of the foe. Of such defeat there is no evidence, and positive affirmations about it, such as are found in the New Testament and in the writings of the early Fathers, can only be described as naïve and as originating in a mental world very different from that of the twentieth century.

Nevertheless, it would appear that the occurrence of demoniacal possession in the sense in which we have used the terms is regressive. 'As regards the extra-European world,' Oesterreich writes, 'manifestations of possession are everywhere in regression in primitive peoples in places *where the Christian missions have struck root*', the reason for this being that 'they inspire the natives with trust in God and free them from the fear of demons and their attacks on the souls of the living'.[1] To that extent it may be claimed that the Lordship of Christ, when acknowledged, means that the demons withdraw or that, when people cease to fear them or to believe in them, they are seen to have no existence or at any rate no power. It may mean, on the other hand, that the powers of evil have taken up new positions, and, in some way which cannot be defined, pervert scientists into inventing incomparable methods of mass-destruction and the politicians into devising new methods of disrupting nations and enslaving sections of their people, and deep below the conscious life of any person there lurk forces whose potency for evil is unpredictable, though only in a relatively few instances do these forces emerge with full and devastating power. Quite apart from the question of demoniacal possession the problem is given greater depth by the fact that, where rational restraint no longer operates, as for example in senile degeneration of the brain, a patient who was formerly kind and loving becomes violent, foul-mouthed, and abusive towards those whom he most loved. Anyone such as Berdyaev who denies the possibility of an ontology of evil is left with the question of what it is which predisposes a person thus to degenerate into a condition which is virtually sub-animal and is not only, from the medical point of view, pathological, but evil in its manifestation and consequences.

The Christian prayer, moreover, remains: Deliver us from evil. It is a prayer with continuous relevance to the human predicament precisely because evil has *not* been conquered but on the contrary is still there and apparently inexhaustible. It is not in the least 'mythical', despite the picturesque language with which it has been clothed. There is nothing mythical about arrogance, greed, lust, and vice, which are not exorcized in the same way as one possessed of the devil. Jesus himself was far less successful with them than with the demoniacs, who, according to the Gospel narratives, were more amenable to treatment. Even though the investigation of forms of evil such as possession opens up many vistas into the fields of anthropology and parapsychology, the thing itself does not disappear. The mystery remains, and the

[1] Op. cit., p. 379. Italics mine.

ultimate question seems to be unanswerable and the problem is insoluble in rational terms.

Further: even though it may be granted that the New Testament thinks 'mythologically' about evil, objectifying it naïvely in the form of demonic beings able to usurp the place of reason and to break up the unity of personality, it should also be stated that there are good reasons for believing that its representation of evil is far from being a fiction of the superstitious imagination. Possession is an observed phenomenon, and it always assumes an evil form. Psychoanalysis may describe the phenomenon in non-religious terms, yet, however accurate its description, it does little more than describe it and offer a methodology of treatment. The evil still remains evil, and its character and impact are such that the New Testament categories are as satisfactory a means of accounting for it as any. The insights of Jesus, explicable no doubt as reflecting the ideas of the age, may be profounder than the explanations offered by psychologists; for it is at least possible —to put it no higher—that man is set not only in a material but in a spiritual world: one which is actually peopled by evil forces of whose origin nothing is known yet whose existence is nevertheless real.

If this is so, it is in the realm of the spiritual that evil forces are to be defeated, and the declaration of the New Testament— however repugnant this may be to the modern man who considers himself to be emancipated from 'mythological' thinking—is that victory over them can be assured only by belief in the Cross and Resurrection. Nevertheless, in the final instance the field over which the Lordship of Jesus is exercised is the moral world of the individual. It is through the defeat of evil in him that his Lordship is practically acknowledged and exercised. The problem of evil—the problem of the demonic, of sub-human evil, of the tragic —is, and is likely to remain, intractable. Why it is there at all is a question to which no satisfactory answer—least of all a non-mythological one—can be given in the present state of knowledge. It is a mystery as great as the ultimate mystery of what lies beyond evil and tragedy, of what lies beyond death.

4

The Lordship of Jesus, then, does not mean that evil has been abolished. It does not even mean that it has been brought to a standstill as an army is fought to a standstill. It does not mean that man can sit down in his 'border situation', as Tillich calls it, and contemplate the retreating forces of evil, the dissolution of the sinister, and the demonic perversion of the good. The Christian belief in the Lordship of Jesus does not mean that there is no more to be done just because the 'final' or decisive battle has been fought. Rather does it mean that the war continues and will be waged effectively on the human level only by those who acknowledge his Lordship, for they alone have an understanding of evil for what it really is: a form of rebellion against God or, as the *Nichtig*, that which God does not desire and which exists in defiance of Him.

According to the New Testament it is the 'armour of God' which provides the Christian with protection. His strength in the Lord is the assurance that, even though he does not put the powers of evil to flight, he will at least be able to withstand them, even if, in the last resort, he appears to succumb to them. It may be that, *for the Christian*, the decisive battle has been fought, on his behalf, by Jesus, but that the rest of time will be required before the full strategic consequences are realized. But this, too, is translating the problem into mythological, or at any rate into metaphorical, terms.

In point of fact, however, it would seem that only in so far as man deals personally with evil in individual situations can it be successfully encountered, just as Jesus, in the 'mythological' language of the Gospels, deals with the demons personally and individually in terms of an actual situation. Whether demythologized or not, evil confronts man with its full vigour in the most malignant forms, no matter by what names he may call it. The Karamazovs will recur, though an Alyosha may be exempt from the taint. Alyosha is untouched both by the Karamazov heritage of evil and by the glamour of Grushenka, the *femme fatale*. Whether Dostoievsky intended his novel to be understood in this way or not is not known; but it seems clear that the one who is capable of withstanding the tremendous onslaught of evil is he who receives strength from the divine-human *agape* by means of which he transcends both the evil and the tragedy of his family's destiny.

It is in such transcendence that the so-called 'victory' over evil consists, not in some imagined 'battle' as a result of which 'evil' is defeated. Sub-human or microbic evil is not 'defeated' in this sense by the Cross, although it is a substantial part of the total picture of evil. Some forms of evil will be removed by various scientific techniques and other secular methods. The evil of disease will be removed, if at all, by scientific research operating independently of any acknowledgment of the Lordship of Jesus, even though many of those who have been concerned in the attack on disease in the primitive communities of Africa and the East have been led to dedicate themselves to the work by their Christian faith. And if Barth really means that the Cross represents the defeat of evil,[1] he is using 'mythological' terms which are manifestly not true, and Cullmann's idea of D-day may mean very little when subjected to close examination; for there is little analogy between a D-day followed by Victory day after a year or two and the D-day of the Cross followed by 'victory' after an interval of time so great that it cannot be calculated. Cullmann admits that the war 'must still be carried on for an undefined time';[2] but it is the undefinable character of the time which weakens the force of his metaphor. Only in retrospect, when the war is over, can the decisive battle be recognized, and even so each battle, as part of a pattern or series, even a lost battle, may be seen to possess decisive significance as a nexus in a continuous chain of events. In so far as Barth and Cullmann have created the impression that what they mean is that evil has been defeated on the Cross and that from that time on all that has happened is a series of mopping-up operations and skirmishes, their thought has been misleading; and Brunner has been guilty of the same kind of exaggeration in saying that 'the hostile forces have been thoroughly deprived of their power by the Cross and

---

[1] Barth, for example, describes the *Nichtig* as the 'monster' which 'has passed away in Jesus Christ' (*K.D.* III/3, p. 419) and adds that the Kingdom of the *Nichtig* 'is destroyed'. On no showing can this be said to be the case, nor can it be said that the *Nichtig* should be considered as 'abolished' (p. 421).

[2] *Christ and Time*, p. 84.

Resurrection', a statement so manifestly untrue that he hastens to modify it by adding that 'their actual resistance still continues. It continues in those who do not "bow the knee" to Jesus, who do not believe in him, who do not obey him; it continues in those invisible regions which form the background of human sin; it continues most evidently in the still unbroken dominion of death, the Last Enemy'.[1] That is to say, the 'hostile forces' have not been 'thoroughly deprived of their power'; indeed, they continue their operations on as large a scale as ever. It is erroneous of Brunner, too, to regard death as the 'last enemy', for, as we have already stated, it is as natural as a conclusion to life as is birth as its beginning. It is an 'enemy' only in certain circumstances; for it is part of the divine order of creation and is the gateway to eternal life. Although such sentiments have been frequently expressed in theology and in piety, they are nevertheless misleading and require more careful examination than has hitherto been accorded to them. Evil is still rampant: it has not been defeated. For what Brunner really admits is that there is no such thing as an automatic overcoming of evil *in general* and that the Cross cannot be thought of as working *ex opere operato*; evil is defeated only in him who acknowledges the Lordship of Jesus. There is no vicarious defeat of evil. The 'battle' is not won by proxy, even if that proxy is the Lord himself. The conflict continues, for the demons, to use language which may or may not be mythological, are still active. The *Nichtig* may give ground, the demons may shudder, but they do not disappear.

It is clear that it is the 'mythological' language of the New Testament which represents Jesus as Lord of the demons which has led to so much false thinking about the relation of the Cross to the dominion of evil. If the Lordship of Jesus over evil is a notion to which content can be given, it is in its relevance to the personal world, for neither the incursion of the Kingdom of God nor the Resurrection will prevent the stoat from killing the rabbit or the malaria parasite from battening on man, and it is difficult to see what relationship the Lordship of Jesus has to the fact of the syphilis spirochete, a form of microbic evil whose depredations are cured not by the sacrifice on the Cross but by penicillin

[1] *Dogmatics*, II, p. 301.

treatment. In case this kind of criticism is thought to be trivial, let it be said that it arises from the too literal acceptance of mythological thinking of the New Testament and of conventional theology particularly by the biblical theologians. Of this the quotations from Barth and Brunner should be sufficient evidence. For it is by means of the transcendence of evil rather than through direct onslaught, through the power given to resist and rise above it, that the conquest of evil is achieved.[1] Stated paradoxically, it means that even in being overwhelmed by evil the Christian may at the same time be victorious over it. Indeed, the problem cannot be approached without paradox, for the Cross, as the New Testament realized, is itself the supreme paradox.

It is this paradox of victory through submergence, through the transcendence of the very predicament which engulfs the victim, the paradox of Gretchen and Antigone, that throws light on the 'victory' of the Cross and the 'defeat' of the demons. It is, indeed, inherent in all great tragedy and distinguishes it, in its literary expression, from mere melodrama or disaster. Karl Jaspers contends that it is this factor of transcendence which differentiates it from a mere story of grief, misery, misfortune, and failure, and that in order to be distinguished from them tragedy, or the tragic point of view, must be 'anchored in metaphysics'. In other words, the tragic situation is not entirely meaningless and is such that the victim is not only the victim but also he who transcends it. Doom is not empty, meaningless doom: it has to do with the atonement of guilt if it is truly tragic doom. In Jaspers' view disaster as such is not tragedy, and tragedy is not wholly disaster. It is only disaster when it excludes the factor of transcendence, and then, by definition, it ceases to be disaster. Tragic knowledge, however, is deeper than mere knowledge of the fact of evil, for it knows that 'even in his last and most important strongholds of ostensible success and ostensible security man is forsaken and abandoned to the bottomless',[2] though tragic visions and perspectives 'contain a hidden philosophy, for they lend

[1] Dr. Elie Cohen, in his book *Human Behaviour in the Concentration Camp* (1953), has stated that the victims best equipped with the qualities which enabled them to survive the horrors of the camps were the Christians and the Communists: that is, those who possessed an attitude of mind which made it possible for them to transcend the immediate evil from which they could not escape.

[2] *Tragedy is not Enough*, 1953, pp. 96, 97.

meaning to an otherwise meaningless doom'.[1] In this sense the cry of dereliction on the Cross, like the psalm from which it is a quotation, is expressive of true tragedy. It is the cry of one who knows that he is completely at the mercy of the bottomless, the *Nichtig*, the hosts of the demons, and that there is no escape from it. It is not the cry of one who knows that he is the victor, though *we* know that the victory is won through forsakenness. Even though superseded and, so to speak, rectified by the Resurrection, the tragedy remains real. It is more than an incident, though a painful one, in the inter-cosmic existence of a divine being. In its very finality it is the supreme example of transcendence over evil.

5

Now, we have agreed with Bultmann that the New Testament representation of evil in terms of personalized demonic beings over whom Jesus triumphs and exercises his Lordship is mythological, for it offers a naïve picture of the world which few today, rightly or wrongly, are able to accept. We have also questioned the conventional belief that in the Cross evil has been defeated: a statement which is manifestly untrue to our knowledge of facts. With the rest of Bultmann's description of the cosmological aspect of evil which the New Testament shared with the Hellenistic world we have dealt only incidentally, as it is so obviously mythological as to merit little consideration.

As far as the ontology of evil is concerned, however, the matter cannot be allowed to rest at this point; for if the demonology of the New Testament is *not* merely descriptive of how things are but, in spite of being mythological, points to something beyond itself, we are required to adopt a definite attitude towards it. If, on the other hand, it is merely descriptive of phenomena, and descriptive in a manner which can no longer claim validity, it should nevertheless confront us with the questions: 'What is it telling us about human existence? To what is it a pointer? What has it to say about the structure of being? How does this New Testament representation of evil speak *existentially*?' For the New Testament conception of the world and of the evil which

[1] *Tragedy is not Enough*, 1953, pp. 96, 97.

is manifest in it, if it is to be demythologized, must be either dissolved into some such questions or explained satisfactorily in some non-mythological manner. 'Existentially', however, whatever we do with this problem of evil, it leaves us where we were; for in Bultmann's terms the 'self-understanding' or the 'understanding of existence' which it offers is confrontation with the same fact of evil, which leaves us no nearer to an explanation of the thing itself. Man is just that being who, being 'in the world', experiences evil as a form of menace to his existence. Whatever names we give to them, evil powers are a reality, and the study of man in his world shows how greatly under their dominion he is and reveals the extent to which their operations are observable in his experience. When Bultmann, therefore, describes the primitive Christian (primitive in the sense of belonging to the primitive Christian community) he does so in terms designed to reveal his 'existential' situation: man in relation to time, and the situation of man in his world.[1] The man of the New Testament age is enslaved to the 'powers' as they were conceived by Gnosticism; but although they are 'mythical' their presence is actually discernible in the powers of the 'flesh', the 'law', sin, and death.[2] Both the Pauline and the Johannine writings exemplify this analysis of the human predicament, and it is indeed a gloomy picture that they offer, though they do not wholly exclude the other side. However, the Christian of the Apostolic age differed from the Hellenistic man oppressed with the sense of fate in what Bultmann calls 'freedom from the past' and 'openness to the future':[3] deliverance from the former and guidance into the latter is the work of the saving event in Jesus. Man is so delivered from the wickedness of the present world that his past no longer enslaves him or holds him back, nor does the future frighten him.

Such, as interpreted by Bultmann, is the 'existential' situation of man in the New Testament when faced with the 'powers' as conceived in contemporary myth, and we assume that, whether he considers them as myth or not, modern man is like the as yet unredeemed person before he feels release from the burden of the

[1] *Das Urchristentum*, pp. 200 ff.
[2] Ibid., pp. 213 ff.
[3] Ibid., p. 210. Cf. *Kerygma and Myth*, p. 205.

past and while he still thinks of the future in terms of 'closed-ness' rather than of 'openness'. He knows, if he is a Christian, that the Cross and Resurrection have not objectively deprived evil forces of their factual power, and that no automatic victory over them has been won. He knows that he and his kind may be crushed by them at any moment and he cannot accept the affirmations of pious conventional theology that things are not as he knows them to be in his experience and from his observation of the world. Yet he knows, too, that the Cross and Resurrection are the key which, if used, will open the door in the direction in which victory lies, so that neither will the past be a burden nor the future the object of fear. But completely demythologized the New Testament conception of evil cannot be; for evil then becomes purely subjective, in which case, it seems, violence is done to experience, for too often evil is 'felt' as something palpable and external. What is seen to count is not the fact of evil so much as the analysis of feelings which awareness of evil-ness stimulates. To demythologize the picture of evil 'existenti-ally', if this is what is meant by it, weakens the force of the evil, or dilutes the presentation of it, without getting rid of the evil.

An alternative form of demything, that which is offered by psychology, also leaves us more or less where we were, for to deny the demonic causation of a psychosis and offer a psychological one is to reject the 'mythological' explanation and at the same time to submit one which still leaves a person at the mercy of the irrational. The irruption of disruptive 'evil' forces into the world both as dysgenic factors such as the collective will to power and as forms of personal evil may be attributed, according to Jung's psychology, to the disturbing uprush of archetypal images from the collective unconscious, that primal, pre-natal repository of the emotional experiences of countless generations. Indeed, the evils which might be attributed by the New Testament to 'demons' are attributed by Jung to the powerful emotional effects of irrational qualities in the racial unconscious.[1] Such an explanation is satisfactory up to a point, but it falls short of accounting for the fact of evil, unless the 'collective' unconscious is to be considered as leading back through infinite regression to

[1] *The Integration of the Personality*, p. 293.

the moment of primal 'fall' and the consequent 'vitiation' of the life-force suggested by N. P. Williams or to some 'mythological' conception of the fall such as is found in Genesis; or it may be thought of as a depth-dimension of a fluid character in which contact is made between people at a level below that of consciousness. In any case, evil is not robbed of its power, though the field in which it may be dealt with is extended to the realm covered by psychopathology. In any case, we have still to explain why what is retained and transmitted in the collective unconscious is predominantly evil in its effects, and why it has not, as an inheritance from a sub- or pre-human form of life, worked itself out during the long history of man's existence. In any case, all that has been done is to postulate instead of evil spirits a 'collective unconscious', the existence of which cannot be finally demonstrated though there may be good grounds for believing in it.[1] Nor is there much to choose, from the practical standpoint, between being menaced by the upsurge of Jung's archetypal images, which may occur at any moment with devastating consequences no longer controllable, and being at the mercy of demons whose operations are equally unexpected and uncontrollable. In the first case a psychological 'myth' is invoked, whereas in the second the 'myth' is theological. As Schniewind has observed in his reply to Bultmann, the real issue is that evil has a 'trans-subjective reality' and that 'the opposition of the whole universe to the will of God is so deliberate and so well-organized that it is more than the product of the human will',[2] and, we might add, of the racial unconscious, though it is questionable if the opposition of the 'whole universe', a rather comprehensive term, is as total or as well organized as Schniewind believed. For there are limits to the demythologizing of myth, and they are reached perhaps at this point. The terms used—principalities, powers, the

[1] Dr. J. A. Hadfield, in commenting on Jung's notion of archetypes, doubts whether a 'racial unconscious' as the deposit from which the archetypes are transmitted has any 'existence' such as Jung suggests. He does not question the existence of archetypes or archetypal images but only the source from which they are derived, which may, in Hadfield's view, be personal experiences. On the other hand, there is no reason why these images may not be derived from 'ancestral patterns of existence' (*Dreams and Nightmares*, 1954, p. 59). If a psychological explanation of a religious cult is sought, an example may be found in the occurrence of the Virgin Mary cult in a church whose clergy are celibate. The Virgin may be a religious projection of Jung's *anima*.　　　　　　　　　　　　　　[2] *Kerygma and Myth*, p. 92.

world-rulers of this darkness—may be those of Gnostic mythology and sound like nothing more than the rhetorical titles of objectified irrational or sub-personal forces, and the extent of their rule should be understood within the context of the cosmology of the time. Nevertheless, they are designations of an appalling and, apparently, a most persistent and elusive reality.

The Christian belief is that, if the overcoming of evil is to be a reality and not merely a phrase, it will be through the germinating force of Christian obedience and through the liberation of such forces as have their source in the Christian knowledge of God. How far the germination will proceed is unpredictable. Human destiny may be like progress: not a straight line, or even a zigzag, but a spiral where new nihilistic powers oppose the divine resources on ascending levels. Evil, so far, has proved to be an ineradicable phenomenon of all existence, human and sub-human, and, perhaps, super-human, if the 'mythological' thinking of the New Testament is considered to correspond to reality. Disaster and tragedy will remain, as far as one can see, as part of the structure of existence. The problem which faces man is not that of their elimination but rather of victory over them and his appropriation of the power which enables him to transcend them even while he is being overwhelmed, though this transcendence by himself does not eliminate evil elsewhere; and even if, by some miracle, one generation were to succeed in eradicating evil, or at least forms of physical and social evil, there is no assurance which our knowledge or experience can provide that this achievement will be transmitted to the next generation. Evil *locally* eradicated can yield to the virtue of kindness, humility, meekness, long-suffering, forbearing one another, forgiveness (Col. 3: 13; Gal. 5: 22, etc.), the bond of charity. In these qualities, called by St. Paul the fruits of the Spirit, is to be seen the occasion on which evil is defeated: not impersonal, irrational, sub-human evil, but the power of the lie over the individual life. Evil is *locally* destroyed, the demons are defeated, where it is replaced by these qualities, though it may, and will, emerge again elsewhere. There is no metaphysical solidarity in evil which compels it to retreat all along the line when a considerable blow has been struck at one point. On the contrary, evil acts by means of continuous pressure which demands ceaseless vigilance, and in some instances its menace can be met only by the physical extermination of those in whom it is embodied. Its most spectacular expression in the twentieth century is political, and it is at the same time its most diabolical expression, for in this field it is least possible to impose restraint upon it, and it suggests something far more radical than a diseased imagination or the temptation of power as its source.

The Gospels, indeed, shed but little light on this dark problem if what is desired is a definite word of Jesus, who seems to have envisaged the collateral existence of good and evil until the moment of final, eschatological reckoning. This, at any rate, is what is suggested by the Parable of the Tares, which gives no indication as to when the culmination of history will be. It is true that in a moment of insight Jesus has an apocalyptic vision of Satan falling like lightning from heaven, whatever is meant by this vivid, if enigmatic, saying. The Apocalyptic discourses do not suggest that the Crucifixion was to be tantamount to the defeat of evil, but rather imply the indefinite continuance of evil until a mounting period of troubles reaches its highest point of intensity to be terminated by the appearance of the Son of Man at an unascertainable moment. 'But of that day knoweth no man, no, not even the angels in heaven, but my Father only' (Matt. 24: 36). If the setting of the Discourses is the period immediately preceding the Crucifixion (even allowing that some passages may be of later date), and Jesus is aware of the impending tragedy in which the nation will in due course be engulfed, there is no suggestion in his recorded words that he regarded the Cross as the final blow struck against the dominion of evil. The end would come, but after the Gospel had been preached in all the world for a witness to all nations. In any case, the Parousia itself is a striking instance of mythological thinking, and even if it is thought of symbolically as implying God's ultimate victory over evil, it presents further difficulties, for something ultimate has little meaning for the generations which are unable to participate in its benefits, and a victory 'outside' time has no conceivable relevance to a victory within history. For if the notion of the ultimate victory of the Cross over evil refers to some dimension other than the historical, we are still left with the problem of its significance as a sign of victory over evil in this world. Victories there are, but there is no victory.

Nevertheless, it is of the essence of the Gospel that Jesus transcended tragedy and that self-transcendence even in the tragic moment comes to those who accept his Lordship with all the consequences of this acceptance. 'In the world you shall have tribulation, but be of good cheer: I have overcome the world.' The Christian faith implies this transcendence over the world rather than the progressive and 'objective' defeat of demonic powers, though there is no assurance that in each individual life the tragic situation will be overcome or that every person will see his predicament against the trans-temporal background which will deprive it of its apparent meaninglessness. We say that there is no assurance, but there is hope and there is faith, though if the words of forsakenness uttered on the Cross are intended to mean what we naturally understand them to mean, Jesus experienced neither hope nor faith but only utter desolation and disillusionment. Nevertheless, it is through self-transcendence and transcendence over evil by means of Resurrection and Exaltation that the tragedy of Holy Week achieves its true significance; and if Jesus is the Lord of life he is in some way Lord and conqueror of evil, too, whatever the degree of mythological thinking is involved in this affirmation. But in what sense—the question recurs insistently—does this Lordship extend over evil so that when we use the phrase we are not merely expressing a pious sentiment? In the Gospels Jesus rebukes the demons and they depart. In such concrete situations, given the belief in demoniac possession, he remains the victor on the field. The problem is how to discover a general meaning in such victory so that the Gospel not only depicts a historical incident in the sense of *historisch* or (as Bultmann would also express it) *faktisch*, but also as *geschichtlich*, as possessing this universal *historic* content which makes an 'existential' impact far outside the circumscribed range of the immediate event.

In answering the question—as far as such a question can be precisely answered—it is necessary that we should again distinguish between actuality and potentiality, between what can happen and what does happen, and also that we should limit the scope of the Lordship of Jesus over this field.

The first stage in attempting an answer consists in avoiding general terms or pious general phrases such as 'mankind has been saved by Christ', for 'mankind' is aware of no such deliverance, and nothing is further from reality than this 'mankind' which has been 'saved'. Although individual Christians have had this awareness, it is by no means the case that the majority of Christians so-called are personally aware of such deliverance or salvation or whatever word is used in this connection. Man is still to be delivered from fear of death, from unfruitfulness of life, from sin, self-hood, and the dominion of evil things and the desire to commit evil, and from ignorance of the sovereignty of God. Deliverance is, for the most part, *in spe* rather than *in re*. It is something which can be rather than that which is, a promise and an assurance rather than a universal present fact somehow brought about automatically by the Cross and Resurrection. Salvation does not occur automatically, independently, as it were, of whether the offer is accepted or not. A man in danger of drowning is not saved by exhortation or by the assurance that the life-belt is within his reach. He must reach out for it and grasp it. It is individual persons, who enter upon a new life and thereby *accept* the free gift of divine grace in Jesus Christ, who are 'saved', not man in the mass or an abstraction such as 'mankind'. While the divine offer is universally available, it must first of all be accepted. To use the term which Berdyaev employed in an existentialist context, there must be 'participation'. The antithesis of object and subject must be overcome. The Cross as a historical event is a mere object. 'Historically' the dead man nailed to it is just a dead man. The Cross becomes 'historic', *geschichtlich*, when we appropriate what it has to offer. We have to participate in the 'event' by personal commitment, for those who do not thus participate are not 'saved': they are merely spectators. To *know* Christ, in Melanchthon's phrase, is to know his benefits, that is, to appropriate the salvation offered. The 'whole-making' must be experienced if it is to be effective. It is therefore through the personal acknowledgment of the Lordship of Jesus Christ that 'salvation' takes meaning. If, in the words of eighteenth-century evangelicalism, 'his blood availed for me', it is not because something has been done which is efficacious apart from my acceptance of it, but because it evokes from me a particular kind of commitment. It 'avails' only in so far as there is a direct relationship between myself and what is done, and appropriation by myself, through acceptance, of the potentially effective 'atonement'. Man and God are not reconciled as long as man remains a rebel, for only when he *sees that he is a rebel* is there a basis for reconciliation. What is offered does not become in the fullest sense a gift until it is accepted. It is freely offered out of gladness of heart, but it may be left lying on the table. To be in the fullest sense a gift it must be appropriated. The demons are overcome, we are delivered from evil, at the point where and at the moment when the gift is accepted and the reconciliation is complete.

In the last resort the victory of Jesus over the demons and the Christian's belief in the conquest of evil through him mean, as Berdyaev has said, that 'the final victory over evil cannot be achieved by the natural powers of man in separation from God'.[1] Organization, administration, and technical equipment may mitigate the consequences of breakdowns which bring evils in their train, and science may soften the worst effects of physical affliction. But there is an ultimate affliction of the soul, a *malheur*, as Simone Weil has pointed out, beyond human remedy, the unrelieved deep-level anguish from which merely human assistance offers no means of escape. Into this condition even the divine fails sometimes to break because the sufferer feels himself to be completely overwhelmed and beyond deliverance. This is the ultimate state of despair in which the soul is submerged and the sufferer shares with the Son of God (to borrow Simone Weil's telling metaphor) the harrowing agony of the blow concentrated in the point of the nail which transmits the full force of the shock at the point to which it is applied.[2] When man has reached this depth of suffering which is scarcely distinguishable from evil he is at one with Christ on the Cross, and it is through sharing in his victory that he himself will be victorious and transcend the moment of dereliction.

It is this experience which is symbolized by the 'mythology' of the Cross.

[1] *Freedom and the Spirit*, p. 171.
[2] *Waiting on God*, p. 77; cf. *Gravity and Grace*, pp. 62–76.

PART IV

THE MYTH AS LOGOS

SUMMARY OF ARGUMENT

In this enquiry the terms 'myth', 'mythology', and 'mythological thinking' have been employed, often without marked
differentiation. It is necessary, however, to distinguish between
them in order to avoid confusion of thought; for 'mythological'
thinking should be understood as indicating a *type* of thought
rather than a rigidly archaic view of the world. Though
'mythical' thinking implies religious thinking on a primitive
level, it is evident in non-primitive societies, and in its New
Testament manifestation has affinity with the Hellenistic rather
than with the Hebraic constituents of Apostolic Christianity.
Certain inherent characteristics of authentic mythical thinking
however, such as the mythic conception of time, space, and
number, are prominent throughout the New Testament.
Ultimately mythical and mythological modes of thought are
pictorial, symbolic, and archetypal.

The psychological importance and necessity of primordial
images and archetypes are considered. Karl Mannheim has
emphasized their sociological and religious value, and A. J.
Toynbee sees in them an objective truth about the genesis of
culture and even about cosmogony. Some of the Christian
archetypes are mentioned and their significance for the continuity of Christian experience remarked upon.

The 'myth' is both symbol and a norm providing faith with
a permanent point of reference without which Christianity
would dissolve into metaphysics or ethics. It is therefore a valid
expression of Christian truth and an indispensable form of
symbolic language. Even for Bultmann it has an 'objective'
function in so far as it addresses man in his existential situation,
and in this way it may be thought of as the divine 'logos'

speaking in a challenging and decisive manner. It transcends the 'historical' by raising it to the level of the 'historic' and relates what happens in time to the eternal purposes of God. In this way the *mythos* is seen to be a *logos*.

─────────────────────────────────

CHAPTER ONE

MYTH AND MYTHOLOGICAL THINKING

I

In his important study of the mystery religions Reitzenstein[1] distinguishes between two distinct types of near-eastern religion: the one, represented by Babylonian and especially by early Old Testament religion, consisting of the historical conception of God as establishing a relationship between himself and a particular nation, with its emphasis on the 'covenant' or external 'bond' and on the divine transcendence; and the other represented by the sacramental mystery religions with their ritual and emphasis on the intimate mystical relationship between man and his deity. The distinction is important, for it corresponds, roughly, to the difference between the comparatively non-mythological and the mythological elements in biblical religion. Reitzenstein concedes that the distinction is not absolute, for the one type influenced the other and absorbed some of its characteristics. The distinction, nevertheless, is profound and is significant for our estimate of the various factors involved in an assessment of the extent and value of the 'mythological' element in New Testament Christology.

Our analysis of this Christology against the background of mythological thinking has shown that both types of religion are in evidence in the New Testament and are represented, roughly, by the Synoptic Gospels (and perhaps by the Epistle to the Hebrews, notwithstanding its frequently neo-platonic cast of thought) on the one hand, and the Pauline-Johannine writings on the other, though the latter combine both in varying degrees. As for the influence of Hellenistic ideas and cults on St. Paul, no final agreement has been, or is likely to be, reached by those who have investigated it. Some have tended to minimise the extent of Hellenistic influence on his thought, while others, especially the exponents of the 'religious-historical' approach, doubtless

[1] *Die Hellenistischen Mysterienreligionen*, 3rd ed., 1927, pp. 5–6.

exaggerate it, though the evidence which they adduce in support of their contentions is considerable.[1] It is clear that Paul's attitude towards the Law and the sacraments is quite out of keeping with the Hebraic tradition, and his indebtedness to Platonic, Stoic, and other forms of Hellenistic thought is unmistakable. The admission that he was 'debtor both to the Greeks and to the Barbarians' shows that his was a complex mind with many facets, and that, despite his orthodox Pharisaic upbringing, he was familiar with current intellectual and religious modes of thought and willing to learn from them.

The 'mythological' element in the Synoptic Gospels is confined almost wholly to two Christological titles, belief in demons (which does not seem to extend to disease as such but only to mental and epileptic disorders), and eschatological hopes. In the rest of the New Testament the field is wider, and includes such conceptions as the heavenly man, the visible self-realization of the Logos, the manifestation in time of a pre-existent divine being, the spirit-flesh and light-darkness antithesis, the Hellenistic cosmology, sacramental conceptions which have analogies in the mystery religions, and the widely diffused Stoic terminology which appears so frequently in Paul and to a lesser extent in the Fourth Gospel and the Epistle to the Hebrews. The preponderance of mythological conceptions is found in the Hellenistically-influenced strands of the New Testament, though it should be added that the Birth-narratives in Matthew and Luke are Hebraic in style, despite the fact that the idea of the incarnation of the Son of God is foreign to the Hebrew tradition. It is, however, mainly in the Hellenistic background that we should seek the sources of New Testament myth, even if this is not consciously borrowed, and it is in a Hellenistic environment at the end of the first century that the deification of Jesus is on its way to completion.

---

[1] *Die Hellenistischen Mysterienreligionen*, 3rd ed., 1927, pp. 332 ff. 'Paulus als Pneumatiker'; pp. 174 ff. Reitzenstein (p. 357) states that the phrase $\mu o \rho \phi \grave{\eta} \; \theta \epsilon o \hat{v}$ was widespread in Hellenistic mysticism and supports his contention with a persuasive amount of evidence, while Dieterich, in commenting on Romans 8: 14 and Galatians 4: 5, says that the notion of 'adoption' into 'sonship' would be easily understood by Hellenistic readers (*Eine Mithrasliturgie*, pp. 152 ff.), and the group of ideas associated with 'dying' and rebirth he describes as 'absolutely un-Jewish' (ibid., p. 175). Lohmeyer, however (op. cit., p. 91), in commenting on Reitzenstein, is disinclined to believe that the 'vague use' of the term $\mu o \rho \phi \grave{\eta} \; \theta \epsilon o \hat{v}$ has any particular significance or philosophical implication.

In turning to the Old Testament we find that, despite the so-called myths of the Creation, the Flood, and the Tower of Babel, the curious passage in Genesis 6 describing the marriage of angelic beings with the daughters of men, and the mixture of folklore and primitive ideas such as are to be found in any heroic literature, it is, on the whole, non-mythological and even anti-mythological. Gunkel suggests that the Hebrews did not favour myth because of its polytheistic associations,[1] and in a volume devoted to the study of the relation of Hebrew myth and ritual to the cultic pattern of the ancient east, Dr. T. H. Robinson seemed to experience difficulty in finding a genuine myth, with the exception of the Creation story, in the Old Testament.[2] The line separating legend from myth is not clearly drawn.

Moreover, the comparison even of the Hebrew cosmogonic myth with the cosmogonic myths of other eastern cultures or with the elaborate myth in Plato's *Timaeus* shows how far removed from one another the two types are. In one of the Rigveda hymns, for example, the world is described as issuing from the body of a man, the Purusha, of whose body the parts of the world are the organs and limbs. The moon originates in his spirit, the sun in his eye; the navel is the source of the atmosphere, the world proceeds from his feet, and so on. According to one Egyptian creation-myth the source of life was the primordial abyss, Nun, whence emerged the primeval hillock from which Rē was born. In the Brahmanas as well as in Egyptian mythology the cosmic egg occurs. In Egyptian lore there are also found pre-creation gods: Nun and his consort Naunet, Hum, Amun, Kuk (darkness) and Kauket, and several others. According to another creation myth Shu and Tefnut (air and moisture) produce the sky, the earth-god and the earth-goddess, Geb and Nut, who in turn produce Osiris and Isis.[3] The mythic

---

[1] *Religion in Geschichte und Gegenwart*, IV,[2] 381 ff.
[2] *Myth and Ritual*, ed. S. H. Hooke, Oxford, 1933, pp. 172 ff.
[3] Cf., *inter alia*, H. Frankfort (ed.) *Before Philosophy*, pp. 51 ff., 138 ff.; E. A. Wallis Budge, *From Fetish to God in Ancient Egypt*, pp. 235 ff.; S. Langdon, *Tammuz and Ishtar*, pp. 159 ff.; Baudissin, *Tammuz und Osiris*; J. G. Frazer, *Adonis, Tammuz and Osiris*; M. Jastrow, *Aspects of Religious Belief and Practice in Babylon and Assyria*, etc.; W. K. C. Guthrie, *The Greeks and their Gods*, pp. 205 ff.; H. J. Rose, *A Handbook of Greek Mythology*, chaps. 2 and 4; M. P. Nilsson, *A History of Greek Religion*, p. 38, for the origins of Greek mythology. See also Andrew Lang, art. 'Mythology' in the *Encyclopedia Britannica*; J. G. Frazer, *Folklore of the Old Testament*, I, part 1.

cosmogony of Greece was equally far from the Hebrew religious world. Whereas these other cosmogonic myths are fantastically mythological, the Hebrew story is characterized by an austere and transcendent conception of God which is wholly absent from other ancient myths of the same kind. Even if God 'walks' in Eden, or 'goes down' to see what is going on on the plain of Shinar, it is the invisible God who does so, not a grotesque or anthropomorphic representation. When God 'speaks' He is never seen (Exod. 30: 20 ff.): to this extent the Hebrews rejected a mythical conception of God in favour of the non-mythical, the difference between the two being exemplified by the contrast between Moses on Mt. Sinai and the Israelites worshipping the Golden Calf, an instance, no doubt, of the 'bull' archetype so frequent in mythical religion. Some of the most violent denunciations of the prophets were directed against syncretism, a sure sign of the penetration of a non-mythical religion by extraneous and alien mythical ideas and practices. It is significant, too, that whereas the sacrifice of Jephthah's daughter might have provided the foundation of a cult similar to that of Tammuz, it actually appears to have become no more than an occasion for commemoration.

Further, the Commandments as well as the prophetic writings are evidence of the strongly non-mythological character of the Old Testament tradition as compared with non-Hebraic and Hellenistic religions. Indeed, the Old Testament is virtually the story of the emancipation of thought from myth, and even the eschatological words of Jesus are seen to be rooted in a kind of historicized eschatology. The Twelve are to be the successors of the Twelve Tribes, and the Messianic banquet is to be eaten in the Kingdom of God, that is, within the total framework of the Hebrew notion of the Chosen People and the sovereignty of God; and in order to realize the extent of the transformation brought about by the second type of religion mentioned by Reitzenstein we have only to compare the simple words of Jesus at the Last Supper with the sacramental discourse in John 6, where there is implied, if not a theophagy, at any rate something very near it which scandalized Jesus' interlocutors and which is quite alien to the Hebraic tradition in which Christianity was born, but not to its later Hellenistic environment. What we are suggesting is that it was through its transplantation into the Hellenistic world that it became impregnated with mythological character and idiom. Historically this may have been inevitable, for the Gospel and the Church were destined to leave the land of their origin in order to gain universality; but even though this may be so, it does not follow that the Hellenistic accretions should necessarily be regarded as permanent or valid constituents of Christian thought.

It is significant that a characteristic emphasis of the Reformation, at any rate in its Calvinistic form, was on the Hebraic, non-ritualistic, non-sacramental and non-mystical elements in Christianity and on the transcendent majesty of God, His divine righteousness and will, on election and the establishment of the bond between God and man through ethical obedience, on the Word of God and the permeation of the common life by His law. The non-Hebraic Hellenistic elements continued and grew in Roman Catholicism, with its sacramentalism, mysticism, and reverence for the saints and the Virgin which are barely distinguishable, and in popular Catholicism indistinguishable, from their worship. Indeed, one of the achievements of Catholicism has been the progressive mythologizing of Christianity, and in it myth as well as mythological thinking reaches its maximum intensity. 'Every religious idea and experience,' writes Friedrich Heiler, an ex-Catholic, 'every form of cult and of piety that has ever existed in mankind is found again in Catholicism' (*Der Katholizismus*, p. 16). It might be said that all the characteristics of mythic religion, that is of primitive religion, are also exhibited in Catholicism to the full, though, as Heiler observes, the crudest forms of heathen cultism and magic remained outside when popular religion passed through the 'filter' of Christian church-thinking (ibid., p. 164). It is questionable, however, if this statement is applicable to popular Catholicism in Sicily and Mexico. Catholicism has always encouraged and protected a popular piety which has throughout been, and still is, compounded chiefly of myth with all its sense-imagery and materialistic representation of Catholic dogma and doctrine. Belief in holy or even magic powers resident in the object, mascots[1], the cult of Mary, which is in a sense an invented mythology in that it has achieved the apotheosis and cultic transformation of a human person, of whom very little is known, into an elaborate myth. Heiler even goes so far as to say that 'the Mother of God of Catholic piety is not the same person as the mother of Jesus of Nazareth' (p. 183), which, notwith-

---

[1] 'On the lowest levels of mythical consciousness,' writes Cassirer (*Das Mythische Denken*, p. 103) in commenting on the forms of the mythical, 'power or holiness appears as a kind of "thing", as a sensuous-physical quality which is attached to a particular person or object who is its bearer.' This admirably describes this aspect of popular Catholicism which, according to Cassirer's observation, brings it into the category of the mythical.

standing the identification of the Queen of Heaven with the mother of Jesus, is quite true. The title *Theotokos*, Mother of God, is mythological, and the parallels between the Virgin-cult and the cults of Isis and Artemis have often been indicated.[1] Even the veneration of the Black Madonna at Einsiedeln and Altötting would seem to be the survival of the worship of Diana, of whom (according to Heiler) many black representations have been found in Asia Minor. Mechthild of Magdeburg even addressed Mary as 'goddess' (Heiler, ibid., p. 184).

In art and architecture the same distinctions between Protestantism and Catholicism are apparent. In Troeltsch's opinion Protestant art reached its most typical expression in the 'abstract' art of Bach's music. Contrasted with this is the profuse and proliferating character of baroque religious art, particularly as exemplified in ecclesiastical decorations in Austria and Bavaria, though baroque has also a strongly naturalistic aspect so forceful that it can be repulsive. Examples of this are the Pietà in the Cartuja de Miraflores at Burgos, the Crucifixion by Gixon in Seville Cathedral, and the *matres dolorosae* so frequently found in southern baroque churches.

These two great and opposed Christian traditions, then, the Protestant and the Catholic, correspond, roughly, to the Hebraic and the Hellenistic, not only in content but in basic attitude. It is the contrast between the prophetic word and ritualism, between the non-mythical and the mythical type of religion. Whatever else the two kinds of faith may have in common, they belong to two different types of religion. That which divides them is, predominantly, the degree in which is manifested the attitude of mind which is described as mythological. Such 'mythological' thinking as there is in Protestantism is derived from the Bible only and lacks both the syncretistic and primordial character of the mythical element in Catholic belief and ritual.

Now, it should be clear that mythological thinking and myth are not necessarily the same thing, and that myth is not the same as mythology. Mythological thinking may mean no more than thinking in a mythological manner by analogically applying the category of myth, as a symbol or metaphor, to religion. There can be myth without mythology, for whereas we have spoken

---

[1] Cf. E. Norden, *Die Geburt des Kindes*, pp. 76 ff., 112 ff.; Sir William Ramsay, *Pauline and other Studies*, 125 ff. and especially p. 127, where Ramsay considers the rise of the Virgin-cult at Ephesus to be a continuation of the ancient Diana religion in Christian guise. Norden maintains that there was sufficient contact between Egypt and Palestine to account for Egyptian influence on the Lukan Birth-narrative, and draws attention to several similarities between the Christian and Egyptian stories about the birth of the Child.

about myth in the New Testament it would be inaccurate to speak of 'the New Testament mythology' as we might speak of Scandinavian or Greek mythology, for there is no such body of mythological material in the New Testament. The term 'mythology' implies a definite classification relative to either the study of myth, the existence of a body of myths, or the religious activity of the primitive mind. The study of mythology is akin to that of anthropology and comparative religion and suggests a special, rounded-off mental approach to the world which can be studied and empirically observed at work in the religious life of undeveloped communities.[1] Primitive peoples think mythologically, but not all who so think are primitive; indeed, mythological thinking may be evident in the most fully developed religion and in advanced civilizations and may, as we are endeavouring to establish, be an indispensable mode of religious perception. Although we began this enquiry by quoting definitions of myth and mythological thinking, it is necessary before proceeding further to clarify our ideas about the nature of myth and the kind of thinking which is associated with it.

2

There are several kinds of myth.[2] First of all there are cosmogonic and ethnogonic myths, primordial myths through which the primitive mind endeavours to picture the beginnings of the world and of the race. Whether these are actually intended to be accounts of what the 'authors' (using the term to cover whoever may have been individually or collectively responsible for the genesis of the myth) thought about the origin of the world is difficult to ascertain, though the sacredness attaching to them may have given them the prestige of truth. It has been held, too, that all genuine myth is aetiological. But whether the Egyptians

---

[1] For example, Andrew Lang's *Myth, Ritual, and Religion* (1887), and Grimm's *Deutsche Mythologie.*

[2] For a fuller classification see E. A. Gardner, Hastings' *E.R.E.*, art. 'Mythology'; and Andrew Lang, art. 'Mythology' in the *Encyclopedia Britannica.* Robert Graves defines myth as the 'reduction to narrative shorthand of ritual mime performed on public festivals', which severely limits the scope of the term. He is, however, writing chiefly of Greek myths, and gives a list of twelve things from which myth in the strict sense should be differentiated (*The Greek Myths*, vol. i, p. 10, 1955).

actually believed, according to one myth, that the primeval water, Nun, actually produced an egg which in turn produced the sun-god Rē, we can only conjecture. Compared with Egyptian and Mesopotamian cosmogonic myths the Genesis myth is sophisticated, and because of its reduced mythological character it is nearer to a credible account of creation than other more grotesque narratives. How the myth-symbols came to be is a question for anthropology and psychology and is outside the field of this enquiry, though the fact that some symbols recur in most mythologies may suggest something like the racial or collective unconscious, the deposit of primordial archetypes, postulated by Jung.

Secondly, there are religious myths which also represent a fantastic world of anthropomorphic deities who are projections of human beings, and are engaged, usually, in doing what human beings do, or ought not to do. These myths belong to the heroic ages of peoples and are generally replaced later by more abstract conceptions, as Plato, for example, while using myth analogically, replaced myth by philosophy. Socrates' references to 'gods' are never quite convincing.

A third type of myth, such as that of Theseus and the Minotaur, deals with the deeds of heroes in a form which represents fancifully what may well have had a historical basis. The bull in the Theseus story may have been an archetypal symbol or a real bull, imaginatively mythologized, especially kept for combat with the young men and women who were surrendered as tribute to Minos.

A fourth type of myth is exemplified by the story of Prometheus. It belongs neither to the second nor third type but contains elements of both.

A fifth type should be described as a pseudo-myth to which reference has already been made: the 'myth' of the Proletarian Man, the Myth of the State, the Myth of Blood and Soil; by which is meant an emotive ideology designed to organize a nation or class round some representative and evocative symbol.

Of these types of myth (if we exclude the Apocalypse) there are no clear traces in the New Testament. Nevertheless, the idea of a divine being who becomes man may be considered to correspond to the second type, with which the Gnostic cosmology may have something in common. Corresponding to the third kind of myth are the two Birth-narratives which are founded on fact in the sense of having a historical person as their subject. But the New Testament possesses no 'mythology' in the sense of a coherent, fixed collection of mythical material such as we have in mind when speaking of Greek or Scandinavian mythology as body of folk tales about gods in the form of men. It is apparent, therefore, that this is not what is meant in speaking about New Testament 'myth'; for if 'myth' is to be equated with pre-scientific thinking rather than, in Lévy-Bruhl's phrase, with pre-logical thinking, the term loses its more precise meaning. Whatever it is considered to cover, in the New Testament context it does not refer to 'mythology' or represent the deeds of the members of a pantheon.

Moreover, our analysis of the New Testament language has shown that conceptions are prominent which cannot be considered to apply to mythical phenomena as these are apprehended by the primitive-mythological mind. While a notion, for example, such as that of the creation of the world by (say) Zeus or Odin or the Purusha belongs unambiguously to the field of myth, the mytho-poetical Christology of the creation of the world by the pre-existent Logos-Son does not, for it is not so much a statement about creation as about Jesus. It is Christological, not cosmogonic or cosmological. The great passage in Colossians and echoes of the same kind of thought elsewhere are not primarily cosmogonic or aetiological in intention: they are designed primarily to affirm a truth about the relationship of Jesus to God and about God to the world *through* Jesus which is not conditioned by time, and about Jesus' relationship to man as one to whom the attribute of Lordship over the human order is given. This is not myth; it is not part of a mythology; but it is mythological thinking if we understand by this the attempt to convey a truth about existence as transformed by Christ in terms of the 'descent' of the Son of God. This 'descent' is not described pictorially and has no space content as has a 'descent' from Olympus. Yet it is not the expression of abstract thought nor is it a merely propositional statement. Nor does the so-called mythological thinking of the New Testament involve the complete lack of clear division between mere imagining and 'real' perception which is reflected in the part played by dream-images in the mythic consciousness; for the mythic mind does not make this distinction between appearance, mythical symbols, and reality.[1] Further: because the New Testament is about a historical person his mythopoetical attributes do not strike us as belonging to an unreal world as do those of mythical personages whom we know not to have existed. The nearest Christology comes to myth is in the conception of the 'self-emptying' of the Son of God (though this can be non-mythologically interpreted) and the ascending-descending Son in the Fourth Gospel, which, there are good reasons for believing, is not without contact with Hellenistic modes of thought. Yet in each case the 'mythological' thinking draws attention not to a fiction resulting from the activity of the mythopœic imagination but to a unique quality in a historical person.

As for the miraculous and the demonic, it must be frankly admitted that not enough is known of the physical or para-physical world to be dogmatic about it. While the language suggests mythological thinking, the things about which it is used may not belong to the sphere of myth, though it is true that demonology and angelology reflect an attitude of mind which is not consistent with modern man's conception of nature.[2] The attribution of epilepsy and mental illness to demonic causes can be described as mythological thinking because demons are generally believed to belong to an imaginary world of super-human beings; yet this world, as conceived in the New Testament, is not a mythical world as is that of the savage living in an animist state. Nor can the notion of Jesus' victory on the Cross over the combined hosts of evil be described as part of a mythology, even though those hosts have no perceptible or measurable existence or objective being as have the soldiers who carried out the execution. The Crucifixion is a historical event with historical consequences. And though the story of the Temptation is mytho-logical in form, the theme is not Satan but the rejection by Jesus of current Messianic conceptions and of short cuts to success.

[1] E. Cassirer, *Das Mythische Denken*, p. 48.
[2] 'Whatever is seen or felt,' writes Cassirer of the mythical consciousness, 'is sur-rounded by a special atmosphere of joy or grief, of anguish, or excitement, or de-pression. All objects are benignant or malignant, friendly or inimical, familiar or uncanny' (*Essay on Man*, pp. 76–77).

The New Testament is not myth: still less has it a consistent mythology, though often it shows evidence of a 'mythic' stage of reflection which has left a primitive stage of society and cults far behind. Mythical thinking, as understood by Cassirer and others who have studied this aspect of human activity, is essentially that which is disclosed by anthropology, ethnology, and the study of primitive religions to be a mode of apprehension and expression peculiar to primitive man or to the survival in more advanced cultures of such modes which are no longer fully characteristic of them. Yet New Testament society is not primitive: it is civilized and sophisticated and has no social relationship to the primitive *Weltanschauung*, even though its authors share the presuppositions of pre-Copernican cosmology. Whatever of the mythical is found in it has to be examined from quite a different standpoint from that which is adopted in examining the workings of the genuine 'mythical' mind. Yet evidence is not lacking of 'mythological' thinking which has survived, despite the historical, religious, and social evolution of Israel.

Of the current demonological and cosmological beliefs which the New Testament people shared with the rest of the contemporary world no more need be said,[1] though it may be added that it is doubtful if the Hebraic tradition entertained such dubious beliefs as could be described as polytheistic. The Five Elemental Spirits and the Seven Cosmocrats were not part of the Hebrew cosmology, for, though late Judaism believed in various angelic and demonic hierarchies, the Jews were monotheists. One has only to read documents such as Psalm 115 and Jeremiah 10 to realize how profound was their hostility to any kind of polytheism and its concomitant mythology. Nevertheless, though mythological thinking was perimetrical to the Hebrew mind, it did not fail to influence it.

An instance of this mythological thinking is the New Testament conception of space, time, and number, which Cassirer[2] considers to be typical of this mode of thought. Biblical time, space, and number are not mathematical but often mythological terms.

[1] For an account of these beliefs within the framework of the time see Dr. Edward Langton's *Essentials of Demonology*, 1949, pp. 145 ff., 183 ff., 198 ff.
[2] *Das Mythische Denken*, pp. 95 ff.

New Testament time, for example, is eschatological rather than strictly chronological, for the evangelists appear to be somewhat indifferent to chronology.[1] The Fourth Gospel, moreover, re-arranges the order of events as conceived by the Synoptists, as though such freedom of treatment were of little account. The events of Acts are narrated without creating the impression that they covered a period of some three decades, and Luke appears actually to foreshorten the time-span. The notion of pre-temporal existence provides Paul and John with no problems: it is accepted without demur. Time and eternity interpenetrate. Eternal life is here and now.

So, too, with the New Testament conception of space, which exists on two planes, the historical and the mythical. The historical dimension is that within which the Synoptic 'chronicle' and the history of the Acts are enacted. The mythological dimension is that which is inhabited by angels and demons; it is the realm of 'above' and 'below', of the ascent and descent of the Son of Man, of light and darkness (which belong, in Cassirer's view, to the concept of the mythical) and of the man caught up into the 'third heaven' by which St. Paul presumably means himself in a moment of ecstasy (II Cor. 12: 1–4). Indeed, being 'in' Christ is a mystical and mythical dimension, for the mystical experience transcends both time and space. The mutual in-dwelling of the Father and the Son in the Fourth Gospel is con-ceived in terms of 'mythological' space such as are encountered in the Hermetic writings and elsewhere.

Thirdly, only on very few occasions in the New Testament have numbers any arithmetical significance. Number, like time and space, is mythological, and frequently possesses for the evangelist an ulterior meaning which is not always apparent to the reader. Seven, with its multiples fourteen, seventy, and seventy times seven, are among the most frequent examples of this stylized numerology; then comes forty (days and nights), ten, half of ten, three with its multiples twelve, thirty, and sixty. In very

---

[1] Although there is some doubt about the value of the Markan order of events, Dr. C. H. Dodd, in criticism of K. L. Schmidt, believes that the Markan framework follows a roughly chronological sequence (*The Expository Times*, xliii, p. 396). It is scarcely necessary to observe that Luke provides definite historical points of reference, though this does not invalidate the general contention.

few of the many instances in the Gospels where these numbers occur should they be thought of as indicating precision. The seven, for instance, was a particularly significant number in the ancient world, and the time-span was indicated by such stock terms as forty or 'after three days'.[1] The most elaborate example of this mythological conception of time, space, and number, is the Apocalypse, with its bewildering arithmetic and its completely mythological imagery which has nothing to do with historical time.

A yet further instance of mythological thinking is the difficulty which the primitive and mythical mind encounters in distinguishing the self from the group and in conceiving of the ego as a clearly delineated entity. Thus, when Jesus asks the disciples 'Whom do men say that I am?' the reply is that some think he is Elijah, or John the Baptist, or 'one of the prophets', when it was obvious that he could not have been any of them; and if there is any justification for the somewhat questionable interpretation of the term 'Son of Man' as having a both collective and individual connotation, it may gain some support from reference to a mythological (or mythical) conception of personality.[2]

There are evident, then, indications such as these (to select but a few examples) of the kind of thinking peculiar to the 'mythological' mind.

Nevertheless, mythological thinking does not *in itself* constitute a basis for mythology. That which is characterized by it is not necessarily authentic myth; for if myth is the mode of thought, contemplation, and life of primitive man—or to use Cassirer's

---

[1] See C. Taylor Smith in Hastings' *Dictionary of Christ and the Gospels*, II, pp. 247 ff. In his *Study in St. Mark*, A. M. Farrer has fancifully analysed the Gospel material in a manner suggesting that Mark was a mathematical wizard as interested in figures as was Plato's Timaeus. The ingenuity displayed in Mark's arithmetical symbolism must, if Dr. Farrer is right, have been phenomenal. The cyclic patterns are certainly ingenious. Cf. Philo, *On the Creation (de Mundi Opif.)* 88–102, where the author rhapsodizes on the virtues of numbers, particular the number seven. See also R. Reitzenstein, *Das Iranische Erlösungsmysterium*, pp. 161 ff.

[2] Cf. *inter alia* T. W. Manson, *The Teaching of Jesus*, pp. 227 ff.; C. J. Cadoux, *The Historic Mission of Jesus*, pp. 100 ff.; H. H. Rowley, *The Relevance of Apocalyptic*, where Jesus is described as the Son of Man who came to bring in the Son of Man (p. 145) and it is stated that Hebrew thought never conceived of man 'as an individual but as a corporate personality' (p. 150), a judgment which would hardly apply to Job or to many other instances of Hebrew individualism.

terms, a *Denkform*, *Anschauungsform*, and *Lebensform*—then what we have in the New Testament is not genuine myth, of which there is probably only one example, the myth of the Woman Clothed with the Sun in the Apocalypse, though, to those who are inclined to question their historicality, the Birth narratives as recounted by Luke might fall within this category. Mythical thinking is *sui generis*, with its own laws, organic development, and psychological characteristics within a special field of reference.

> The genuine myth [writes Cassirer] begins just at that point where not only a conception of the universe and its individual parts and forces are given the forms of particular pictures or of demonic and divine figures, but where there is predicated of these figures an origin, a continuous development, and a life in time. Only where there is no longer any passive contemplation of the divine, but where it explicates its nature and being in time, where there is progress from the mere conception of divine figures to their embodiment in history and narrative, are we concerned with 'myths' in the narrower and special meaning of the word.[1]

It is possible, of course, to apply this as a methodology of mythology to the New Testament narrative, and thus to mythologize it; but what is being then mythologized is not the substance of myth but of history.

We are confronted, therefore, with a kind of ambiguity which arises from the application of the term 'mythological thinking' to what is essentially historical or to the point at which a *historic* factor makes its impact on man. The myth, as a form of primitive *Weltanschauung*, as something which comprehends man's relation to the 'other' world, to his cosmos, and to his community, is a method of total apprehension of reality on a level prior to discursive thought. In this sense the New Testament cannot be said to express mythical thinking except by using the term analogically. For in all the instances of the kind of thinking which we have examined we have seen that the intention has been to convey some thought about Jesus or some spiritual conviction or experience, in a mode to which ordinary language might be deemed inappropriate and insufficient. What we encounter is really the

[1] Op. cit., pp. 132–133.

problem of language as symbol and of what kind of symbol is to be considered adequate to the communication of religious belief. For in contrast to the mythic imagination in its authentic form the minds of the New Testament people were not objectifying symbols of an apparently irrational character in an apparently rational form: they were giving actual intellectual form and content to living religious ideas. The origin of what is being mythologized about is not to be found in the mists of the pre-logical mind or of pre-history or in man's primitive attempt to express his idea of his place in the cosmos but in the Gospel story and in the conflict of historical personalities and interests.

Yet this very historical scene has been elevated to the 'mythical' dimension so that it is possible to describe it in what are manifestly mythological terms and also visually in sacrament, ritual, and art, that is, in terms of archetypal or primordial symbols. The pious imagination has succeeded in creating the myth out of what is non-mythical, as has occurred in Roman Catholicism; and when it is reduced to intellectual terms, this 'mythological' manner of thinking still remains. We are left with the Birth-narratives, the story of the pre-existent Son of God coming 'down' to redeem man from the malignant power of the demons, conquering them on the Cross, and eventually 'ascending' to the 'right hand of God'; and we are offered the picture of Last Things in terms and images which bear no relation to the historical reality which they of necessity transcend because they speak of what lies outside historical time. These mythological representations of the Christian story contain an emotional potential which is absent from theological statement, and the very symbols and pictures have impressed themselves upon the Christian consciousness just as the parables and the imagery of the Apocalypse impress themselves often through the emotionally evocative power which is less conspicuously present in ethical precept or theological definition. That is to say: what might be described as Christian archetypes have a function of *Gefühlsdynamik* and can penetrate to depths which lie below the level of ratiocination. To that extent Cassirer is right when he says that mythical perception is always impregnated with emotional qualities.[1]

---

[1] *Essay on Man,* p. 76.

What, in effect, we are called upon to do is to detach the notion of mythological thinking from authentic primitive myth and to consider it as a form of metaphor. That the mode of thinking is mythological we are not disputing; but it is the mythological thinking of a socially and politically post-mythological society in which a deposit of the mythical apprehension of the world still remains. What we have now to decide is how far such thinking is legitimately applicable to Christology, how far it is descriptive rather than, so to speak, substantive or constitutive, and how far it embodies a truth about reality which cannot be conveyed by other means. In other words, the crucial question to which our investigation has led is that of the understanding of the terms employed and of their interpretation. Ultimately, as Bultmann has said, what we do with the 'myth' is a question of hermeneutics, though the character of the interpretation will depend upon the point of departure and the principle of interpretation which the interpreter brings to his task.

For it is clear that religious truth can be expressed in more ways than one, though first of all we have to be sure of what it is that we are expressing when we employ a certain kind of language. The aesthetic experience requires one method of communication, that which is provided by art in its various forms. Physics requires a different kind of language, metaphysics yet another. The Bible indicates throughout that transcendental truth can be best expressed in terms of myth and quasi-myth, for even the story of Creation is not an authentic myth in the sense in which the word is applied to the primitive cosmological and cosmogonic myths of other ancient cultures. It is rather the result of the mythopoetical creativeness of a mind capable of contemplating, in terms of advanced ethical and theological ideas, the human situation as confronted by a by no means mythically-conceived God. It uses the method of myth but reflects the thought of a post-mythical age. In so doing it so employs the technique of vivid imagery that this operates in the more advanced religious consciousness as do primordial images in the religion which has not yet broken away from myth. These images are archetypal concepts drawn from the depths of the religious consciousness and persist even when 'mythical' religion has been superseded and a culture-religion has been placed by a universal faith. To these archetypal forms of 'authentic' myth correspond the symbols and images of a developed religion, so that side by side with surviving archetypes there exist new symbols, images, and mythical conceptions which play the same part in the new religion as did their prototypes or paratypes in the old. This 'mythological' thinking, as Cassirer has observed, has its own dialectic by which a religion is enabled more objectively to reflect upon its mythological content and conceives of it analogically or metaphorically instead of as identified with it. It thereby evolves a new attitude towards the 'mythical' picture of the world which it has outgrown and adopts a new relationship towards the totality of the empirical world.[1] The identity of form and content is replaced by a symbolical understanding of the mythical content. 'Mythical' thinking becomes 'mythological' thinking. It is the relevance of this latter type of thought, the validity of its use, the permanent significance of the language used (which includes the archetypal idiom), and the importance of its conservation, which will form the concluding stages of this enquiry.

[1] Op. cit., pp. 286 ff.

CHAPTER TWO

THE MYTH AS ARCHETYPE

I

In an essay entitled *Towards A New Social Philosophy* Professor Karl Mannheim drew attention to the importance of what he called 'Christian archetypes', 'primordial images', or the expression of 'paradigmatic experience' as necessary both for social integration and for the continuity of the religious tradition. They are necessary because theoretical or propositional statements or formulations are inadequate to the task of representing religious ideas as living and creative forces. The modern age, in his view, has become despiritualized because of the 'evaporation of primordial images or archetypes which have directed the life-experience of mankind throughout the ages'. Mannheim mentions as examples of these primordial images which dominate the Christian imagination Baptism, Absolution, Agape, the Eucharist, the Good Shepherd, the Cross, and Redemption.

> They are not fully understood [he says] if they are taken as mere relics of a pre-scientific stage of development. It is their disappearance without anything else to take their place which leads to the disintegration of modern life-experience and human conduct. Without paradigmatic experiences no coexistence and co-operation are possible. Without them our universe of discourse loses its articulation, conduct falls to pieces, and only disconnected bits of successful behaviour-patterns and fragments of adjustment to an ever-changing environment remain.[1]

Fundamental Christian attitudes are not laid down as rules but in the form of 'paradigmata' which present a demand in enduring concrete pictures to which men can adjust themselves in different periods and in varying ways though still responding to the original stimulus. The parable, for example, is for this reason more helpful

[1] *A Diagnosis of Our Time*, Kegan Paul, 1943, p. 136.

than the precept, and makes possible the transference of Jesus' intention into varying situations. A paradigm conveys a wealth of experience, whereas a rational formulation of a principle can even be misleading.[1] Relative to this approval of the usefulness of paradigmatic symbols Mannheim writes about the 'presentness' in the idea of progress by which he means a dynamic element making necessary the 'return' to central experiences which transfuse their spirit into new situations. Thus it means a continual rebirth, a continued revaluation and reinterpretation of the same substance. The preservation of primordial images means, in the modern age, the conservative element preserving the basis of a diffused pattern of thought and behaviour while permitting a plastic re-interpretation in the light of the changing needs of the time.

What Mannheim has said about religion in relation to social patterns is applicable to religion as such. Without its archetypal images it would soon dissolve into either idealism on the one hand or ethics on the other, the one lacking dynamic and without a living clothing, and the other hardening into a group of moral imperatives without persuasive ultimate sanction.

Now, whether the Christian story of Redemption is to be described as 'myth' in the sense in which the word is generally understood, or as 'mythological' in the sense of being presented in what Dr. Rawlinson briefly calls 'pictorial metaphor', it is clear that the story is told in terms which have become archetypes and 'primordial images', some of which are not peculiar to Christianity but are common to other forms of religion. The 'primordial image', for example, of the Divine Mother and the Mother and Child, older than Christianity and representing a fusion of it with surviving or adapted elements of other religions, is among the most ancient and widespread of its kind, and satisfies a primitive religious need which no mere statement of doctrine is able to do. This particular 'primordial' image has been mainly instrumental in preserving the pattern of Roman Catholic piety and has been such a potent force that, in contrast

---

[1] Ibid., p. 118. Mannheim's observation may be regarded as lending support to the idea of myth as *Lebensform* (Cassirer). Malinowski, in his *Myth in Primitive Psychology* (in *Frazer Lectures*, 1932), emphasizes this relation between *mythos* and life.

to Protestant piety, Catholicism has assumed the form of mother-and-child cult in which the Mother has been given a mediatorial function no less conspicuous than that assigned to the Son. A complex of archetypal associations is deeply engrained in popular Catholicism, and, through official policy, has become normative for the Roman faith. That this is so is demonstrated by the universality of the plastic and pictorial representation of the mother-and-child-*motif* as an archetypal image capable of evoking psychological phenomena of a complex and far-reaching character.

On a deeper level, too, that of the biblical picture of the history of Redemption, the 'myth' is inseparable from the theological scheme of traditional Christianity. It begins with Creation and the place in it of the archetypal man in whom sin entered into the world through the primordial 'Fall'. This could, in such a form, be described only in terms which could hardly have been intended to be understood otherwise than mythologically. Until the nineteenth century the mythological expression of primordial experience dominated Christian anthropology, and even in the twentieth century theologians have been unable to resist what still appears to them to be the necessity to 'interpret' mythological categories whose relevance either to knowledge or to a modern approach to the question of sin, is to say the least, somewhat questionable. Although the rest of the Old Testament exhibits little familiarity with the Adamic myth, the traditional view of biblical inspiration conferred upon it an authoritativeness which it would otherwise not have possessed; yet it contains a truth which, if interpreted non-mythologically, corresponds to our empirical knowledge that sin, sorrow, anguish, and evil are universal in extent, are temporally embedded in human history and in pre-history, and are therefore radically inalienable factors in the 'existential' situation. Neither the age of the Adamic myth nor the depths of its roots in the Hebrew religious conscious-ness is it possible to acertain, for the Mosaic law shows no know-ledge of it, nor does the Book of Job, the only other document in the Old Testament (apart, possibly, from some of the Psalms) which deals with the problems of evil and suffering. But whether this is relevant or irrelevant to its significance, it was given a fundamental place in the Christian scheme of Redemption through its occurrence in a body of literature considered to be divinely inspired, and also through St. Paul's association of the Adam in whom all died with the New Man, the New Adam, who reversed the doom overhanging human destiny. In the Pauline picture of Redemption Jesus has been given a 'mythical' significance through his attainment of a position complementary to that of Adam. The New Adam as the image of God is not, however, a 'mythical' conception but rather a metaphor based on religious experience and the encounter of the Christian with the Redeemer in his redemptive function as Lord. The idea of the first Adam as the 'image' of God *is* mythological, for it has no basis in history or anthropology, and is a falsification of history in that it represents man as having 'fallen' from a state of unverifiable perfection. Whatever truth the Adamic myth contains has not to do with the 'fall' of man but with his 'fallenness'. Nevertheless, though the Adam-image has been woven into the pattern of the plan of Salvation, it is questionable *how much* of it is capable of reinterpretation in any sense compatible with either psychological knowledge or theological integrity.

Moreover, within the completed design of this pattern, or as its consummation, there are other images, experiences, or theological concepts which have assumed the significance of archetypes or primordial symbols and which are given the ambiguous character already mentioned of being a metaphysical mythologization of the historical. They can be understood only through the impact of the historical on man's experience, which they not only reflect but condition and re-shape within the Christian context. The Sotēr, for example, whether purely mythological as in the mystery-religions, or historical, as in the New Testament, is a primordial concept whose efficacy is dependent upon the correspondence of man's plight to his situation as mythologically described in the Adamic myth. 'Saviour' is both a mythical and a historical conception: myth in that the 'Saviour' of antiquity had no real existence, and historical in so far as the Christian Saviour, the *Kyrios* of the Church, is he who has been personally involved in history.

For the New Testament the notion of Redemption and the cognate ones of Atonement and Reconciliation were rooted in

Hebraic archetypal thinking which centred in the idea of sacrifice and the efficacy of blood-letting. This, again, is a universal and primitive religious idea, and for the writers of the New Testament was given direct paradigmatic form in the story of the historical sacrifice on Calvary. That Jesus' own interpretation of his mission was conditioned, at any rate in part, by this archetypal way of thinking, is clear; and the author of the Epistle to the Hebrews interpreted it by referring to the prefigurative Melchizedek, who belongs to the realm of mythological thinking. Jesus has 'become' a high priest for ever after the order of Melchizedek (Heb. 6: 20); as a 'priest' he entered the sanctuary offering 'his own blood, thus securing an eternal redemption' (9: 12). 'Without the shedding of blood there can be no forgiveness of sins' (9: 22). The Epistle is an outstanding example of the way in which not only analogical but typological thinking had so penetrated the early Christian mind that it thought of the 'present' without effort in terms of the past whose distance in time was curiously foreshortened by this inability to distinguish clearly between history and myth. Jesus 'is' Melchizedek; he 'is' Adam, the second Adam, because he is the consummation of humanity as Adam was its representative prototype. Recent study of the so-called unity of the Old Testament and the New has shown how this kind of typological thinking permeated the thought of the Apostolic writers. Even if their principles of interpretation appear somewhat arbitrary to the modern reader and their lack of clearness as to the difference between myth and history is perplexing to the modern mind, they throw much light on first-century habits of mind. Jesus 'is' the Son of Man, he 'is' the Messiah, though these are futurist 'persons'. His sacrifice, and therefore the method of redemption, is to be understood in terms of primordial and paradigmatic concepts, or at any rate of picturesque thought-forms which had become archetypal determinants through long incorporation in a religious tradition.

If it is difficult for the modern mind to appreciate this dependence on archetypal-primordial thinking some illumination may be derived from the insight of the world of literature. In this connexion further mention should be made of Thomas Mann's *Joseph and his Brethren*, where Mann, with great learning and creative insight, has tried to penetrate into and to reconstruct imaginatively the primordial deposits of the primitive mind in the context of this confusion of history and myth. Joseph 'goes down' into Egypt and emerges into a new life, which is the symbol of death-and-resurrection. Like Osiris, he is the 'mangled one'. He renames himself Osarsiph (Osiris-Joseph). Mann sets out the intellectual and religious presuppositions of Joseph's world, which is furnished with the lore and mythology of Babylon, Canaan, and the Osiris-cults. He 'becomes' Osiris; Abraham is for him a kind of grandfather, having been brought by a foreshortening of time into the present. Jacob's well is a womb of time, symbolical of the human consciousness, the repository of the 'primitive mythical inheritance of all peoples'. Joseph eats of the lamb whose blood has soaked his dress: through this haemophagy it is made clear that 'the blood is the life'. In *Joseph the Provider* Pharaoh utters a speech which is a deliberate parallel, through an adaptation of the phraseology of the Hermetic writings, to the mystical words of Jesus in the Fourth Gospel. Throughout great sections of his tetralogy Mann seeks to show how the thought of the biblical world was inseparable from archetypal concepts and primordial images. It should be borne in mind that the same deposits were most likely present in the minds of the Apostolic writers, though the symbols may not have been in all instances the same. (See further, K. Hamburger, op. cit., pp. 43–142, especially p. 96 ff., on *Der Mythus und Joseph oder Der Mythus als Symbol*, and my article on *Joseph and his Brethren* in *The Congregational Quarterly*, Oct., 1947).

The place of archetypal symbols in modern art might prove to be a subject of profitable enquiry. One instance is the place of the bull in Picasso's work. The bull is given a prominent place in his *Guernica*, his *Minotauromachy*, and *The Death of the Bull*. As the function of the bull in the first of the three pictures is not clear, it would appear that it possesses some symbolic significance, especially in view of the facts that the Bull is one of the signs of the Zodiac (the sign of Taurus), and the symbol of the first Evangelist. It is given prominence in the Mithraic ritual of the Taurobolium, and the cow occurs in the Egyptian cosmogony. The Golden Calf was presumably the symbol of the Bull, that is of the principle of generation. I have mentioned Picasso in order to show that one of the most 'abstract' of artists painted as his most impressive work one which seems to include archetypal symbols (of which the horse would appear to be one) possessing a certain significance for the painter. The question of their significance for religion as indicated by its comparative study is of considerable interest. While the Cross, for example, as one of the Christian symbols, is 'historical', it has affinities with the mythology of the 'world-tree', which occurs in many mythologies and religions. Osiris was associated with the tamarisk, Attis with the pine; Odin hung on the tree Yggdrasil. This suggests that the mythopoeic imagination lingered on the tree-symbol, which is also the *axis mundi*; and Jesus made use of the figures of the vine and its branches and of the tree as the symbol of the Kingdom of Heaven (cf. A. W. Watts, *Myth and Ritual in Christianity*, pp. 158 ff.). Within the same context of archetypal images are Jesus' words: 'For as Jonah was three days and three nights in the whale's belly, so shall the Son of Man be three days and three nights in the heart of the earth.' How much of the Jonah story was a comparatively recent fable, and how far it embodied very ancient traditions cannot easily be ascertained; but it is quite possible that its manifest symbolism covers the latent primordial symbolism of the return to the womb (descent into the hold of the ship and into the darkness of the 'whale's' belly—cf. Erich Fromm, *The Forgotten Language*, p. 28).

Indeed, the more the subject is studied in depth, the more difficult does it become to escape the conclusion that both the Old Testament and New Testament archetypes are incapable of being fully understood in isolation from the expression in other religions and cults of the basic images from which all are derived. Thus the words 'spoken' on the occasion of Jesus' Baptism—'Thou art my beloved Son in whom I am well pleased': a composite reference to Isaiah 42: 1 and Psalm 2: 7, with the omission of the 'this day I have begotten thee'—are paralleled in Amon-Rē's words to his son Horus: 'You are my beloved Son whom I begat' (E. Norden, *Die Geburt des Kindes*, p. 75) and by the moment in the Mithraïc Fire Greeting in which the initiate is declared to be 'born again today' (A. Dieterich, *Eine Mithrasliturgie*, text pp. 10, 12). H. Gressmann goes so far as to say that 'the blood-goblet which Osiris offers to his nearest before his death, and the blood-goblet of Jesus on the night in which he was betrayed can no more be separated from one another than the sacrament of the Lord's supper itself from the sacramental meals of Osiris' (*Der Messias*, p. 414): no doubt a sweeping statement but one which implies that the same root-conception is present in both and is derived from something ulterior: the primitive belief in the efficacy of a theophagy. C. H. Dodd states that the place of theophagy in Hellenistic cults has been exaggerated, and gives it as his judgement, in relation to the Fourth Gospel, that the most we may say is that 'theophagy belongs to a deep stratum of primitive thought and practice which, lying submerged in our minds, generates a natural and more or less universal symbolism; and such symbolism is capable of being revivified on a higher level'. Dodd adds that the background of John's Gospel is not in the cruder paganism but in Philo and the Hermetica and in developed Gnostic systems from which theophagy is absent (*The Interpretation of the Fourth Gospel*, p. 339, footnote).

Further, though the birth of Jesus is that of a historical person, the Messianic background to the New Testament conception of it is much wider and deeper than at first appears. The birth of the wonderful child (Isa. 9: 6–7) and the Messianic thought-world which it represents is surprisingly similar to the theme of Virgil's Fourth Eclogue, which Gressmann (op. cit., pp. 462 ff.) expounds and which was the starting-point of Norden's investigations into the myth of the birth of the Child which, in its parallels in Egyptian myth, also presupposes an encounter between a deity (Helios) and a woman (Selene). Norden's view is that there was sufficient cultural contact between Egypt and Palestine to account for the spread of the story of the miraculous birth. Nevertheless, as W. M. Urban says (*Humanity and Deity*, p. 93), 'similarity of form does not mean identity of essence'. The point is that the stuff out of which religious symbols are made represents something universal in the human psyche. A historical parallel is no less historical because it shares the same kind of symbolism or mythical concept as the non-Christian cults or mythologies. If it means anything, it is that the history is the fulfilment of the ultra-mythical impulses which are objectified in myth. For accounts of the formation of archetypal symbols and their appearance in ritual and belief see, inter alia, A. W. Watts. op. cit., E. O. James, *Christian Myth and Ritual* (1933), C. G. Jung, *Psychology and Alchemy*, where form-symbols such as the *mandala* sign are dealt with at length, Mircea Éliade, *Le Mythe de l'Eternel Retour: Archetypes et Répétition* (1949)[1] and his article: 'Psychology and Comparative Religion: A Study of the Symbolism of the Centre', reprinted in *Selection* II (Sheed and Ward, 1954).

The Cross, which is the universal symbol of Christianity rather than in the strict sense an archetypal image, stands not only for sacrifice but for resurrection. This, however, is not only a category of mythological thinking (as in the mystery religions), for it describes what for the Christian is the historical act of salvation. It is nevertheless given a mythological colouring by St. Paul's language about dying to sin through baptism into Christ and emergence into newness of life 'through' his resurrection (Rom. 6: 1–12), though it might be unwise to press the analogy too far.

Taken as a whole, then, the pattern of *Heilsgeschichte* is presented in near-mythical form. Through the first Adam sin entered into the world; the evil done could not be put right except by the 'second' Adam who, as the Saviour, effects the reconciliation between man and God through the shedding of blood. This is not only the pattern of the 'myth': it is the dynamic basis of all Christian thinking. If this story is removed and there are substituted for it bare propositional or theological statements, the truth which Christianity proclaims is confined more or less to doctrinal formulae or dogmatic affirmations. The depths out of which emerge new and continually creative re-statements of faith would no longer be fully available, and the faith would be tied to the letter instead of being continually expanded by the spirit, as would appear to be the case with Judaism. Even the concept of salvation may be unintelligible or only barely comprehensible to the modern man whose religious world has gone into dissolution because the archetypal symbols mean little or

[1] *The Myth of the Eternal Return* (Kegan Paul, 1955).

nothing to him, and because he lacks the background which is necessary to the provision of a common Christian experience.

Moreover, once a figure of thought or a religious image has become an archetypal and familiar norm to which religious conceptions can be referred and is at the same time accepted as the source of those conceptions, it is not easy to find a substitute for it. This is especially so in regard to the 'mythical' unity of the whole 'story' of salvation, for in it we are dealing, as Brunner has observed, not with theories but with 'existential statements of the Faith' which are not mere objects of contemplation but matters of faith in which believers share.[1] The 'myth' is a divine word, not a human invention, though the form in which it appears takes the shape which man gives to it. It is, fundamentally, a dramatic representation of human destiny and of the intervention of God in the history which He Himself has motivated. And drama is not only dialogue: it is dialogue with action. Berdyaev is right in saying that only a symbolic and mythological approach to the relationship between God and man can bring us closer to the divine mystery. 'The meeting of God and man,' he says, 'is a mythological representation and not a philosophical proposition.'[2] Reason, philosophical speculation, and what he calls 'theological theism' are inadequate to penetrate to the ultimate reality which faith discloses; and where reason is brought to bear analytically upon myth it is often as a solvent, not as an interpreter. Bultmann distinguishes between 'understanding' and 'rational' interpretation, with which it should not be identified; and an early 'existential', if not in the narrower sense 'existentialist' philosopher, Miguel de Unamuno, intensely critical of all rationalism and conceptual analytical thinking derived, as he believed, through Kant from the Reformation, opposed reason, the instrument of analysis, to imagination, which he regarded as synthetic; and myth is a truth given its form by the mythopoeic and mythopoetical imagination. 'Reason annihilates,' he wrote, 'imagination integrates and gives totality; reason by itself kills and imagination is that which gives life'.[3]

---

[1] *The Mediator*, p. 389.
[2] *Freedom and the Spirit*, p. 195.
[3] 'La razón aniquila, y la imaginación entera, integra o totaliza; la razón por

The great myths are primarily imaginative creations. Even though they may appear to be attempts to rationalize or provide an explanation of experience, they do so as the product not of reason but of imaginative insight. The Creation and Adamic myths, for example, are imaginatively conceived attempts to explain the origin of the world and of evil. They are mythopoetical not scientifically apodictic or psychological, explanations, for these were not available to the writers, whose minds moved easily and naturally in the realms of faith and imagination. They thought of creation as a religious act, and of the facts of sin and pain as aspects of what, had they been aware of such a mode of thought, they might have described as man's 'existential' situation and of his 'existential' reactions to a religiously conceived, though problematical, order. Hence the statement with which Genesis begins is insufficient: it must be amplified by a magnificently imaginative attempt to describe *how* God in the beginning created the heavens and the earth. In this case the theology is prior to the cosmogony, which is expressed in terms of myth. The anthropogonic myth, however, is more 'mythical' than the cosmogonic, and so productive has it been of the archetypal forms which have stimulated Christian theology that, notwithstanding its non-historicity, the pictures and images which have been employed in it have left an impression on the religious imagination which is likely to be permanent. The myth has become a paradigm of Christian thinking, though it is realized that it does not correspond to the actual pattern of events.

Into the relationship between the Christological 'myth' or the mythological thinking of Christology and the archetypal ideas embedded in the sacraments I do not propose to enter, though it is a fruitful field of investigation. As, moreover, much has been written on this matter it is necessary only to state that, in their present form the Pauline references to baptism, in particular, are indissociable from *some* degree of mythological content and association. The conception of the Christ 'in' whom one 'dies' and 'in' whom one is 'raised up' in newness of life ('Therefore

---

sí solo mata y la imaginación es la que da vida' (*Del Sentimiento Trágico de la Vida*, p. 181).

are we buried with him by baptism into death,' etc., Rom. 6: 4) belongs to a group of archetypes which, as Fr. Louis Beirnaert has pointed out in an illuminating essay, must be understood if the writings of the Fathers on baptism are to be appreciated. The archetypal symbolism of water is taken up into the sacrament and shows that the 'mythical dimension' is still present and active in the new dimension which dominates it.[1] Relevant to this aspect of New Testament 'myth', too, is the wider question of St. Paul's indebtedness to the mystery religions, a complicated question on which full agreement is difficult to reach. It is, of course, true that the sacraments have affinity with similar non-Christian cults, though they are in a sense demythologized in their form, and also that the 'myth' must be rationally examined in order to be intelligible or that its value as truth may be ascertained. Nevertheless, behind the sacrament itself is a complexity of depth-symbols which reach back into the unconscious and are made intelligible through mythological pictures. As is well-known, C. G. Jung has given a prominent place to the function of primordial images or archetypes in his analytical psychology, recognizing the importance of the myth, and claiming that there exists in the 'collective unconscious' a vast reservoir of primordial ways of thinking and feeling: archetypes which he describes as 'inherited potentialities of human imagination'. Thomas Mann, as has been noted, gave a complex literary expression to this world of primordial images in the *Joseph* tetralogy, one of which was the concept of 'going down', an image which occurs in the sacrament of baptism and in the descent 'into the lowest parts of the earth' (Ephes. 4: 9) and other similar instances. In the light of illustrations provided by Fr. Beirnaert in the essay alluded to it seems that there is much more in the original sacramental symbols than is immediately apparent, though the primordial images have long been forgotten or superseded by the historical reference of what is being celebrated. Jung, at any rate, believes this hidden deposit of images in the unconscious to be of such importance that he has taken cognizance of them in the clinical treatment of neurosis.

[1] 'The Mythical Dimension in Christian Baptism', Eranos-Jahrbuch, Zurich, 1949, reprinted in *Selection* I, Sheed and Ward, 1953, pp. 43 ff. Cf. also F. W. Dillistone, *Christianity and Symbolism* (1955), chapter 7.

It should be stated that Bultmann's use of the term myth (and the use of it which is made in the present context) differs from Jung's, which is confined to pictures having their roots in the unconscious. 'Myths are original revelations of the preconscious psyche' (*Introduction to a Science of Mythology*, by C. G. Jung and C. Kerenyi, Kegan Paul, 1951, p. 101). In his comments on Kerenyi's study of the myth of the Child, Jung points out that in all child-myths there are three elements: insignificant beginnings and miraculous birth; the helplessness of the child before his enemies; his possession of powers exceeding those of ordinary human nature. The analogies in the Gospels are obvious. What Jung says of archetypes can, however, be applied analogically to 'myth' in the sense in which we are using the term. 'No archetype,' he says, 'can be reduced to a simple formula. It is a vessel which we can never empty, never fill ... The archetypes are the imperishable elements of the unconscious, but they change their shape continually' (ibid., p. 136). He proceeds to express the view that we cannot legitimately repudiate these archetypal foundations unless we are prepared to pay the price of a neurosis (p. 105), to which we might compare the spiritual impoverishment which results from the rejection of Christological and other archetypes in religion. It may be argued therefore that the Christological 'myth' is necessary to the transmission of the faith in order to save it from theological asthenia. Although in their original form the sacraments and the Christological titles contain archetypal foundations which we no longer regard as organic to them, their importance should not be underestimated or disregarded. If, as Jung says, 'an archetype is a dynamic image, a fragment of the objective psyche' (*Two Essays on Analytical Psychology*, Kegan Paul, 1953 (E.tr. collected works, vol. vii) p. 108), the definition has to be adapted to the context in which we are discussing it; though in certain forms, e.g. the 'magic demon', the archetype may be seen as occurring in the New Testament thought-world. Just as the demonic effect 'emanating' from someone may disappear when the mysterious feeling is traced to the collective unconscious (Jung), so the demon is exorcized when it is named.

In his discussion of religious archetypes Dr. A. M. Farrer considers them to be essential as descriptions of God unless He is to be regarded as 'simple pure and infinite essence' (*The Glass of Vision*, Dacre Press, 1948, p. 102), though they may become dangerous in so far as they favour dogmatisms. Archetypes, in his view, have a purely historical justification and may be called 'rhetorical exaggerations', though the exaggeration which they imply has 'huge spiritual consequences' (p. 103). The images which archetypes assume are 'supernaturally formed and supernaturally made intelligible to faith' (p. 110). The safeguard against the false suggestions of archetypes is to be found in reducing them to 'creative intentions' which, if this phrase is broadly understood, is the purpose of demythologizing. Dr. Farrer does not use the term archetype in the Jungian sense but rather as it is employed by Mannheim and as indicating ancient religious images which have come to have a definite meaning through association and through which divine truth is supernaturally communicated (ibid., p. 57).

2

In another field, the study of history and of the forces which contribute to its motivation, Professor A. J. Toynbee has dwelt at length on the significance of myth, which often takes the form of describing an encounter between two superhuman personalities or between one superhuman and one human personality.[1]

> An encounter between two superhuman personalities is the plot of some of the greatest stories and dramas that the human imagination has conceived. An encounter between Yahweh and the Serpent is the plot of the story of the Fall of Man in the Book of Genesis; a second encounter between the same antagonists is the plot of the New Testament which tells the story of the Redemption; an encounter between the Lord and Satan is the plot of the Book of Job; an encounter between the Lord and Mephistopheles is the plot of Goethe's *Faust*; an encounter between gods and demons is the plot of the Scandinavian Voluspá; an encounter between Artemis and Aphrodite is the plot of Euripides' *Hippolytus*. . . . We find another version of the same plot in that ubiquitous and ever-recurring myth—a 'primordial image', if there ever was one —of the encounter between the Virgin and the Father of her Child.

One form of the myth is the story of the wager between God and the Devil, in which the Devil is defeated and an innocent victim is involved, examples of which are the Book of Job, Goethe's *Faust*, the biblical story of the Fall, and the Gospel story, for it is significant that, though the actual wager is absent, it opens with the Temptation, in which the Devil is confounded. Some forms of the doctrine of the Atonement, too, have taken this mythological form in so far as the Crucifixion was regarded as a means of cheating the Devil of his due.

Another theme of the myth is Redemption through Suffering.

> In the New Testament [Toynbee proceeds] the agony and resignation and passion of Jesus achieve the redemption of Man and are followed by the Redeemer's Resurrection and Ascension; in

---

[1] *A Study of History*, vol. i, pp. 271 ff.

the Scandinavian mythology Odin returns to life after hanging upon a tree. . .

Now, this superhuman encounter, according to Toynbee, is the mythical depiction of the challenge and response responsible for the genesis of civilizations. It is conceived as a

> rare and sometimes as a unique event; and it has consequences which are vast in proportion to the vastness of the breach which it makes in the customary course of Nature.

These consequences are exemplified in the results of the encounters portrayed in the book of Genesis and in the New Testament, where the uniqueness of the divine event is the essence of the story.

Toynbee summarises his argument as follows:

> By the light of Mythology, as we have gained some insight into the nature of challenges and responses. We have come to see that creation is the outcome of an encounter,—or, to re-translate the imagery of myths into the terminology of Science—that genesis is a function of interaction:[1]

an interaction which is 'mythologized' even by a scientist such as Sir James Jeans in order to make the process (the description of which is pictorial) intelligible. The purpose of Dr. Toynbee's contention, illustrated by an opulence of examples, is to show that mythological thinking is a natural means of rendering intelligible the great moments of human development, and that it is not purely fictitious but corresponds in some degree to reality. An extraordinary feature of this mythological thinking is the closeness of the parallels between the myths of widely separated cultures and their similarity to a historical narrative such as that which is presented in the New Testament. *Heilsgeschichte* is history; but its underlying structure is remarkably like that of non-historical mythology. Whether this testifies to the unconscious operation in the minds of the New Testament writers of the primordial images of the racial unconscious, or whether these

[1] *A Study of History*, vol. i, p. 299.

images are at the basis of all human action and therefore of history, is an interesting theme for speculation.[1] However this may be, Toynbee regards myth as more than a mere tale: it is a vehicle of truth. It is not itself the truth, but its vehicle.

It is here that some guidance may be found in our attempt to evaluate the importance and usefulness of mythological thinking in its relevance to Christology. Whereas, however, the primordial images of the analytical psychology belong to the sub-rational world, the unconscious depth into which one may on certain occasions gaze, as Jacob gazes into the depths of the well in the first volume of Mann's tetralogy while the perspective dies away in the infinite and obscure distance of what Mann calls *Zeitkulissen*,[2] and whereas the genetic myths of Toynbee's 'encounters' are the literary creations of primitive people, the result, no doubt of an imaginative insight whose operation cannot be intellectually grasped, the mythological idiom of the New Testament is in a somewhat different category. It differs from folk-lore or from ethnic myth in that this does not really concern itself with humanity at all, for the epic heroes are not men like gods but gods like men. The 'failure of nerve' of the ancient world, to borrow Dr. Gilbert Murray's phrase, was due to a considerable extent to the fact that the people of that world no longer took their pantheon seriously but believed in it only formally, if at all.

Because of its concrete historical relevance the Christian 'myth', re-enacted in church liturgy and ritual, is a vehicle of truth in a way in which the pagan mythology was not. Neither the Olympic mythology nor the bizarre world of the Mabinogion, which has been so transformed by literary narrative that the original Celtic deities are now no more than men whose heroic stature is enhanced by their grotesque prowess, nor Osiris, Serapis nor Isis, speaks to man of any truth about his own existence capable

---

[1] It is probable that some of the perplexing images in Revelation, such as that of the Woman Clothed with the Sun (Rev. 12: 1–9), belong to this deep level from which archetypes are drawn. This passage is the only example in the New Testament of the genuine myth and may be a creation-myth to which an apocalyptic-messianic context is given. Gressmann, who deals at length with it (*Der Messias*, pp. 393 ff.) believes it to be of Egyptian origin. See further A. M. Farrer, *The Rebirth of Images*, for a study of the symbolism of Revelation.

[2] '*Zeitkulissen*' may be paraphrased as 'receding time-vistas', literally 'time-scenery' (on the stage-wings).

of remoulding society, regenerating personality, and of providing ethical norms. From the standpoints of psychology and of the paradigmatic interpretation and understanding of religious experience and the conservation of a vivid appreciation of Christian doctrine, mythological expression of the Christian faith is indispensable. The elucidation of its meaning is the task of theological interpretation.

CHAPTER THREE

THE MYTH AS NORM

I

There is one matter to which we must return: the question with which our enquiry began. How far should mythological thinking be retained in an age to which it is foreign and to which mythological categories are likely to be increasingly unacceptable? This mode of thinking, we have seen, is embedded in the New Testament, and the problem with which Bultmann set out to deal was that of interpreting this mythological material 'existentially', so that the 'myth' might be retained while at the same time addressing itself to man in his 'existential' situation. His thesis is that the 'myth' in the New Testament should be considered as having 'anthropological' rather than 'cosmological' reference. In other words, it speaks of what is on its human side rather than of what is beyond itself. Bultmann, it should be observed, does not suggest that the 'myth' should be understood Christologically or theologically, though he implies that it is the task of theology to interpret it. We have already agreed that the myth, like any doctrine, should have 'existential' reference, which in the last resort means little more than that it should be seen to be relevant to personal experience and not, as Schelling interpreted it, as the expression of the self-realization of the absolute.

Although, however, Bultmann explains in his reply to his critics that what he has in mind is 'existential self-understanding' and not 'the existentialist understanding of human existence elaborated by philosophical analysis',[1] it is questionable whether the field covered by New Testament 'myth' can be confined to this. In any case, to emphasize so heavily the subjective factor at the expense of the objective truth behind the myth—assuming

---

[1] *Kerygma and Myth*, p. 203. Bultmann admits here that he was to blame for confusion caused by failing to distinguish between the two things with sufficient clarity.

that it can be disclosed—comes perilously near to substituting one kind of 'consciousness religion' for another, so that the 'feeling of absolute dependence' in Schleiermacher's theology (one of the chief targets of the dialectical theology) is replaced by 'existential self-understanding', a kind of *Existenzgefühl*; though here again Bultmann endeavours to remove misunderstanding by saying that in this self-understanding there is involved the further understanding of the 'object of the encounter'. It is, of course, apparent that there must be two parties to an encounter, an 'it' or a 'thou' as well as an 'I'. Yet Bultmann's emphasis seems to be predominantly on the 'I', on the self and its understanding of itself and of its predicament when confronted with ultimate 'nothingness', an emphasis which is supported by the observation that 'faith needs to be emancipated from its association with a world-view expressed in objective terms, whether mythical or scientific'.[1]

Now, if this means that faith, that is, Christian belief, is not to be tied down to any particular cosmology, whether Hebrew, Hellenistic, or post-Newtonian, we should agree; for it is evident that this faith does not depend on the truth or falsehood of a cosmological pattern into which the 'beggarly elements' or the Seven Cosmocrats are woven. But there is no need to pay any attention to this particular cosmological pattern: it does not even require an existential interpretation; it is, moreover, not conspicuous in the Synoptic Gospels, though these Bultmann appears to exclude from his consideration. The cosmology can be left out of account, for it is of value neither cosmologically nor anthropologically. This kind of picture is part of an obsolete world view, and it is doubtful if anyone would wish to see in it any importance for faith or for man's 'self-understanding', though we have suggested how it might be so interpreted. Barth, quite rightly, asks whether we must deny a proposition *because* it happens to be bound up with an obsolete mythological world-picture, for it would be a *Katastrophenpolitik* to insist on either its acceptance or its rejection for such a reason or its opposite; and he asks, too, if a theological proposition is to be accepted even though it may not be regarded as a genuine constituent of the Christian

[1] *Kerygma and Myth,* p. 210.

understanding of existence.[1] It is clear that the cosmology of the Epistles should be detached from the content of faith.

The 'mythological' constituents of Christology, we maintain, are in a somewhat different category from the cosmological 'myth'. They are not statements about cosmology but affirmations of faith in Jesus Christ. The Christology of Colossians 1 does not seek primarily to state an objective truth about creation: it is an affirmation, in possibly liturgical terms combined with widely current phrases drawn from Stoicism, about the Lordship of Christ: a status which, in the New Testament view, is 'objective' in so far as it is regarded as having been conferred by God upon Jesus, but which is not, so to speak, complete apart from the relation of the believer to it as subject. The cosmological ideas of the New Testament, as Bultmann has said, are those of the time and are not peculiarly Christian. They are no more necessary to the understanding of the Gospel and to Christology than is the astral fatalism of *King Lear* (and the cosmology of the Elizabethan age) to the appreciation of Shakespeare.

While, further, it is evident that a religious 'truth' should have to do with man's self-understanding (this should be self-evident), this is not its only or its primary function, which is to speak to man about God. It is a kind of Logos about God. This is also true of the mythological element in the New Testament which is a special language designed for the conveying of truths about God, Christ, and man: about God the Creator, Christ the Saviour, and man as the subject of salvation. The myth should be regarded as a form of symbolic language, just as the language of poetry is symbolic, and as science and metaphysics have their own kind of symbolism.

For ultimately, whatever its original character or intention, mythological language is symbolic, and if 'myth' is to be retained it is as a symbol. In W. M. Urban's phrase, myth is the 'symbolization of the infinite'[2] and the only language adequate to this symbolization. For this reason the mythical is not merely a primitive type of mentality to be outgrown, nor is it a wholly provisional form of expression later to be dissolved, for the

---

[1] *Kirchliche Dogmatik*, III/2, p. 534.
[2] *Humanity and Deity*, p. 101.

religious and the mythical consciousness are closely allied. Indeed, though the object of belief is not to be formally identified with the stuff of the myth, the religious consciousness nevertheless requires the mythological as its appropriate form of expression.

> It cannot do without this world [of myth, Urban writes], for it is in the mythical consciousness that the immediate intuition of meaningfulness of the world is given. Nor can the religious consciousness express its deepest insights without using the language of myth and employing the mythical categories, as all times and all peoples have discovered. But while they have discovered this they have also discovered something else—namely that the myth has acquired a new meaning and function; it has become symbolic. Religion makes use of sensuous pictures and signs but at the same time it knows them to be such.[1]

Prof. Urban proceeds to speak of the myth as indispensable both psychologically and as a necessary means of preventing religion from becoming an abstraction, for

> myth is indispensable for the reason that it is only from the language of myth that the primary symbols can be formed and only in such language that its deepest insights can be expressed.[2]

It is important that this should be realized, for otherwise myth and mythological thinking appear to be no more than the survival of an archaic and pre-theological mode of apprehension in a world which has outgrown it through its familiarity with abstract formulae on the one hand and a changed view of nature on the other. Even so succinct a statement of belief as the Apostles' Creed is mythological in character: indeed, it may be regarded as the distillation of the *Heilsgeschichte* in 'mythical' form, and it is difficult to see how any liturgy can dispense with this kind of language. Hymns, for example, which are a necessary part of

---

[1] *Humanity and Diety*, pp. 114–115.

[2] Ibid., p. 116, Chaps. II and III ('Religion and the Mythical Consciousness') and VII ('The Literal and the Symbolic in Religion'), as well as other parts of Urban's book, are a valuable contribution to the discussion of the place of myth and symbol as the language of religion. See also Urban, *Language and Reality*, Chaps. IX, X, and XII.

community worship, consist to a considerable extent of mythological thinking. They are the translation of doctrine into poetry, or at any rate into verse, which is essentially a symbolic or metaphorical representation of Christian belief and experience in non-abstract terms. Any attempt to speak of God which renounces picture, myth, symbol, or analogy, tends to result in a negative or apophatic theology in which the term 'God' makes little impression on the mind and little impact on the emotions or the imagination. There is what A. N. Whitehead calls an 'aggregate of inherited symbolism'[1] in all liturgy which seeks to preserve continuity and universality in religious ideas and doctrines which, without it, would be in danger of becoming abstract formulations. The simplest definition or description of God as 'Father' in the teaching of Jesus is analogical, and even a concept such as the Kingdom of God Jesus found incommunicable without illustration and analogy. The Kingdom is not the merchant seeking pearls, nor is it a mustard seed or a tree, though it cannot be brought within the range of intelligibility without reliance upon such symbols or metaphors which, through usage, have become part of the heritage of Christian imagery.

Similarly, a term such as 'Lamb of God', with all its ritualistic associations and adjectival attributes, is deemed necessary to convey a Christological and soteriological truth in a manner to which extended theological statement might be inadequate. The term is symbolical, though in the apocalyptic language of the Book of Revelation it becomes mythological.

Into the difference between symbol, myth, and analogy I do not propose to enter, as it would involve an extended discussion of the questions of the relation of symbol to meaning and of language as symbolism.[2] It must be sufficient to state that, as far as our purpose is concerned, 'myth' is to be considered as a form of symbol and mythological thinking as a form of dynamic symbolism; for a mere symbol is static, whereas a characteristic of myth is that it is symbol expressed in movement. Symbolic representation is present in developed and in undeveloped religions,

---

[1] *Symbolism: its Meaning and Effect*, p. 86.
[2] In addition to the works of Urban and Cassirer already mentioned, see Edwyn Bevan, *Symbolism and Belief*, 1938.

and in its mythological form it should be regarded as containing both truth and fiction: truth in so far as what is symbolized has value apart from the symbol, and fiction in so far as an imaginative form is created in order to express the particular truth. Thus, to take an example from our field of enquiry, the representation of the 'story of salvation' as the descent and ascent of a pre-existent divine being may be a fiction with analogies in other non-historical religions which the Christian regards as myth, whereas the 'truth' consists in the statement that the transcendent God became personally immanent in the world of His creation through Incarnation in Jesus of Nazareth. How this occurred can only be described mythologically, for even if the Divine Conception and the Virgin Birth are accepted as historically factual, they can be described only in non-biological terms, that is to say, in terms which are taken from some other field of reference and so applied that the result is that narrative partakes of the character of myth. For the mythological content of the Birth-narratives consists of the familiar story of the encounter between a deity and a human person. The divine-human encounter is the basic substance of the myth. The truth can be explicated only by means of the theological interpretation of the myth. Indeed, this encounter, in one form or another, is of the essence of experiential religion and, it should be added, of Old Testament prophecy. The Bible is the story of such encounter, though its modes vary according to the cultural level of those who describe or experience it.

Cassirer observes[1] that the language of religion is to be distinguished from that of logic in that, whereas for the latter 'reality' and 'appearance' are two opposites which provide for no alternative, for the former the antithesis does not exist in such a sharp form: there is a middle term between 'appearance' and 'reality'. Hence, when the religious consciousness has developed beyond the mythical stage, the rejection of the mythical as merely 'appearance' does not mean that the conceptual reality behind it requires no other kind of non-logical representation. The myth is not to be considered to have no value simply because it is superseded, though the prophetic-monotheistic religion rejects

[1] *Das Mythische Denken*, p. 291.

mythology in order to make possible the direct inter-communion between God and man;[1] and Cassirer correctly observes that in Christianity the dissolution of the mythical world-picture becomes all the more difficult because the mythical mode of perception (*Anschaulichkeit*) is so implied in its basic teaching and dogmatic content that this content would be jeopardized if deprived of its mythological expression.[2] As an illustration of this, let anyone try to describe the Christian *Heilsgeschichte* in any manner which excludes the divine-human encounter which is, ultimately, the main substance of most mythologies and that which the New Testament has consistently set forth through the mythological language of the Birth-narratives, the symbolic description of the Baptism, the terminology of apocalyptic and eschatology, the 'Pauline' mythopoetry of Colossians, the Transfiguration, the sacraments, and the Resurrection itself. An encounter with evil (that is, a superhuman, demonic, spiritual cosmic power) is expressed through the confrontation of Jesus with the demoniacally possessed, and in the overcoming of the power of darkness through the weapons of faith placed in the hands of the Christian. It may, further, be with justice claimed that it is the 'mythological' expression of the Gospel rather than the more objective character of the Synoptic narrative which raises it from the level of the merely 'historical' (*historisch*) to that of the historic (*geschichtlich*).

Symbol, metaphor, analogy, mythological thinking: these constitute the language most appropriate to the conveying of religious ideas; the ultimate question of how far what is conveyed by them is true is one for apologetics and lies outside the scope of this investigation. What is being contended is that universal experience lends support to the thesis that religion deprived of its mythological expression loses its creative and dynamic power, and also its roots in man's deepest psychological needs. Here we are not directly concerned with what Urban calls the 'ontological import'[3] of the religious symbol but rather with its efficacy and necessity as a means of expression. 'Symbolism,' A. N. Whitehead has written, 'is essential for the higher grades of life, and the

---

[1] *Das Mythische Denken*, p. 293.   [2] Ibid., p. 296.
[1] *Language and Reality*, pp. 436 ff.

errors of symbolism can never be wholly avoided.'[1] If in these 'higher grades of life' Whitehead includes the religious conscious- ness, what he says is true of theological thinking, and it applies to its mythological expression, which is closely related to sym- bolism. But the warning sounded in the second half of the statement should be taken seriously, for the symbol, like the myth, may even obscure the truth if it is misunderstood or misapplied.

Moreover, the myth, the crystallization of mythological think- ing in picturesque, concrete form with emotive power, is more than a symbolic form of apprehension and expression: it is a mythopoetical norm giving permanence to the particular concept or doctrine to which it corresponds, thus providing an enduring point of reference.

For the great symbols of the Christian faith cannot be dis- pensed with without leaving its formulation to the mercy of changing intellectual and philosophical habits of mind which confine it to terms which may be acceptable to one age and unacceptable to another. That is the danger inherent in the endeavour to give philosophical expression to religious doctrines. In any case, it is mythological thinking, the archetypal symbols, which are themselves retranslated into these changing intellectual expressions. Incarnation, Atonement, the sacramental meal, the Cross, the overcoming of darkness by light, the Logos assuming the 'likeness' of sinful flesh, the pre-existence of the creator Saviour-Kyrios, the birth of the wonderful Child by divine conception, the personalized creation awaiting its deliverance in anguish, the death and resurrection of the saviour-victim, belief that the 'world' is evil and lies in the power of the Devil, the voice from heaven at the Baptism and Transfiguration, the story of the Temptation itself: these are instances of mythological thinking, many of which have close affinities with an extra- biblical thought-world but are nevertheless inalienable forms of expressing the 'salvation-event', the *Heilsgeschehen*. They are so embedded in the New Testament that they cannot be removed from it, and because they have to do with history, with both *Historie* and *Geschichte* and not with a mythological world-view

[1] *Process and Reality*, p. 259.

or a cult centring in a mythical or fictitious personage, they remain as enduring representations of moments in the Christian story and expressions as well as creators of faith, paradigmata, in Mannheim's term, which are capable of continual reinterpretation. They remain when the reinterpretation is found not to be final and are capable of stimulating new patterns of piety and experience, rescuing Christian belief from the subjectivism into which it is likely to fall when they are deprived of objective validity. The mythological thought of the New Testament is intended not only to be understood in terms of 'existential' experience or 'self-understanding' but also to be about an ultimate reality; not about cosmology but about revelation. This does not mean, however, that all such thought is of equal value or validity, but that it is a form of language appropriate to the theme. Although in its New Testament context the word 'myth' ($\mu\tilde{\upsilon}\theta o\varsigma$) is equated with fiction and is therefore opposed to $\lambda \acute{o}\gamma o\varsigma$, namely a true narrative,[1] as symbolical language, describing what cannot be otherwise adequately represented, it is a vehicle of a divine Word and is therefore itself a Logos. It speaks of God and man in relationship to one another and of the forms which the divine-human encounter takes.

For it is necessary to have some permanent standard of reference, some biblical norm, to which theological conceptions can be referred, though this does not mean that the pictorial and the irrational should have primacy over the definable and the rational or that the historical should be subjugated to the mythological. It does, however, mean that myth can communicate something which conceptual thought cannot. Dr. Toynbee has made this clear with reference to the mythologically described process of encounter and movement which lies, in his view, at the genesis of history.

The event can best be described in these mythological images because they are not embarrassed by the contradiction that arises

---

[1] The New Testament references are to 'myths which promote private speculations rather than the divine training that is in faith' (I Tim. 1: 4); 'godless and silly myths' (I Tim. 4: 7); 'Jewish myths' (Tit. 1: 14). There are those who 'turn away from listening to the truth and wander into myths' (II Tim. 4: 4), and the author of II Peter assures his readers that 'we did not follow cleverly devised myths' (1: 16). Cf. Philo, a 'myth of the men of old' ($\tau\tilde{\omega}\nu$ $\pi\alpha\lambda\alpha\iota\tilde{\omega}\nu$ $\mu\tilde{\upsilon}\theta o\varsigma$, de Plantatione, 1: 30).

when the statement is translated into logical terms. In logic, if God's universe is perfect, there cannot be a Devil outside it, while, if the Devil exists, the perfection which he comes to spoil must have been incomplete already through the very fact of his existence. This logical contradiction, which cannot logically be resolved, is intuitively transcended in the imagery of the poet and the prophet, who give glory to an omnipotent God yet take it for granted that He is subject to two crucial limitations.[1]

Dr. Toynbee proceeds to say that the contradictions cannot be resolved by translating its terms into impersonal and abstract language.

The context of this passage does not matter to our argument; what is of importance is the principle which it propounds. Moreover, Christian belief cannot undergo continual restatement without the danger of serious loss if the original forms which are to be restated are not given some objective importance. In any case, unless a major surgical operation is to be performed on the New Testament, or it is to be abolished or ignored, the mythological element cannot be eliminated either from the Christian picture of human destiny or from the endeavour to describe what Christ means in the totality of existence, which includes man's understanding of himself and of his world. If the *Kyrios* is what the New Testament says he is, he is not, so to speak, on the same 'level' as ordinary humanity. If history with him is totally different from history without him, some terms must be employed, or devised, to indicate in what this superiority and difference consist; but whereas no Christology can be wholly satisfactory which does not take account of the thought-forms of the age, it may not be easily understood by men of another age if it is too deeply bound up with them.

2

The essence of myth is that it is not, formally, history. The inventor of myth is not a historian. Mythological thinking may be 'historic' but it is not historiographical. How far, then, can demythologizing proceed without depriving the historical

[1] *A Study of History*, I, p. 279.

Christian faith of such non-historical symbols as approach archetypal or primordial images? Probably not very far, for a radical demythologizing will doubtless result in the discarding of the essentials of the *kerygma* as well as of what is peripheral to it. It is also difficult to devise a procedure which is calculated to make a demythologized New Testament acceptable to the modern age, to which such deference is shown, if that is really what is required. Jaspers frankly states that the Bible and the antique conception of the world are insufficient for today, and that the metamorphosis of biblical religion is a vital question for the immediate future.[1] If such a radical reinterpretation or adaptation of the religion of the biblical source of Christianity implies the excision of the mythological material from the New Testament, who is to perform the operation, and what assurance is there that, this having been done, our hypothetical amputator will thereupon proceed to attend to what the Gospel has to say? It is likely to remain a stumbling-block and a foolishness as it was to the Greeks and Barbarians and Jews who shared the cosmological worldview of the age. Paul's philosophical discourse at Athens, which made full use of the current Stoic conception of natural theology, seems to have been his greatest failure. Notwithstanding Paul's familiarity with the thought of his age, the proclamation of the Resurrection was not received with approval. There is no evidence to show that the commendable preaching of the Gospel on the lowest common level and in terms most acceptable to the intellectual mood of the time, that is to say, when deprived of all its supposed incredibilities, its distance, its transcendent demands, and its supernatural background, will be any more successful as long as the stumbling-block is not the mythology alone but the very substance of the Gospel and the conception of a spiritual universe which 'scientificism' (to use again the term employed by Miguel de Unamuno and F. A. Hayek), or the popular misunderstanding of science debased into an emotional prejudice against religion, is unable to appreciate.

The essence of the Gospel is that God personally intervened in history. What the New Testament writers sought to do, aided

---

[1] In *Europa der Gegenwart*, p. 51, Vienna, 1947; *Rechenschaft und Ausblick*, Munich, 1951, p. 260.

by the intellectual apparatus of their time, was to show *how* He did so: *how* He 'came' into the world which He had made. As man is not omniscient he cannot achieve precision in answering the question 'How was it done?' If the answer given by Christian theology is 'Through the Incarnation', we are only a step further on, for the major theological and Christological problem during nineteen centuries has been that of describing *how* the Incarnation represents divine intervention 'for us men and for our salvation', though it has been described by such conceptions as the Virgin Birth, the Messiah, the self-emptying of the Son of God, the Logos becoming flesh, and the exaltation of the Son of God to supreme status in the universe at the right hand of the Father and Creator. To him who rejects this, which is the substance of the Gospel, it is the fundamental affirmation, not merely the world-view of antiquity, which is unacceptable.

In Brunner's view Bultmann has failed to distinguish clearly between the antique picture of the world and the 'mythology' of the New Testament. There is some justice in this criticism, for the cosmology of the ancients is one thing: the Gospel is another. It does not depend on whether the earth is round or flat or whether it is supported on the backs of elephants or 'on the waters under the earth', or on whether the universe is finite or infinite, expanding or contracting. The spatial terms of the New Testament, the 'up' and the 'down', do not affect the validity of the Gospel which was proclaimed in that world any more than it has been substantially affected by the change from the physics of Newton to that of Einstein. As far as precision of location is concerned, it does not matter whether Christ sits 'at the right hand of God' or whether he is diffused throughout space. The efficacy of the Atonement and the proclamation of Salvation are not affected by whether, depending on the point of observation, the earth goes round the sun or by whether, as may well be possible in relativity physics, the sun goes round the earth.

Moreover, it is not wholly accurate to say, as Bultmann says, that 'the presentation of God's saving act corresponds to the mythical world-view'. The most that can be said is that it grew up within it and used some of its terms. 'Can Christian preaching,' Bultmann continues, 'really expect the man of today to recognize the mythical world-picture as true? That is absurd and impossible; for the mythical world-picture as such is not specifically Christian but that of a past age.'[1]

Of course it is absurd and impossible to expect this. But the 'modern man' is also unable, according to Bultmann, to understand the doctrine of vicarious satisfaction or atonement through the death of Christ. 'What primitive mythology to imagine that a divine being can atone for human sin through the shedding of blood!' Yet, he says, the mythology should be neither selectively omitted nor excised as a whole. It is the task of theology to interpret it. Bultmann, therefore, favours the retention of the myth as a point of reference for the purpose of stimulating man to a further understanding of himself; but it should be retained on condition that the preacher leaves his congregation in no doubt as to his attitude towards it. The *kerygma* is capable of being disentangled from the myth, in Bultmann's view, through being interpreted existentially. It can in this way speak through, or in spite of, the obsolete cosmology, through the metaphor, to man in his situation.

That is precisely what the Gospel has always done, and it still does so through the myth, whether it is understood literally, or as metaphor and mythopoetry, or whether, with Bultmann, we try to get behind the myth to the understanding of existence which underlies its language. To have any relevance to human needs the 'myth' must speak *to* man in his situation; it must speak *of* man in so far as it discloses what man is as the centre of his situation. But it must also be understood as speaking to him of that which transcends his own position in the world and as pointing away from him to the *Kyrios* to whom, in its Christological form, it testifies. As a form of perception or expression the 'myth' of the New Testament can either be ignored or it can be interpreted, existentially or mythopoetically, not by exact exegesis which implies a literal understanding of it, but in general terms which disclose the basic thought and experience which underlie it. Where this myth is cosmological it can be disregarded. Where it is Christological different treatment is required, for in this case what is necessary is an assessment of how far the form of the

[1] *Kerygma und Mythos*, pp. 16–17; E. trans., p. 3.

mythological affirmation indicates not factual truth about Jesus' mode of existence but rather his significance for history and faith.

A Christianity which jettisons the so-called mythological element in the New Testament Christology instead of retaining it *in the knowledge that it is mythological* not only impoverishes itself but weakens its own historical-biblical roots. The biblical witness is, after all, as near to being final as any witness can be, though not necessarily infallibly so in the sense that its accuracy as *logos* is such that we are committed to its literal acceptance. It is final in the sense that it is extremely improbable that what it says about Jesus will be superseded by anything better, certainly not by accommodation to any philosophical system or intellectual mood. As Dr. Dodd has written of the *testimonia*:

> If theology seeks an accommodation with temporary fashions of thought by cutting loose from its firm foundations in *kerygma* and testimonies, as it has sometimes done, it declines into insignificance, and has in fact nothing to say to the world which the world may not learn elsewhere. The challenge of a new period with its peculiar problems should force us back into the pit from whence we were digged and the rock from whence we were hewn.[1]

That a terminology is 'valid' does not mean that we are committed to its literal form or that there is no need to reinterpret it. It means, rather, that it remains the permanent anchor of faith and the fixed point to which any age may turn for an objective statement of that which, though it may be differently understood by people of different historical periods, remains substantially unchanged.

The unchanging substance is the New Testament affirmation that Jesus is Lord.

[1] *According to the Scriptures*, p. 138.

APPENDICES

1. *Note on the non-mythological character of the Synoptic Gospels.*

I have implied above (pp. 55 f., 88 ff., 116, 162 ff., 235 f.) that a distinction should be drawn between the mythological assessment of Jesus in the Synoptic Gospels and that which is found in the Pauline Epistles and the Fourth Gospel. A considerable amount of recent work on the New Testament, however, including much that has been written about the 'unity of the Bible', and that of New Testament scholars whose approach has affinities with or has been influenced by form-criticism (though without necessarily accepting all the conclusion of the form-critics), suggests a denial of this distinction to any substantial extent, or at any rate a reduction of it to a negligible minimum. Hoskyns and Davey, for example, in their cogently argued book *The Riddle of the New Testament* (1931), demonstrated (though Wrede had done something of the same kind thirty years earlier) that it is no longer permissible to regard the Synoptic tradition as uninfluenced by doctrinal and Christological motives but that the form and even narrative-content of the Marcan Gospel are saturated with and conditioned by Old Testament archetypal and Messianic Christology. That is to say, there is an underlying and unifying Christological interpretation of the Gospel story, not superimposed upon the tradition, which derives from the faith of apostolic circles that Jesus was the Messiah promised in the Old Testament as they interpreted it. The Gospel history was written within the framework of Old Testament prophecy; none the less, the evangelists wrote 'as historians and not as theologians' (p. 207). The theologians, however —Paul, John, the author of Hebrews—do not 'move in a world of their own ideas' (p. 244) inconsistent with that of the evangelists. Even in the Marcan Gospel the tension between history and interpretation is presented in an acute form. One should not, therefore, seek a 'reduced' Christology at any stage in the Synoptic tradition which is not, as it were, embryonic of later apostolic developments. Thus R. H. Lightfoot, who deals with the history and its interpretation from a similar point of view, says that the Marcan history is 'concerned with a divine being, a pre-existent Son of God' and indicates a Christology essentially the same as Paul's, which represents the life of Jesus as a temporary episode between two existences (*History and Interpretation in the Gospels*, 1935, pp. 210-11); though in discussing Philippians 2 Lightfoot observes that 'only pre-existence seems to be wanting in the Synoptic Gospels' —an important qualification which should not go unnoticed.[1] According to Dr. A. M. Farrer, the structure of Mark is even more complicated and artificial, and almost every detail of the Gospel story is connected with an Old Testament prototype and is given its place in a complex design of symbols and

---

[1] It should be observed, however, that a Son of God/Son of Man Christology such as that which is evident in Mark is not necessarily 'mythological'; for from the Johannine standpoint, as C. K. Barrett has said, Mark could be easily interpreted as inadequate and favourable to an Adoptionist point of view (*The Gospel According to St. John*, 1955, p. 43).

numbers until there emerges a bewildering pattern of cycles and anti-cycles and still more cunningly contrived subdivisions. Dr. Farrer's thesis (which was in some respects modified and renounced in a later work, *St. Matthew and St. Mark*, 1954) has not won general acceptance, though he elaborated it in another form in an essay in which he claims that sections of the Matthean Gospel are modelled on the Hexateuch ('On Dispensing with Q' in *Studies in the Gospels*, 1955). C. F. Evans, too, has followed the same kind of method: the central portion of Luke, it is alleged, was written with passages of Deuteronomy in mind ('The Central Section of St. Luke's Gospel' in the same collective work). These analyses of the Synoptic tradition, when shorn of their more fanciful trappings and of the desire to find some complicated or obscure references or implications in the Gospel narratives, show that the 'history' is not a straightforward biography but a work shot through with the doctrinal presuppositions of the apostolic age which constitute the underlying Christological unity of the New Testament. Even if the evangelists' method and the tradition which they took over appear quaint to the modern mind, when various allowances are made and certain exaggerations discounted, there is substantial truth in the conclusions of the exponents of their methods. Archetypes, patterns, and doctrinal intention cannot be excluded from the Synoptic Gospels, though in this one should not assume that the purpose of the evangelists was as non-historical as is often alleged. The inference from these instances of this approach to the study of the Gospel tradition is that the 'mythological' presuppositions of Paul and John were already present in the earliest tradition and informed it.

A similar conclusion follows from Bultmann's form-critical method of dealing with the Synoptic tradition,[1] according to which it is not possible to turn to the Gospels in search of evidence of a non-mythological Christology or in support of the supposition that *Jesus himself* considerably demythed Christological archetypes, for little of historical value survives his microscopic analysis of the Synoptic tradition; in any case, few of the sayings of Jesus (except the eschatological ones) can be regarded as authentic. The Gospels are collections and redactions of fragmentary traditions which are given their form as popular *Kleinliteratur* or by the doctrinal requirements of the primitive Hellenistic churches. The earliest strata are not free from the 'mythological' outlook of the formers of the tradition. Dr. Vincent Taylor has described his ingenious, lucid, and brilliant work as 'a study in the art of the conceivable' (*The Formation of the Gospel Tradition*, p. 15). There is much capriciousness and pure conjecture in Bultmann's dismissal of historicity.

Martin Dibelius, however, may be cited in support of the view that, in comparison with the other literature of the New Testament, the Synoptic tradition embodies a soberly non-mythological Christology. The letters of Paul, he says, 'are an unambiguous proof that there was a *Christ-mythology*' and adds that 'at the same time they are a proof that this mythology could not

---

[1] *Die Geschichte der Synoptischen Tradition*, 2nd ed. 1931.

be supported from the tradition of the life of Jesus' (*From Tradition to Gospel*, 1934, p. 267),[1] and of the Pauline myth of the descent and ascent of the pre-existent divine Son of God there is in his view no evidence in the Synoptic tradition (ibid., p. 268). In this tradition a 'thoroughgoing mythological formulation has not been carried out', which shows 'how firmly at bottom the tradition kept its feet upon the ground. A mythology of Christ only gained place very incompletely within the description of the life of Jesus' (ibid., p. 269). Whatever Christological presuppositions may be assumed to have been present in the minds of the compilers of the various strands of the tradition, the mythological motive, evident in Paul and John, does not appear to have taken charge of the 'entire material of the gospel history. . . . But this,' he goes on to say, 'corresponds to the general development of primitive Christianity which passes from a historical person to his formal worship and finally to the cosmic mythological Christ of Gnosis'. Dibelius is inclined to limit the mythological material to the stories of the Temptation, the Baptism, and the Transfiguration (p. 271), though there are mythological elements in the Birth-narratives. The full mythological assessment of Jesus in Paul and John is in contrast to the mythological tradition in the Synoptics which is assembled 'only to the smallest extent' (ibid., p. 279). Dibelius nevertheless regards the Q logion Matthew 11 : 25 ff. as the utterance of a mythological person. In the Fourth Gospel 'everything is mythological'; 'the tradition has entered into the realm of mythology' (ibid., p. 286). Whether Dibelius takes a too limited view of myth (ibid., p. 266) is beside the point; a 'legend' is not necessarily a 'myth' because it has Hellenistic parallels, nor is it necessarily unhistorical; but that it reflects a 'mythological' way of thinking if elaborated as the description of the acts of a divine being goes without saying, though we have to turn to the non-canonical 'gospels' in order to see how far the mythopœic imagination could go when ignoring the restraints imposed by respect for history.[2] Occasionally, however, Dibelius is guilty of the same kind of exaggeration as Bultmann when he cites Mark 9 : 10 ('You unfaithful generation! How long shall I be with you, how long shall I bear with you!') as having a 'powerful mythological background' because the words are those of 'a God only temporarily in human form'. What is important to note is Dibelius' belief that there is a Christological growth in the New Testament and that the Pauline Epistles and the Fourth Gospel testify to an increasingly mythological conception of the person of Jesus which is not in evidence to any great extent in the Synoptic tradition.

Further, Dr. B. S. Easton, an earlier exponent (and critic) of form-criticism, observes that St. John's Christology shows how 'archaic' the Synoptic Christology was regarded in later circles, and 'the absence of almost every trace of the more developed doctrine from the post-Pauline Synoptists is a powerful guarantee of their historic conscientiousness' (*The Gospel Before the Gospels*,

[1] English translation of *Die Formgeschichte des Evangeliums*, 2nd ed. 1933.

[2] Cf. the fully mythological character of the legendary tales in the non-canonical Proto-Gospel of James and the Nativity Gospel of Thomas, which show how possible it is that the Birth-narratives may also be fictitious though more soberly so.

p. 100). He concludes that the 'primary historic value of the Synoptists is not for their own age but for the tradition of the teachings of Jesus' (p. 109).[1]

I am not disputing the general correctness of the position of Hoskyns and Lightfoot and others who have demonstrated the strongly Christological structure of the earliest Synoptic tradition, though they are often inclined to read interpretation into the history when this is unnecessary and to complicate what seems to be straightforward enough. The influence of Old Testament archetypes and of the interpretation of prophecy on the minds of the evangelists and the traditions which they took over is undeniable. There doubtless was a consistent, though by no means static, apostolic Christology. But the Synoptic tradition does not represent Jesus as a pre-existent divine being, nor is there any association of him with the mythically-conceived Messiah-Son of Man of Jewish apocalyptic. Despite repeated statements of the kind that the Synoptic Gospels are 'not primarily an effort at biography' and that their composition was less prompted by the desire for historical reminiscence than by the need for 'representative and significant signs and deeds of the Lord which could be used in preaching, teaching, and worship' (Lightfoot, op. cit., p. 126), they are nevertheless biographies in a sense, and also historical because they can be presumed to have been written in order that the Church might have a permanent if fragmentary record of what the Lord did and said. There has been so too much disparagement of the *historical* purpose of the Gospels that they have come to be regarded in some circles primarily as theological documents with a merely subordinate historical importance. In the last analysis it may be that, as B. S. Easton suggests, the so-called 'mythical' ingredients of the Synoptic tradition are only a heightening of the impression that the Jesus of history actually produced and represent 'merely . . . a terminology which myth-makers used as well' (op. cit., p. 162). In view of divergencies between the views of New Testament scholars themselves perhaps the most adequate comment is that of Hoskyns and Davey: 'there are no "assured results" of New Testament criticism' (op. cit., p. 159).

11. *The Synoptic reduction of myth and the demything of Christological archetypes* (*pp. 12, 37.*)

It is significant that, whereas the Epistles and the Johannine Gospel reveal a heightening of the Christology of the Synoptics and even features which are not present in them, the Christology of the latter indicates a considerable reduction, in terms of Jesus' own interpretation of them, of the Messianic titles with their mythological ingredients. The two most important titles of Jesus referred to directly or indirectly in the Synoptic Gospels—Messiah and Son of Man—had come to represent a futurist personality possessing qualities of more than epic transcendence over human dimensions. They are numinous

[1] See, further, Vincent Taylor, *The Formation of the Gospel Tradition* (1933, 1945), E. F. Scott, *The Validity of the Gospel Record* (1938) and *The Purpose of the Gospels* (1945), and L. J. McGinlay, S.J., *Form Criticism and the Healing Miracles of the Gospels* (Maryland, 1941), for fair and informed appraisals of form-criticism.

terms, though their precise meaning is still in dispute, and there is no complete agreement as to how far Jesus used them and, if he did, what exactly he meant by them; whether they were attributed to him by the apostolic age, and, if so, in what sense. On the whole, however, there are general lines of agreement, and as the ground has been traversed so often and so thoroughly little is to be gained by covering it again in detail. Some of the main issues only will be touched upon.

In the first place, it should be observed that if Jesus was convinced of the Messianic character of his mission it was in terms quite other than those which were popularly believed to describe the Messianic person and which, both in allegedly Messianic passages in the Old Testament and in current apocalyptic, he considered false. Indeed, it is not overstating the matter when it is said that what Jesus did was to retain the concept of Messiah while rejecting the Old Testament and apocalyptic notions of Messiahship out of hand. Otherwise the story of the Temptation is meaningless. If, as is generally agreed, he gave priority to the prototypical symbol of the Suffering Servant of Yahweh as described in Isaiah 53 over other expressions of the redemptive character of his mission, he was adopting a model which was not considered Messianic until the time of the apostles.[1] There is a basic incompatibility between the figure envisaged in Isaiah 9: 6-11, 11: 1 ff. (who is not designated as Messiah) and the apocalyptic fantasy of Jewish expectation on the one hand and Jesus' conception of his mission on the other. Nor, according to the Synoptics (which distinguishes them from the Fourth Gospel), did Jesus in the first place use the term Messiah of himself, though, as Dr. Vincent Taylor has remarked, that he did not speak of himself as the Christ does not mean that he did not believe himself to be the Messiah (*The Names of Jesus*, p. 20). Dr. C. J. Cadoux even maintained that the 'Servant' concept was 'another proo that for [Jesus] the conception of Messiahship was not itself primary, but was governed by other considerations' (*The Historic Mission of Jesus*, p. 52), while Prof. W. Manson inclines to the view that Jesus held a *functional* conception of Messiahship and adopted the Messianic thought of Israel as a 'reagent' or medium in which he brought out 'the true colour and significance of the revelation of God of which he knew himself to be the bearer' (*Jesus the Messiah*, p. 97). Dr. G. S. Duncan concludes that the Synoptic record of his sayings 'yields only precarious evidence of a claim to the Messiahship' (*Jesus Son of God*, p. 126).

By, roughly, the New Testament period the Messianic figure, slightly prefigured by a few Old Testament passages, had become a mighty, semi-divine, semi-military or political, numinous and mythologically conceived figure, sometimes (as in the Enochic apocalypse) regarded as pre-existent, but always as future and as one whose function was to put an end to the age of oppression and usher in a new age of equity and peace after the total rout of Israel's

---

[1] The field has been thoroughly surveyed by Dr. H. H. Rowley in *The Servant of the Lord*, chapters 1 and 2. Dr. Rowley sums up the vast amount of literature on the subject by concluding that there was no pre-Christian identification of the Messiah with the Servant.

enemies. Doubtless the precise form of the expectation was based to some extent on the military successes of the Maccabeans, for the period 220 B.C. onwards was the classical age of Jewish apocalyptic, which took the place of prophecy, and to all the apocalyptic writings the hope for the coming of a great national leader-deliverer is common. As in Jubilees and the Psalms of Solomon the ideal was noble and spiritual as well as political. Sometimes the Messianic kingdom was thought to be as of only short duration, or as a terrestrial kingdom; sometimes it was conceived in transcendent terms because the world was thought of as unfit for the manifestation of divine righteousness. By the time of IV Ezra apocalyptic had reached a fantastic baroque-like level and finally disappeared when it was seen that the great 'woes' did not bring with them the reign of the mythical vice-gerent of God. There is nothing of this, nor of any kind of Messianism, in the Suffering Servant, and by Jesus the notion of the futuristic reign is largely rejected; its place is taken by the Kingdom of God which is here and now as well as future. The mythical, super-human Messiah has been completely demythologized: the very expectation, belonging to the world of picture and hope, has become a present reality.[1]

The same attitude on the part of Jesus towards current conceptions is seen in his treatment of the term 'Son of Man'. Although there is apocalyptic-eschatological material in the Synoptic Gospels, such as, for example, the 'little apocalypse' of Mark 13 with parallels in Matthew and Luke, and passages such as Matthew 25: 31 ff. and Luke 17: 22 ff., the mythical-futuristic idea of the super-human, trans-historical figure is almost absent. The Synoptics contain little suggestion of the extravagant exuberance of the vision of the Son of Man of IV Ezra 13, where this figure comes on the clouds of heaven and destroys his enemies with the fire breathed from his mouth: a passage which is closer to the Johannine Apocalypse than to any words of Jesus which can be accepted as authentic. The comparative absence of vividly eschatological material and of eschatological teaching generally from Q and L and the 'paradigms' should also be remarked upon. In assessing the 'genuine' eschatological matter in the Synoptics it would seem that Mark 13 should hardly be cited because of its composite character and stylised form. (See on these points, *inter alia*, R. H. Charles, *Eschatology*, p. 384; B. H. Streeter, in *Foundations*, *The Four Gospels*, pp. 491 ff.; C. W. Emmet, *The Eschatological Question in the Gospels*, p. 144; F. C. Burkitt in *Cambridge Biblical Essays*; A. T. Cadoux, *The Theology of Jesus*, pp. 26 ff.; C. J. Cadoux, *The Historic Mission of Jesus*, pp. 16 f.; C. H. Dodd, *The Apostolic Preaching and its Developments*, p. 84; Vincent Taylor, *The Gospel According to Mark*, pp. 638, 664; A. T. Cadoux, *The Sources of the Second Gospel*; W. L. Knox, *Sources of the Synoptic Gospels*, I, pp. 103–14; F. C. Burkitt, *Jewish and Christian Apocalypses*, pp. 23–5; R. Otto, *The Kingdom of God and the Son of Man*, pp. 176 ff. Dr. G. R. Beasley-Murray's

---

[1] The subject of Messianism and Apocalyptic during the New Testament period and that preceding it is thoroughly dealt with by Bousset, *Die Religion des Judentums im neutestamentlichen Zeitalter*, pp. 233–46. See also, among other studies in this field, R. H. Charles, *Eschatology Hebrew, Jewish, and Christian*, pp. 247 ff.; J. Klausner, *Die messianischen Vorstellungen des Jüdischen Volkes im Zeitalter der Tannaiten* (1904).

exhaustive survey of what has been written on Mark 13 does not bring us any nearer to a decision as to the genuineness or otherwise of the apocalyptic material in the Gospels (*Jesus and the Future*, 1954).

The question of what Jesus meant by the term 'Son of Man'—whether it was used in the individual or collective sense or both—lies outside the present purpose (see, e.g., T. W. Manson, *The Teaching of Jesus*, p. 218; C. J. Cadoux, *The Historic Mission of Jesus*, pp. 71 ff.; V. Taylor, *The Life and Ministry of Jesus*, p. 73). Two of three classifications of the use of the term have no apocalyptic connotation (Mark 8:31; 9:31; 10:33; 14:21; Luke 7:34; 12:10, etc.). The 'Son' is a human person living in the present.

The 'source' of the concept is usually considered to be Daniel 7:13, though the words in Mark 14:62 = Matthew 26:64 are not an exact quotation but a telescoped paraphrase as stereotyped as in the other instances where the Son of Man is mentioned together with the clouds of heaven. Dalman (*The Words of Jesus*, p. 257) holds this view. The 'Son of Man' of Daniel, however, is a simile indicating the 'saints of the Most High' and is much more likely to be the source of the 'Son of Man' of I Enoch and IV Ezra than of Jesus' use of it. For if Jesus found in prophecy, namely in Isaiah 53, the source of his 'Messianic' conception, it is equally probable that that was where he found the most congenial use of the term 'Son of Man'; for in Ezekiel the phrase occurs some ninety times. Jesus' awareness that he was sent first to the 'lost sheep of the house of Israel' and his reply to the Syro-Phoenician woman are similar to the commission given to Ezekiel: 'Son of Man, get you to the house of Israel, and speak my words to them. For you are not sent to a people of foreign speech and hard language, but to the house of Israel' (Ezek. 3:4–5); and 'I am come to seek and to save that which is lost' is an echo of Ezekiel 34:16, 'I will seek that which is lost'. Indeed, the 'Son of Man' who is 'sent' has much more affinity, in the Synoptic Gospels, with prophecy than with apocalyptic, though the latter also doubtless exerted *some* influnce over his mind.

The phrase 'Son of God' was not used by Jesus of himself in the Synoptics. There is no evidence that he thought of his Sonship in progenitive terms such as those in which later Christianity, or the 'mythical' Birth-narratives, came to understand it. It is conceived by Jesus in terms of spiritual relationship, not analogically with any biological notion of father-son relationship. Any use of the term 'Son of God' would most likely have provoked comparison with the popular conception of divine sonship familiar in the Hellenistic world. That Jesus *regarded himself* as the incarnation of the Son of God or of God Himself in the sense in which orthodoxy has understood it is nowhere indicated in the Synoptic tradition.

It would appear, then, that Jesus had little place for 'mythological' conceptions and that he actually demythologized current ones by his own interpretation of his mission. The 'mythical' Son of Man of apocalyptic has been brought down, so to speak, from the clouds of heaven to Galilee and Judea: the futurist-mythical figure of eschatological symbolism is now present as a contemporary figure, though what is presented is not the incarnation or realisation of the myth but a kind of mythological kenosis.

INDEX OF NAMES

INDEX OF SUBJECTS

INDEX OF FOREIGN TERMS

GEORGE ALLEN & UNWIN LTD
London: 40 Museum Street, W.C.1

Auckland: 24 Wyndham Street
Sydney, N.S.W.: Bradbury House, 55 York Street
Cape Town: 109 Long Street
Bombay: 15 Graham Road, Ballard Estate, Bombay 1
Calcutta: 17 Chittaranjan Avenue, Calcutta 13
New Delhi: 13–14 Ajmere Gate Extension, New Delhi 1
Karachi: Haroon Chambers, South Napier Road, Karachi 2
Toronto: 91 Wellington Street West
São Paulo: Avenida 9 de Julho 11388–Ap. 51